MAKING TRANSNATIONALS ACCOUNTABLE

A Significant Step for Britain

David Bailey, George Harte and Roger Sugden

London and New York

First published 1994
by Routledge
11 New Fetter Lane, London EC4P 4EE

Simultaneously published in the USA and Canada
by Routledge
29 West 35th Street, New York, NY 10001

Typeset in Garamond by
J&L Composition Ltd, Filey, North Yorkshire
Printed and bound in Great Britain by
Mackays of Chatham PLC, Chatham, Kent

British Library Cataloguing in Publication Data

A catalogue record for this book is available from the British Library.

Library of Congress Cataloging in Publication Data

Bailey, David, 1966–
Making transnationals accountable: a significant step for Britain
David Bailey, George Harte, and Roger Sugden.
p.   cm.
Includes bibliographical references and index.
ISBN 0–415–06870–3. – ISBN 0–415–06871–1
1. International business enterprises—Government policy.
I. Harte, George, 1954– . II Sugden, Roger. III. Title.
HD2755.5.B337 1994
338.8'8—dc20   93–38033
CIP

CONTENTS

List of tables		vi
Acknowledgements		ix
1	THE POSSIBILITY OF A STRATEGY	1
2	BRITAIN'S RECENT ATTITUDE	10
3	CONTRASTING ATTITUDES ELSEWHERE	23
4	A MONITORING STRATEGY	53
5	ISSUES OF CONCERN	68
6	THE FORM OF ACCOUNT	79
7	TOWARDS AN ECONOMIC AND SOCIAL ACCOUNT: A CASE STUDY	100
8	DISCUSSION OF THE GLAXO CASE STUDY	183
9	CO-OPERATION BETWEEN COUNTRIES	197
10	A SIGNIFICANT STEP FOR BRITAIN	216
	Bibliography	227
	Index	240

TABLES

1.1   Share of foreign enterprises in the sales of total UK manufacturing, 1975–89, %   4

1.2   Share of twenty-eight leading UK transnationals in the sales of total UK manufacturing, 1975–81, %   4

1.3   Share of foreign enterprises in the employment of total UK manufacturing, 1975–89, %   5

1.4   Share of forty-five leading UK transnationals in the employment of total UK manufacturing, 1975–81, %   6

3.1   The French legislative position on inward direct investment as of June 1992   35

4.1   Criteria for assessment of investments, and for subsequent 'monitoring', under Canada's Foreign Investment Review Act   60

5.1   French, Japanese and US Government concerns regarding transnational corporations, 1963–93   71

5.2   Analysis of the issues of concern   72

6.1   Typical contents of a transnational's annual report and accounts   81

6.2   Percentage of respondents ranking the annual report/financial statements as their most important source of information, and ranking as a source   87

7.1   The contents of the 1990/91 Glaxo annual report and accounts   106

7.2   Analysis of ordinary shareholdings in Glaxo, at 30 June 1991   109

7.3   Size and value of average shareholdings in Glaxo   110

7.4   Glaxo directors' shareholdings and options at 30 June 1991   111

7.5   Principal subsidiary and associated undertakings – where Glaxo shareholdings are less than 100%   112

7.6   Segment information (geographical analysis) for Glaxo   118

7.7   Profit margin and return on capital employed of Glaxo   119

7.8   Geographical analysis of turnover of Glaxo   119

7.9   Therapeutic analysis of turnover of Glaxo   119

7.10 Major patent expiry dates of Glaxo products   121

7.11 Growth in Glaxo's pharmaceuticals salesforce   123

7.12 Reported sales growth of Glaxo   125

7.13 Therapeutic analysis of Glaxo group pharmaceuticals and food turnover   126

7.14 Leading pharmaceutical markets and Glaxo product shares   127

7.15 World-wide R&D staffing of Glaxo   130

7.16 Exploratory development drugs of Glaxo   132

7.17 Full development drugs of Glaxo   134

7.18 Classification of new drugs stage of development   134

7.19 Glaxo's 1990 Research and Development pipeline status   135

7.20 Glaxo's research and development expenditure over the last twenty years   137

7.21 Contingent liabilities in Glaxo   137

7.22 Directors' remuneration and other employees' wages in Glaxo   140

7.23 Index of average earnings of all employees in Coalite   140

7.24 Rate of exploitation in Glaxo   141

7.25 Incidence of reportable accidents in Coalite works per 1,000 employees, 1970–3   143

7.26 Analysis of employment changes in Glaxo, 1972–91   144

7.27 General Motors US employment at 31 December 1981   146

7.28 Numbers of full-time male and female Avon employees   148

7.29 Female average earnings (and hours worked) as a percentage of male earning (and hours) at Avon companies, 1972–4   148

7.30 Employment of registered disabled people by Avon companies   149

7.31 Glaxo's principal subsidiaries and associated undertakings' operations   150

7.32 Glaxo's exports from Britain 1982–91   154

7.33 Index of UK exports of Tube Investments   154

7.34 Segmental sales and investment data of Glaxo   157

7.35 Avon's donations to charity expressed as a percentage of
     pre-tax profits by various companies   159
7.36 Tube Investments' charitable donations   160
7.37 Dow Chemicals' charitable donations   160
7.38 Value added of Glaxo   165
7.39 Value added per employee of Avon   166
7.40 Index of output (sales) per head of Coalite   167
7.41 Index of output per head of Tube Investments   168
7.42 Corporation tax details of Glaxo   170
7.43 Corporation tax charges of Glaxo   171
7.44 Taxes generated by General Motors' activities   175
7.45 The cost of government regulations to General Motors   176

ACKNOWLEDGEMENTS

A number of people have helped us in producing this volume. Thanks go to Lorna Aitkin (Department of Accounting and Business Method, University of Edinburgh) for typing earlier drafts. Special thanks go to Valerie Nash (Department of Commerce, University of Birmingham) for her patient, accurate and speedy typing.

We would particularly like to thank those closest to us for their support. They are: Stephanie O'Donohoe, Sarah Blowen and Nicky, Rachael and Stuart Sugden.

Our grateful thanks are also due to the following companies:

County NatWest, Dow Chemical Corporation, Extel Financial Ltd, General Motors Corporation, Glaxo Holdings plc, Morgan Stanley, Social Audit, and EIRIS.

1

THE POSSIBILITY OF A STRATEGY

The overall aim of this volume is to provide a solid intellectual foundation for a particular economic strategy; we will be advocating monitoring of transnational corporations as a means of appraising and influencing the activities of such firms in Britain.[1] The argument will be developed throughout the volume in chapters which build upon each other. Our specific concern is Britain but the argument is generalisable to many, perhaps even most other countries.

The subject of transnational corporations has spawned a vast amount of literature and aroused fundamental controversy. The key characteristic of such firms is their international production. They are involved in capital accumulation on a global scale, operating global strategies to produce continued growth (Sklair, 1991). Various theories of the transnational have been put forward, for instance, the monopolistic advantage approach associated with Hymer (1960) and Kindleberger (1969), and the eclectic analysis of Dunning (1977, 1979, 1980 and 1981).[2] Particularly influential has been transaction cost analysis (see, for instance, Buckley and Casson, 1976, and Hennart, 1991). This has its roots in Coasian theory of the firm (Coase, 1937). The basic argument is that a transnational is a firm in which the co-ordination of production without using market exchange takes the firm across national boundaries, and that transnationals arise from the desire to save transaction costs, achieved by using non-market transactions to bypass imperfect markets.

However, an alternative view can be taken. This is rooted in the analysis of monopoly capitalism (Baran and Sweezy, 1966; Cowling, 1982). It criticises the Coasian assumption of an even distribution of power, going beyond the Coasian superficial obsession with markets and focuses on distributional issues rather

1

than Pareto efficiency (Cowling and Sugden, 1987a). Under the monopoly capitalism approach, a transnational corporation is seen as 'the means of coordinating production from one centre of strategic decision making when this co-ordination takes a firm across national boundaries' (ibid.). This definition emphasises the importance of control rather than market exchange. The monopoly capitalism view sees firms becoming transnationals in order to defend against or attack oligopolistic rivals (ibid.). Transnationals may arise from opportunities to strengthen their position *vis-à-vis* rivals, or because of the need to match the actions of rivals. Moreover, transnationals are argued to behave in a manner of divide and rule (Sugden, 1993, drawing on Marglin's analysis (Marglin, 1974)). In this respect transnationals are seen to be in a powerful position in relation to nation states, communities, and employees. Transnationalism gives firms additional leverage and leads to such problems as monopolisation, deindustrialisation and the under-mining of democracy (Cowling and Sugden, 1987a and 1993b).

Moreover, concern has also been expressed about transnationals' homogenising effects, their (lack of) sensitivity to local needs, stifling of local initiatives, sovereignty and autonomy (Hood and Young, 1979) and their power to erode the state's capacity to control its economic future (Held, 1988; Wilms-Wright, 1977). Thus there is a view of transnationals which suggests that largely as a result of their pursuit of private profit, their size and their transnational flexibility (where they are at least potentially highly mobile), they pose problems for nation states.

Recognising this vast literature and fundamental controversy, however, our aim is nevertheless to cut through much of the existing debate. We will bypass disputes about the precise definition of such firms and avoid becoming bogged down in disagreements over their alleged pros and cons. Instead, we will concentrate more directly on policy issues.

Our intention is to advocate a strategy of monitoring trans-national corporations by a series of steps designed to maximise appeal and acceptance amongst policy-makers. This softly-softly approach will be taken because it appears that Britain's policy-makers are reluctant to question and change their current attitude towards transnationals. The approach is typified by the fact that this opening chapter merely aims to establish that the possibility of a government strategy for approaching transnationals is an issue that needs to be examined very closely. In itself this is not a very ambitious task and is not something which will occupy too much space. We are only looking to demonstrate that the possibility of a strategy warrants close attention, which is in no way to focus on monitoring or indeed any specific strategy, let alone suggest that any particular strategy is actually needed. Those concerns will come later.

To establish our point that the possibility of a strategy should be on Britain's agenda this chapter will focus on two considerations. Firstly, on data showing that transnationals are very important players in the British economy. Secondly, on the broad consensus that at least in some respects the impact of a transnational on an economy may be negative. Both of these considerations will receive brief attention. Nevertheless, it will be argued that either the data or the consensus persuasively support our point, and that taken together they are conclusive.

TRANSNATIONALS AND BRITAIN: SOME DATA

Without attempting to be anywhere near exhaustive in presenting data on transnationals' activities as regards Britain, it is easy to show that they are significant players in the British economy. To do this we will focus on aspects of manufacturing sales and employment. The concern with manufacturing does not deny the importance of transnationals in other areas, such as banking. Nevertheless, we take the view that, whilst the nature of economies and the relative importance of particular sectors changes over time, manufacturing remains a vital concern. Hence it is not unreasonable to focus on manufacturing data.

Manufacturing sales

Tables 1.1 and 1.2 give the most recent evidence of transnationals' share in the sales of total UK manufacturing. Table 1.1 refers to 'foreign enterprises'. Their share was 18.80 per cent in 1975 and 24.06 per cent in 1989; in between it consistently hovered around the 20 per cent mark each year.

These high amounts are all the more significant given a major drawback with the data.[3] 'Foreign enterprises are defined as those controlled or owned by companies incorporated overseas',[4] which effectively means UK producers with at least 51 per cent of their shares owned by overseas companies. To base a definition on

Table 1.1 Share of foreign enterprises in the sales of total UK manufacturing, 1975–89, %

Year	%	Year	%
1975	18.80	1985	20.33
1977	21.21	1986	19.43
1979	21.70	1987	21.00
1981	19.41	1988	20.66
1983	20.37	1989	24.06
1984	21.34		

Source: Derived from Census of Production Summary Tables and Summary Volumes.

Table 1.2 Share of twenty-eight leading UK transnationals* in the sales of total UK manufacturing, 1975–81, %

Year	%	Year	%
1975	16.08	1979	15.13
1977	15.34	1981	16.72

* The firms included are: Pilkington Brothers plc, Thomas Tilling plc, BICC plc, The General Electric Co plc, Thorn EMI plc, Associated British Foods Ltd, Cadbury Schweppes plc, Hanson Trust plc, Rank Hovis McDougall plc, Rowntree Mackintosh plc, Tate and Lyle plc, Unigate Ltd, United Biscuits (Holdings) Ltd, Beecham Group plc, Reckitt & Colman plc, Babcock International plc, Hawker Siddeley Group plc, IMI plc, Johnson Matthey & Co plc, Metal Box plc, Rio Tinto Zinc Corporation Ltd, TI Group plc, BL plc, Guest Keen & Nettlefold plc, Lucas Industries plc, Reed International plc, Coates Paton plc and Courtaulds plc.
Source: Cowling and Sugden (1987a).

control is appropriate but the concern with 51 per cent equity holdings is very restrictive and therefore the sales shares attributable to companies controlled overseas are underestimates. Although there is considerable debate about the precise proportion of shares required to control a firm, there is widespread agreement that in publicly-quoted companies less than 51 per cent is needed. Even Berle and Means (1932) only required a 20 per cent holding and the focus of more recent discussion has been on far lower figures (for instance, Pitelis and Sugden, 1986).

Table 1.2 turns the spotlight on 'domestic firms', for which data is considerably more scarce. (This illustrates the fact that, unlike much of the literature on transnationals, our concern is the activities of such firms in general; it is not merely the British activities of overseas firms and the overseas activities of British firms.) The data in the table is intended to indicate the importance of domestic transnationals but again provides lower bounds. Indeed here the problems are far more acute.

The table refers to the sales of a mere twenty-eight leading firms. The data is derived from information in the abbreviated company accounts in Stopford, Dunning and Haberich (1980) and Stopford (1982), two directories of transnational corporations. The twenty-eight firms are all of the UK-registered transnationals for which the directories give sales information for each of the years 1975, 1977, 1979, and 1981 This is clearly a very limited sample. For instance, Stopford (1982) lists 500 leading transnationals from across the world,[5] sixty-nine from the UK. Nevertheless, the table shows that a mere twenty-eight of these UK transnationals alone had a sales share of approximately 16 per cent in the late 1970s, early 1980s. For such a small number of firms this is a very high figure.

Manufacturing employment

The impression that transnationals have a significant presence is reinforced by the evidence of transnationals' share in the employment of total UK manufacturing. This is reported in Tables 1.3 and 1.4, which again present lower bounds on the shares of foreign and domestic transnationals. Between 1975 and 1989 foreign enterprises accounted for roughly 14 per cent of employment. Over the same period a mere forty-five leading UK transnationals accounted for approximately 27 per cent. (Again, information on these firms comes from Stopford, Dunning and Haberich, 1980, and Stopford, 1982. There are forty-five firms rather than twenty-eight, as in Table 1.2, because the directories contain different information for different firms.)

Table 1.3 Share of foreign enterprises in the employment of total UK manufacturing, 1975–89, %

Year	%	Year	%
1975	12.40	1985	13.98
1977	13.92	1986	13.01
1979	14.07	1987	13.37
1981	14.85	1988	13.16
1983	14.49	1989	14.86
1984	14.84		

Source: Derived from Census of Production Summary Tables and Summary Volumes.

Table 1.4 Share of forty-five leading UK transnationals* in the employment of total UK manufacturing, 1975–81, %

Year	%	Year	%
1975	27.47	1979	27.12
1977	26.39	1981	27.71

* The firms included are those in Table 1.2 except Thorn EMI plc and Courtaulds plc, plus: British Aerospace plc, Consolidated Gold Fields plc, RMC Group plc, Turner and Newall Ltd, Bass plc, The Plessey Co plc, Brooke Bond Group plc, Glaxo Holdings plc, BOC Group plc, Imperial Chemical Industries plc, British Steel Corporation plc, The Bowater Corporation plc, British Petroleum Co plc, The Burmah Oil plc, Royal Dutch/Shell Group of Companies, Ultramar plc, Dunlop Holdings Ltd, Imperial Group plc and Rothmans International Ltd.
Source: Cowling and Sugden (1987a).

On the basis of these tables, we can see the importance of transnationals to manufacturing employment in Britain. Alongside the sales data, this strongly suggests that the possibility of a government strategy for approaching transnationals needs very close examination; it would be wrong to ignore such firms to the point of even refusing to give the possibility of a strategy close attention.

POSSIBLE EFFECTS

As noted earlier, there is an extensive literature on transnational corporations and much of this is devoted to the alleged pros and cons of these firms for particular economies. The precise identification of proven disadvantages and whether or not these are offset by benefits are not issues we wish to address in this chapter. They are the quagmire in which much debate on transnationals becomes firmly stuck, often preventing detailed consideration of policy options. This alone would cause us to avoid giving these issues substantial attention at the outset of our discussion. However, from the viewpoint of the volume as a whole, it will become clear that at no point do we need to identify and prove particular pros and cons in order to advocate government monitoring of transnationals as a means of appraising and influencing the activities of such firms. Indeed, that is a very important attribute of our proposal. Moreover as regards this chapter, our concern is the view that at least in some respects the impact of a transnational on an economy may be negative. This is a heavily qualified view. For example it only refers to the possibility of some disadvantages from transnationals' presence and, without implying the need to explore what they may be, does not deny that there are advantages. It does not even say that the disadvantages outweigh the advantages.

We suggest that although it could become very controversial to attempt a precise identification of proven costs and offsetting benefits, there is widespread agreement that there may be some disadvantages to transnationals' presence. This is reflected, for example, in the still very relevant Hood and Young (1979), Caves's (1982) explicitly neo-classical treatment and the more wide-ranging Dicken (1992). Possible disadvantages that have been discussed include adverse effects on economic development, employment and the balance of payments. Queries have been raised over trans-nationals' impact on competition, industrial concentration, techno-logical progress and working conditions. Concern has been expressed about their homogenising effects, their lack of sensitivity to local needs, stifling of local initiatives, sovereignty and autonomy. Some argue that there are problems over tax avoidance bordering on evasion, and over political interference (Gray, McSweeney and Shaw, 1984). Their size and, because they are essentially firms which produce in various countries, their flexibility, have led to disquiet about transnationals' net impact.

The point is not whether everybody can be convinced that each of these worries is justified. Rather it is that there is extensive acknowledgement of potential drawbacks, even if there is disagree-ment on exactly which issues matter and to what extent. There is a widespread view that at least in some respects the impact of a transnational on an economy may be negative. This alone suggests that a government strategy for approaching such firms should be considered.

CONCLUSION

By looking at evidence on manufacturing sales and employment we have shown that transnationals are significant players in the British economy. We have also pointed to the widespread agreement that there may be some disadvantages to transnationals' presence, with-out disputing the possibility that these may be outweighed by advantages. Taking these points together it can be concluded that the British economy is characterised by significant players, trans-national corporations, whose presence may have some disadvantages. For instance we have seen that foreign enterprises and a mere twenty-eight leading UK transnationals accounted for 36 per cent of manufacturing sales in the early 1980s. At the same time, foreign enterprises and only forty-five leading UK transnationals had a 43 per cent share of manufacturing employment. We conclude that one of the most important types of firm in Britain – perhaps the most important type – is also one where widespread opinion recognises potential drawbacks.

Faced with this there can be no doubting that the possibility of a government strategy for approaching transnationals needs careful examination. It would be a closed mind which reached any other conclusion.

From this basis, we will now build up to and explore the idea of monitoring transnationals. Our next step, in Chapter 2, is to analyse Britain's past policies, questioning their appropriateness and looking for possible deficiencies. We will in fact be raising doubts about government's knowledge of transnationals' impact, identifying disagreement over claimed benefits from transnationals' presence, and querying the absence of policies to minimise their disadvantages or maximise their advantages. In doing this, contrasting attitudes in other countries will be noted and then, in Chapter 3, explored in considerable detail. Particular attention will be on Japan, France and the United States. Again governments' information on transnationals' activities will be highlighted, as will be willingness to act against transnationals' alleged disadvantages.

Whilst Chapters 2 and 3 study approaches towards transnationals that have already been pursued or suggested in various countries, Chapter 4 is a turning point in our analysis. Building on the doubts and queries surrounding Britain's recent approach, the chapter will propose and begin to explore something different, a monitoring strategy. More specifically, we will advocate creation of a British Centre on Transnational Corporations, designed to collect information on transnationals' performance and impact, to prepare accounts, and to use these to influence economic policy and attitudes of and towards transnationals. It will be suggested that this simple strategy is potentially of significant direct benefit and would allow a government to progress at its own pace. We will explicitly address the views of both policy-makers who fear that monitoring will push investors to other countries and policy-makers with a strong belief in free markets. Chapters 5 to 8 will then explore our proposal in considerable detail.

In Chapter 5 we will present a framework for examining the

performance and impact of transnationals, drawing on our detailed reviews of government concerns in Japan, France and the United States (see, for example, Bailey, Harte and Sugden, 1994). The chapter will identify issues that might be of interest to the Centre. Given these, in Chapter 6 we suggest that any attempt to monitor transnationals will need to involve more than the collection of their annual corporate reports and accounts. We will discuss the alternative approach of constructing an economic and social account and, in the following chapter, use this and the issues framework of Chapter 5 to examine the publicly-available information concerning a particular firm, Glaxo. Our tentative attempt at an economic and social account of Glaxo also draws on social accounting practice, largely to illustrate what could be done. In Chapter 8 we draw together the comments from Chapter 7 and discuss the significance of our attempting to prepare an economic and social account of a transnational corporation.

Following this detailed exploration of the proposal for a British Centre on Transnational Corporations, and without drawing back from the proposal in any way, the volume will then reach another turning point. In Chapter 9 we will move from a strategy designed for one country acting alone to encompass the possibility of countries acting together. Our particular concern will be European Community initiatives; we will suggest that Britain advocates the creation of a European Centre on Transnational Corporations.

Our overall conclusion is that the strategy towards transnationals outlined and explored in this volume would be a considerable improvement on Britain's recent approach. It will be left to Chapter 10 to summarise our argument for what would be a significant step in a more appropriate direction.

NOTES

1 These firms are otherwise known as multinational corporations. For our purposes 'multinational' and 'transnational' are alternative labels for the same entity.
2 A recent survey is provided by Cantwell (1991).
3 See Cowling and Sugden (1987a) for more detailed discussion of the data in Tables 1.1 to 1.4.
4 Census of Production Summary Volume, 1989.
5 It is interesting to compare the number of foreign enterprises that have investments in Britain; in 1989, for example, the Census of Production Summary Volume put the figure at 1,356.

2

BRITAIN'S RECENT ATTITUDE

Before exploring possible strategies that a British government might adopt for approaching transnationals, we consider Britain's past policies towards these firms. This may enable deficiencies to be recognised and queries to be raised. Accordingly, we first examine Britain's attitude towards transnationals over the last 25 or so years.

The first section will consider the attitude towards British transnationals and the second section that towards overseas transnationals.[1] The first section will be very brief, reflecting the relative absence of past initiatives. For many countries it seems to be the case that in so far as transnationals cause any concerns at all, the prime focus is on inward investors; this has undoubtedly been true for Britain. It will be argued that British transnationals have generally been given a free rein but that governments have lacked appropriate information to support their policy. Turning to overseas firms, pages 12–17 will describe the attitude towards inward investors. In line with the discussion in the first section, no attempt will be made to chronicle every event and scrutinize each policy item, details which can be sought in the likes of Hodges's (1974) account of the 1964–70 Labour administrations, in OECD's (Organization for Economic Co-operation and Development) (1987) survey of member countries' policies as of August 1986 or in Bailey, Harte and Sugden (1994). Rather, we draw on these and other studies to characterise Britain's general position. We argue that successive governments have essentially given overseas transnationals a warm welcome, unrestricted and increasingly active in its encouragement. Reasons for this welcome are discussed in pages 17–21, where governments' apparent indifference to collecting and using information is again highlighted; our suggestion is that governments have been seriously hampered by their lack of information.

10

THE ATTITUDE TOWARDS BRITISH TRANSNATIONALS

There has been relatively little discussion of British policy towards British transnationals in the literature. Even such comparatively detailed reviews of government policy towards transnationals as Safarian (1983) have very little to say on the matter. This is a reflection of the lack of concern about the activities of these firms in Britain.

The basic approach of British governments has essentially been to give British transnationals a free rein to do as they wish, other than to influence their activities in the ways applicable to any firm. It is interesting to consider, for instance, the attitude towards outward investment. If any aspect of a domestic transnational's activity is likely to cause particular concern it is often outward investment. Yet according to Labour Party (1977) the only control on outward investment in the mid-1970s was the 1947 Exchange Control Act, which was only concerned with an investment's 'financial implications' and not at all with its 'industrial consequences'. Even with this limited care it seems that the Act was rarely used to control investments. Although Stopford and Turner (1985) observe that the Act 'put the Treasury firmly in the driving seat as far as control of outward investment was concerned', they conclude that 'incidents of negative effect for major investment proposals were . . . relatively rare' and that 'the real effect of the Treasury's work was of limited consequence . . . as far as the multinationals were concerned'. Moreover, the Act was repealed in 1979, leaving no controls whatsoever (Stopford and Turner, 1985; Globerman, 1986).

More recently, in 1988 when the Swiss giant Nestlé made a bid to take over the confectionary manufacturer Rowntree, the then Trade and Industry Secretary, Lord Young, boasted to the House of Lords that British-owned firms were creating an 'empire' by investing abroad, that Britain was 'buying up the world'.[2] He clearly saw outward investment as desirable and explicitly argued that it should not be jeopardised by referring the Nestlé bid to the Monopolies and Mergers Commission for investigation, thereby inviting retaliation from overseas governments. This is consistent with the free rein characterisation and suggests its basis: to allow British transnationals to do as they please is considered beneficial for Britain.

11

This is not an undisputed view. For example, the activities of British transnationals are arguably associated with deindustrialisation. This case is put by Cowling and Sugden (1987a). Drawing on Gaffikin and Nickson's (1984) conclusion that for ten West-Midlands-based transnationals domestic employment fell by 31 per cent over the period 1978–82 whilst overseas employment rose by 2 per cent, and Stopford and Turner's (1985) report that domestic employment in fifty-eight UK transnationals fell by 600,000 over the period 1972–83 whilst overseas employment rose by 100,000, they suggest that domestic transnationals are partly responsible for British deindustrialisation in the 1970s and 1980s. Similarly, for instance, Cowling and Sugden (1987a) raise the possibility of transnationals using 'divide and rule' tactics against a work-force which is not organised on an international basis; they question the effects for society of firms producing in various countries and being able to divide their work-force, thereby reducing labour's bargaining power and consequently obtaining lower labour costs. Nothing in their argument confines such tactics to overseas transnationals.

Moreover, it is also important to observe that allowing a free rein for transnationals has not been based on good information about their activities. Lack of information in the 1970s is noted in Labour Party (1977) and the problem has not gone away more recently. In the Thatcher governments of the 1980s, for instance, the policy's basis was most likely ideological faith in 'free markets'; it was not obviously knowledge of the impact of what British transnationals have been doing.

THE ATTITUDE TOWARDS OVERSEAS TRANSNATIONALS

A description

Overseas transnationals have generally received a warm, unrestricted welcome from British governments in recent years. This is illustrated by the following statement from Patrick Jenkin, then Secretary of State for Trade and Industry, speaking in 1982:

> This government, like its predecessors, welcomes inward direct investment into the UK. Since the lifting of exchange controls in 1979, non-residents have needed no official permission to invest in this country other than those, such as

12

planning consent, which are required of all investors. Foreign investors are assured of receiving equal treatment with their UK counterparts and are eligible for the full range of incentives and benefits provided to investors generally.[3]

When it comes to detail it might be argued that Conservative governments have offered an even warmer welcome than Labour administrations. For instance Hodges (1974) suggests the welcome was 'perhaps even less qualified' in Heath's government than in its Labour predecessor, and the Thatcher years witnessed a growing emphasis on attracting inward investors (see Young, Hood and Hamill, 1988). However, the existence of a Labour or Conservative government has made no substantive difference. This can be seen, for example, in Graham's (1982) discussion of the 1970s. He argues that in opposition the Labour Party criticised the Heath government's encouragement to foreign investors, seeing its attitude as too relaxed, yet the formation of a new Labour government in 1974 caused no genuine policy change; whilst initially the new government at least seemed to be seeking a firmer line this never really materialised and it ended up actively encouraging new investment from foreign-controlled transnationals.

It is not being denied that Britain – like just about every other country in the world – has had some restrictions over incoming investment (see OECD, 1987, the detailed review in Safarian, 1983, Stopford and Turner, 1985, and the more recent Young, Hood and Hamill, 1988). Many of these constraints have focused on non-manufacturing activity. For instance, the restriction of air transport licences to nationals unless the Secretary of State determines otherwise, the reserving of broadcasting for UK and European Community residents, special requirements for insurance companies with their headquarters outside the European Community, and limits on foreign share ownership in recently-privatised concerns such as British Telecom. But manufacturing has not been ignored. For example, when the 1947 Exchange Control Act was in force it was used to secure undertakings from some incoming investors, for instance, in the infamous Chrysler case. Even without this Act performance requirements have been imposed in some sectors, with the motor industry again prominent. Also the 1975 Industry Act provided for the relevant Ministry to stop control of an important manufacturing firm passing to a non-resident if this would serve the 'national interest', and the Monopolies and Mergers Commission has advised against foreign takeovers of British companies. This happened, for example, in the proposed takeover of the Davy Corporation by the US firm Enserch. The Commission apparently saw loss of national control as an important factor in this case.

Nevertheless, the instances of restrictions are relatively isolated and, when it comes to characterising the general policy perspective, pale into the background alongside the attitude illustrated by Patrick Jenkin's statement (although not everybody takes this view).[4]

The essentially warm, unrestricted welcome can be illustrated in a number of ways. More revealing than the fact that foreign takeovers of British companies could be referred to the Monopolies and Mergers Commission is that they have not been in almost every instance. We see some truth in Young, Hood and Hamill's (1988) point that the number of references is a poor indication of the strength of policy, for example, because the possibility of referral may deter bids. None the less they report that there were only ten major references of acquisition attempts by foreign firms between 1975 and 1986. This is recognised as 'a very small percentage of total acquisition cases' involving transnationals. Similarly Stopford and Turner (1985) report that between 1978 and 1981 a mere 2.2 per cent of acquisitions were referred. This is similar to the proportion of referrals involving acquisition by domestically-owned companies, 1.6 per cent. On the admittedly limited basis of these statistics it would seem that foreign firms have had no more to fear than their British rivals and that no firm has been under anything like a considerable threat. It is also telling that when the Conservative government continually referred bids by state-owned foreign firms in the early 1990s – five were referred between July 1990 and June 1991[5] – it was because they were state-owned, not because of concerns about transnational corporations or inward investors. Even this practice has now been abandoned.[6]

Likewise the potential of the 1975 Industry Act has hardly been exploited. It is also limited. Young, Hood and Hamill (1988) document that its provisions had never been directly used. They also note that under the Act 'control' means at least 30 per cent ownership. As we pointed out in Chapter 1, although there is controversy over the percentage of shares required to control a firm it is generally agreed to be far less than thirty for a publicly quoted company; presumably this would have been reflected in the Act if there was real concern about foreign control. As for the performance requirements in some sectors, at least much of the motivation seems to have been concerns over Japanese dominance (Young, Hood and Hamill, 1988[7]). Concerns over transnational corporations or inward investors as such do not appear to have been the main issue. Indeed it can be argued that requirements have been designed to protect and assist transnational firms from Britain, the US and anywhere else, except Japan.

Moreover, it is perhaps even more informing to consider in some detail the operation of the 1947 Exchange Control Act (see Hodges, 1974; Safarian, 1983, also Steuer *et al.*'s 1975 chapter on regulating inward investment). The Act meant that Treasury permission was needed for the import of capital to set up a new firm or to take over an existing one. In principle there were two criteria that determined whether or not permission was given: firstly, concern over the effect on foreign exchange reserves and hence the balance of payments; secondly, the wider implications of inward investment. Potentially the legislation was quite radical; it conferred considerable power to monitor incoming investment and even laid a basis for its control. Indeed it seems that at times control was sought. For example, when the American car giant Chrysler wanted to take over Rootes in the 1960s, the government secured various undertakings as a condition of permission. For instance, Chrysler was to keep a majority of British directors on the Rootes board; confirm expansion plans at various factories, especially Linwood; and achieve an export percentage at least as high as the average for the British motor industry. However, even in cases like Chrysler the government had no effective control; the undertakings attached to permission had no bite because the Act provided no systematic review to ensure they were satisfied and no sanction for breach. Not only did the government have no powers to pull Chrysler into line if it failed to meet its undertakings, the government seemingly did not even know whether or not the undertakings were being met. It appears that no information was collected.

One view is that the government was trying to control foreign-owned firms but that the legislation had a gross omission. The control view is expressed by Wallace (1982). Whilst characterising Britain as 'liberal', she uses the Chrysler case as an example of Britain's allegedly quiet negotiation with major inward investors over the terms of their entry. She does this recognising the absence of enforcement provisions. However, this absence is such an obvious fault that it cannot be convincingly argued that use of the legislation represents a genuinely firm line with foreign investors.

In fact another view is that the omission was deliberate. If correct, this highlights Britain's true policy even more clearly. Hodges (1974) claims that officials from the Treasury and (the now defunct) Ministry of Technology have suggested that one reason for Chrysler's undertakings was that 'they acted as a political escape-valve to reduce the possibility of criticism of permitting UK companies to come under foreign control'. This is plausible and would explain the lack of follow-up: why check what Chrysler has done if it is all a mere public relations exercise and actually giving the undertakings is sufficient to serve this purpose?

Moreover the Chrysler case can easily be taken out of context. It is exceptional. Even ignoring the fact that it was not a genuine attempt to control a foreign-owned firm, it was so unusual that it should not alter the opinion that British governments have generally given inward investors a warm welcome; at best, Chrysler would be an exception that proves the rule. This is certainly in line with Hodges's (1974) opinion, for instance. Following a very detailed analysis of the 1964–70 period he concludes that the Exchange Control Act's balance of payments criteria for determining permission presented little or no barrier to most potential investors and that the more general second criteria was apparently never used to stop any inward investment.

Another very interesting illustration of Britain's perspective and an aspect of policy that warrants recognition is the strenuous and increasing efforts it has made to sell itself to foreign investors. There is a fairly detailed discussion of this in Young, Hood and Hamill (1988), which refers to 'the creation and formalisation of more aggressive UK foreign investment attraction agencies at both national and regional level since the late 1970s'. For example, in 1977 the Labour government set up the Invest in Britain Bureau in the Department of Trade and Industry to promote Britain as a whole.[8] It has advised and assisted particular investors, and produced glossy booklets entitled *Britain The Preferred Location*. These focus attention on Britain's alleged advantages. For instance, the 1991 edition draws attention to labour costs which 'are markedly lower than those in the US, Japan or many other countries within the European Community'. It also echoes Patrick Jenkin's statement by observing that 'foreign firms are warmly welcomed, and they receive equality of treatment with British-owned firms'. Another function of the Bureau has been to co-ordinate the promotional activities of others. Particularly prominent have been certain regional agencies, for instance Locate in Scotland (LIS), Wales Investment Location (WINVEST) and Northern Ireland's Industrial Development ment Board (IDB). These were established by the Conservatives in the early 1980s. As Dicken (1986) points out, they have been very active and have even competed against each other!

Other illustrations could also be given to depict Britain's attitude. For example, no mention has been made of its pro-transnationals stance in the European Community (Hellman, 1977; Robinson, 1983). This is a point we will return to in Chapter 9. Nor indeed has mention been made of Britain's behaviour in international organisations more generally. Nevertheless, little would be gained by pursuing further illustrations as it would simply be labouring the point: throughout the last twenty-five or so years Britain has essentially given overseas transnationals a warm welcome, unrestricted and increasingly active in its encouragement.

Reasons

The overall explanation for this attitude is a simple view that has characterised all governments throughout the period: the presence of foreign-controlled firms is considered beneficial to Britain. We will now explore this view.

Governments' belief that inward investment is beneficial has been on insecure ground because the quality of their information has been very poor. Hodges (1974) argues that to the extent inward investment had its drawbacks 'they were not readily apparent' to the 1964–70 Labour government, 'particularly since there existed no machinery for giving special scrutiny to the activities of multi-national companies, and in most areas there was inadequate information on which to base a co-ordinated policy toward them'. He explains this as a result of divided responsibility for industrial policy across various government departments, none having a significant interest in transnationals. But even accepting Graham's (1982) report that the 1974–9 Labour government concentrated policy towards transnationals in the Department of Trade and Industry,[9] inadequate information has always remained a problem. There has never been a systematic, effective monitoring of inward investment in Britain.

Notwithstanding the lack of information – or perhaps because of

17

it – there is clear evidence that British governments have believed that inward investment is beneficial. For example, Hodges (1974) conducted in-depth interviews with twenty-eight senior civil servants in 1970–1 and concluded that they all saw inward investment as conferring net benefits, in line with the conclusion that he reached from examining the speeches of ministers in the 1964–70 government. Likewise Fayerweather (1982) surveyed legislators and permanent government officials in 1970. He found that they saw inward investors as having a fairly large effect which erred on the good side. Graham's (1982) survey of British Members of Parliament and senior civil servants in 1975 was similar to Fayerweather's and reached virtually the same conclusion; the vast majority of respondents saw the presence of foreign investors as at least to some extent good. Admittedly these results are not confined to the views of the government of the day but they provide a clear indication of beliefs.

More specifically, various sources of alleged benefit can be identified. Among these prominence has been given to the claims that foreign investment directly implies improved balance of payments, greater employment and a superior technology base (see the detailed discussion of the Treasury in Bridges, 1964; also Hodges, 1974, and Graham, 1982[10]). It has also been thought indirectly beneficial because a country which wants to gain from itself investing overseas can hardly be seen to reject investment from other countries. This was recently illustrated very clearly in the Nestlé takeover of Rowntree, as discussed on page 11.

However, these alleged benefits can be challenged, arguably revealing very insecure foundations for Britain's attitude. For instance, Lord Young's empire-building, seen in the Nestlé case, may be thought immoral, no better than a gangland leader advocating that gang wars are beneficial simply because he has the most powerful gang. In contrast the argument about superior technology may be thought to have greater appeal but even there it should be remembered that this is not necessarily a perceived benefit of a specific inward investment. This is revealed by Nestlé's takeover of Rowntree: a view from within the industry was that the takeover would not result in the British confectionary industry gaining better technology. Moreover, left unfettered inward investment's contribution to employment and the balance of payments is arguably beneficial in at most a superficial sense.

When an inward investor sets up a new plant, it tends to be assumed the resultant jobs can only reduce dole queues. But it has been suggested, for example, that such investment tends to be footloose (see Hymer's 1972 pathbreaking vision of the international division of labour and Cowling's 1986 analysis of deindustrialisation). According to this view, an overseas transnational that is enticed into Britain brings no long-run commitment; given a free rein it will be willing in the future to run down British production in favour of development elsewhere. Even such an apparently well-established company as Ford may be accused of this lack of commitment (see evidence in Cowling and Sugden, 1987a, of Ford's threats to cut back English car manufacture in favour of other European countries if workers fail to do as they are told, and in SMMT, 1984, and Jones, 1985, of it actually cutting back in the early 1980s). Thus it may be claimed that inward investment does not provide long-run, stable employment, at least in the general case, because this is arguably something which needs the development of firms with a commitment to a particular country. Furthermore, it may be similarly thought that whilst short-run balance of payments problems can be mitigated by financing industrial development using foreign currency, firms with the potential to leave a country at the drop of a hat will tend not to provide lasting, secure export potential.

Indeed the dispute goes deeper than an alleged failure to provide long run solutions. An implication of, for instance, Cowling and Sugden (1987a) is that a policy of unfettered inward investment may at least sow the seeds of severe employment and trade difficulties (see, for example, its discussion of monopoly power and stagnation). Consider also GLC's (1985) report of a (local) government fleet car buyer refusing to purchase BMWs because they were made in Germany but instead buying what it saw as British Ford Granadas, not realising that they were also made in Germany. This raises the possibility of an overseas transnational using its time producing in Britain to secure monopoly power in the 'host' market by identifying itself as essentially British and thus by exploiting 'Buy British' sentiments, and then taking advantage of this power using imports and overseas employment!

Thus governments' belief that inward investment is beneficial has been badly founded in terms of the information they have had available and there is dispute surrounding the extent of alleged benefits.

Nor is this the end of the matter. Even if it is accepted that foreign-controlled firms are beneficial to Britain, for the vast majority of people what this means is that their advantages outweigh their disadvantages (Hodges, 1974; Fayerweather, 1982; Graham, 1982). Believing this, yet nevertheless extending inward investors the sort of welcome we have described, is to do very little about either minimising the disadvantages or maximising the advantages.

There are various reasons for people in government supporting this inaction. For some, part of the explanation lies in the belief that any disadvantages are so insignificant they are irrelevant. This was probably the view of some in the Thatcher governments, at least. However, we suggest that the lack of information strongly implies that this is an inadequate foundation. Moreover, believing that the only significant impact of transnationals is beneficial does not excuse a failure to maximise the benefits; policy-makers who only recognise advantages to transnationals' presence should still query recent attitudes. In addition, some will have supported inaction because of their free market ideology, the belief that leaving resource allocation to a set of markets free from government influence is the way to maximise welfare. This ideology was very prominent in the 1980s. Its effect on inward investment policy is suggested, for instance, by comments from the then Industry Minister, Kenneth Clarke, defending the government's refusal to refer Nestlé's bid for Rowntree to the Monopolies and Mergers Commission; he reportedly upheld the operation of a capital market where the best use of resources is determined by the free flow of capital.[11] Of course few, if any, believe that markets should be totally free of government influence and it is ironic that the 1980s saw government more actively encouraging inward investment. To some extent this might be seen as government merely oiling market mechanisms, but in fact the encouragement has included subsidies and so on, initiatives undoubtedly intended to increase government influence over markets!

Another reason for inaction – and the one that has been more prominent within Labour rather than Conservative administrations – is the fear that if inward investment is not given a free rein it will disappear, i.e., that the cost to a country making any attempt to control overseas transnationals is that the firms will take their investment elsewhere (and as the advantages of their presence are thought to outweigh the disadvantages this would be undesirable). The fear is suggested by the comments of Sir Richard Clarke, then Permanent Secretary at the Ministry of Technology:

The government of the recipient country must accept that the multinational company must lay out its resources as it thinks right; and that if the performance of the local subsidiary is bad, nothing can stop the multinational company from drawing its own conclusion. . . . If governments get sensitive about this, they might be put in a quandary if they put pressure on a multinational company and that company refuses to cooperate. . . . The basic question is: do we want foreign investment? If we do we must accept the consequences.[12]

Again, the rationality of this view is not beyond dispute, a point implied by contrasting attitudes in other countries. We will shortly explore these contrasting attitudes in some detail.

CONCLUSION

This chapter has examined Britain's attitude towards transnationals over the last twenty-five or so years. We have suggested that both British and overseas firms have been given an essentially free rein. As regards the former we focused on outward investment. The attitude towards inward investors was explored in greater depth. We noted the argument that Conservative governments might have offered overseas firms an even warmer welcome than Labour administrations but suggested that the general attitude has always been warm. Having recognised that Britain is typical of just about every country in the world in so far as it has had some constraints on incoming investment, it was argued that these have been relatively isolated and transnationals have essentially been unrestricted. This was illustrated by considering Monopolies and Mergers Commission referrals, the unexploited and limited 1975 Industry Act, performance requirements and, in particular, operation of the 1947 Exchange Control Act. We also discussed the strenuous and increasing efforts Britain has made to sell itself to foreign investors, and indeed highlighted increasingly active encouragement as a general characteristic of Britain's recent policy.

The broad explanation for the attitude towards both British and overseas firms was put in terms of alleged benefit to the country. However, we raised doubts about governments' knowledge, for example suggesting that the assessment of inward investment has been badly founded on inadequate information. We also identified disagreement over claimed benefits, for instance, referring to the alleged association of British transnationals with deindustrialisation, divide and rule tactics, and the arguably superficial contribution of inward investors to employment and the balance of trade. Finally we commented that the sort of welcome inward investors have been given has done very little about minimising these firms' disadvantages or maximising their advantages. This was explored. For instance, we looked at free market ideology and the fear of discouraging investors. We suggested that contrasting attitudes in other countries raise doubts about the rationality of this fear. It is to these contrasting attitudes that we turn in the following chapter.

NOTES

1 The second section draws heavily on Sugden (1990a).
2 See *Financial Times*, 26 May 1988.
3 Quoted in Stopford and Turner (1985).
4 For instance, Government of Canada (1976) seems to believe Britain has not been very open; rather Britain seems to be seen as a country which has wished to attract foreign investment but which has bargained about terms and conditions of entry. In truth bargaining has occurred but to see Britain as having been anything other than very open is mistaken.
5 *Financial Times*, 11 June 1991.
6 *Financial Times*, 13 June 1991.
7 They point out that investments subject to performance requirements 'have been largely Japanese'.
8 See also the discussion in Dicken's (1986) survey.
9 Young, Hood and Hamill (1988) argue that 'Almost all the major government departments have some involvement with matters pertaining to inward investors, invariably by coincidence rather than by design'.
10 See also *Financial Times*, 25 March 1987.
11 *Financial Times*, 31 August 1988.
12 Reproduced from British North-American Committee (1970), emphasis added.

3

CONTRASTING ATTITUDES ELSEWHERE

It was suggested in Chapter 2 that some in Britain have feared inward investment will be non-existent if it is not given a free rein. It was also suggested that experiences elsewhere encouraged us to question this fear. Following on from these suggestions and more generally, we could usefully explore attitudes in other countries and contrast these with Britain. That is the task for this chapter.

Whereas so-called developing countries have been far and away the most active in formulating policies with respect to transnationals, for the purposes of exploring possible strategies for Britain it is especially interesting that even many developed countries have not allowed them free rein (see, for example, the surveys in Safarian, 1983; United Nations, 1983; Dicken, 1986; OECD, 1987). This is most notably true of Japan and France, although even the United States – one of the most relaxed countries when it comes to worrying about transnationals – in 1975 introduced the Committee on Foreign Investment (CFIUS) and the Office on Foreign Investment (OFIUS) to monitor, in a broad sense, their impact. This is particularly interesting if only because British policy-makers may be tempted to dismiss experience in developing countries as only relevant to other countries with economies at a similar stage of development, yet contrasting attitudes in the more mature economies of Japan, France and the United States – three countries that British policy-makers are likely to see as, for instance, direct competitors in international markets – may precipitate a reappraisal of Britain's approach and effectively lay a foundation for something new.

Hence the first three sections will consider[1] policies towards transnationals in, respectively, Japan, France and the United States. This will be followed in the fourth section by a discussion of contrasts with Britain's recent approach. Willingness to act against transnationals' alleged disadvantages will receive particular attention, as will the issue of information on transnationals' activities. The basic question that we will be left asking is: if Japan, France and the US can be more bold, why not Britain?

JAPAN

Over the last thirty or so years Japanese policy has responded to international pressures to open up to investment flows yet has maintained an awareness of potential problems associated with transnationals' activities. For example US Senate (1975) refers to an 'instinctive' fear of foreign intrusion upsetting the 'Japanese way' and identifies specific concerns, for instance that inward investors would be unresponsive to the 'informal, subtle but very effective system "administrative guidance"' linking government and business (see also Johnson, 1981). US Senate (1975) also quotes a very interesting comment from an official at the apparently very influential Ministry of International Trade and Industry (MITI):

> the world enterprise typically lets its parent corporation in the home country concentrate on the R&D efforts. If we allow world enterprises with this sort of behavioral pattern to come and operate in Japan as they please, we will likely suffer a critical slow-down of technological progress on our own footing.

On the other hand Japan has also recognised that the presence of transnational corporations can be associated with benefits. Again concerns about technology have been prominent (see, for example, Pearl, 1972b, on the 'facade of liberalisation' that began in 1967[2]).

Before 1967, Japan tightly controlled firms' activities using the 1949 Foreign Exchange and Foreign Trade Control Law and the 1950 Foreign Investment Law. Inward investment required government approval and was virtually impossible, except for joint ventures. This is reflected in the US $900 m of foreign direct investment in Japan between 1945 and 1971; in 1965 alone it was US $640 m in Germany, US $450 m in the UK and US $430 m in France, compared to a mere US $40 m in Japan (US Senate, 1975). Likewise it has been argued that in this period MITI 'had virtually complete control over Japan's external investment' (Robock, Simmonds and Zwick, 1977).

When first introduced, the Foreign Exchange and Foreign Trade Control Law and the Foreign Investment Law were sanctioned by the then occupying United States. This backing gave Japan a strong position when dealing with complaints about restrictions (Averyt, 1986). Nevertheless, pressure for change mounted. As one MITI official candidly admitted:

> MITI's basic approach has been to gain time as long as the opponents are not too angry. [The] frustration of the United States, however, has of late been rising noticeably. We have reached a point where an early liberalisation of capital transactions becomes mandatory.[3]

The result was carefully controlled inward investment policy alterations characterised by Pearl (1972b) as a 'facade of liberalisation which would quell foreign criticism and at the same time import technology and management techniques without endangering Japanese industry'.[4]

A series of alterations began in 1967. For example, without changing the underlying restrictive legislation, for the purposes of greenfield investment three types of industry were established (US Senate, 1975). Firstly, Category I industries, where individual investments were supposedly not screened if foreign ownership was less than 50 per cent and certain other conditions were met, for instance that the investment did not adversely affect existing Japanese business, the proposed venture did not intend a drastic change in Japanese ways of doing business and at least one Japanese partner held at least one-third of the total equity. These conditions encompassed very broad requirements and thus it is unsurprising that Category I investments often entailed 'very heavy negotiations indeed with government agencies' (US Senate, 1975). Secondly, Category II industries, where in principle 100 per cent foreign ownership was allowed but where in practice it seems that proposals were again intensely scrutinised to protect Japanese interests. Thirdly, investment in other sectors and over 50 per cent foreign participation in Category I industries. These still formally required individual approval.

The overall effect of these alterations was that more and more industries were progressively 'liberalised' yet government continued to screen greenfield investment at will, at least where Japanese industry also thought this was a good idea.[5] Moreover, it is revealing that the classification of industries into different types was a planned and controlled process (Johnson, 1982). For example, Category II sectors were initially those where inward investment was highly unlikely anyway, such as saké brewing and wooden clog production; MITI held off 'liberalisation' for industries until they had reorganised in ways suitable for their future development; and vital segments were omitted from the allegedly uncontrolled sectors, for example the television industry was declared liberalised but foreigners were unable to produce colour sets or use integrated circuits!

Furthermore, there were other catch-all barriers that the government could fall back on even in the supposedly uncontrolled sectors. For example, there was 'the screening of every enterprise within the framework of automatic approval, if the Minister so desires, both to gain approval and to insure that the enterprise is not "detrimental"' (Pearl, 1972a). This could be used 'to quash any otherwise impeccable venture which looks as if it might be both foreign-controlled and potentially too successful' (ibid.). Note that this was in addition to the more open screening when a proposed investment fell into a 'non-liberalised' area, or when criteria were not met. Thus approval was anything but 'automatic'. There was also much delay in formal screening. Moreover, another imaginative policy meant that all proposed joint ventures or wholly-owned subsidiaries remained subject to screening and approval by MITI under the Foreign Exchange and Foreign Trade Control Law or the Foreign Investment Law if they involved the introduction of foreign technology into Japan. As Johnson (1982) notes, 'it is hard to imagine a joint venture or subsidiary that would not include the introduction of some form of technology or know-how'. Thus simply by stating that any incoming investment would be screened if it brought in new technology, a quite innocuous policy at first glance, MITI could screen just about any investment it wished.

Hence despite 'liberalisation', Japan's basic approach remained illiberal; it was certainly not giving transnationals a free rein. However, pressure for further relaxation continued, with US complaints again prominent (US Senate, 1975), and thus a further round of alterations began on 1 May 1973 with the government announcing that Japan was '100 per cent liberalised'. This meant that non-hostile foreign bids for Japanese companies would be automatically validated, which in practice meant careful scrutiny![6] It was also supposed to mean that greenfield investment was uncontrolled but Johnson (1982) points out that Japan 'still protected some 22 industries as exceptions, still applied all the old rules about joint ventures and subsidiaries, and still maintained numerous administrative restrictions on both trade and capital transfers'! Seventeen of these exceptional industries were apparently the new strategic sectors MITI wished to nurture. Admittedly their '100 per cent liberalisation' was planned over the coming few years; for instance, computer manufacturing, sales and leasing was set for February 1975, information processing for April 1976 and integrated circuits for December 1976. However, yet again there was a process of controlled change; a pace and direction of change that responded to but was not dictated by outside pressure.

It is also worth noting that at least until the late 1970s Japan screened outward investments by domestically-based firms on a case-by-case basis. Various concerns were in issue; for instance, in the early 1970s attempts were made to encourage outward investment in national resource projects to improve access to foreign raw materials (Robock and Simmonds, 1983; Bergsten, Horst and Moran, 1978). It has been suggested that controls on outward investment were ended in 1972[7] but it would be incorrect to state that all restrictions were lifted. There was still government guidance over outward investment: 'the government maintains an industrial strategy policy that firms are expected to observe' (Robock and Simmonds, 1983). Some kind of review process continued in operation and, with increased sensitivity towards rising Japanese investment abroad, a review of political impact was added to the list of concerns (ibid.). Although approval was 'virtually automatic', denials were made on foreign policy grounds, and to avoid 'grave adverse effects on the national economy' (Bergsten, Horst and Moran, 1978).

Thus we see Japan as having a relatively tight rein on transnationals in the 1970s. As regards foreign firms, this is consistent with Averyt's (1986) view that until 1980 'all inward investment was considered intrinsically suspect unless the applicant provided specific evidence to the contrary', and Birembaum and Zackula's (1988) observation that prior to 1980, MITI and the Ministry of Finance 'retained broad discretionary power to disapprove foreign investment for a variety of reasons – or for no reason at all'.

A different view is presented in OECD (1979). This reports that in the period 1975 to 1977 there were 1,989 inward direct investment applications. Of these, twenty-eight were withdrawn on the initiative of the applicant, and one was rejected outright. The OECD (Organization for Economic Co-operation and Development) states that no inward investment proposals had non-customary or explanatory conditions attached. It concludes that 'restrictions on inward direct investments have been progressively relaxed' and 'such investments are fully liberalised'.

We suggest that this ignores two crucial points. Firstly, as Safarian (1983) notes, one has to remember that there are ways of discouraging applications, or of signalling that they would fail, without formally rejecting them. Birenbaum and Zackula (1988) illustrate this. Pre-1980, prudent foreign investors always consulted officials from MITI, the Ministry of Finance and the Bank of Japan prior to submitting applications. These officials frequently discouraged formal requests for approval of foreign investments, as part of their 'administrative guidance'. Secondly, the OECD is relying on information from the Japanese government, which will be keen to present itself as very liberal, and open to inward investment. We simply do not know to what extent the form and content of investment proposals was influenced by the Ministry of Finance or some other ministry, or indeed how many potential investments were not made because of government policy. This illustrates the problem in assessing countries' policies. Although very difficult, one has to look behind the somewhat bland statement of the OECD and the rhetoric of governments eager to appear liberal, to see what was really going on. Comments in the preceding paragraphs suggest an environment in Japan far from 'fully liberalised'. Indeed, this is implied by the continued pressure from OECD countries to open up, in response to which the Diet urged the Ministry of Finance and MITI in 1979 to amend the foreign investment laws.

In line with this, 1980 saw the government completely overhaul the legal framework, bringing out a new Foreign Exchange and Foreign Trade Control Law. Approval requirements for outward investments were apparently eliminated, although there is some doubt about this (see United Nations, 1988; Levey, 1989). On inward investment, formal entry restrictions on direct investments were generally ended, for example. Majority or 100 per cent foreign ownership was generally possible, whether greenfield or by acquisition, with or without the consent of the company concerned (Safarian, 1983). However, prohibition 'mechanisms were maintained, not abolished, moving in the terminology of government

28

documents from "prohibition in principle" to "freedom in principle"' (Safarian, 1983). If the inward investment was greenfield, or was an acquisition beyond certain limits (over 10 per cent of a listed company and any acquisition of shares of an unlisted company), or involved a substantial change in the business purpose of the company in certain cases, or another of a variety of situations involving control, then the investor had to give prior notice to the Bank of Japan, with the case reviewed by the Ministry of Finance and the relevant Ministry concerned (Safarian, 1983).

MITI and the Ministry of Finance had the power to suspend a transaction indefinitely, or could recommend the proposal be substantially changed under Article 27 of the Law (Birenbaum and Zackula, 1988). Neither an indefinite suspension nor a formal ministry request for amendments have taken place since the Act was initiated. From this, however, it would be incorrect to conclude that the investment climate was made 'liberal'. For instance, as Birenbaum and Zackula (1988) conclude, 'while the scope for exercising administrative guidance to deny foreign investment was reduced by the 1980 changes to the [Law], the practice is still very much alive'. Whilst there has been no formal blocking, there is disagreement over 'whether investments have been blocked informally or 'suspended indefinitely' through the operation of administrative guidance' (ibid.).

This notification system is clearly very flexible. The flexibility was evident in April 1986 when Trafalgar Holdings Ltd and Glen International plc failed to acquire Minebea Co., a high-technology concern and Japan's leading miniature bearing manufacturer (Ishizumi, 1990; Shinmura, 1989). In Shinmura's words, 'legal restrictions seem to have helped prevent Minebea from being taken over'. These included the filing of documents with the Ministry of Finance and other relevant ministries because the foreign firms intended to buy over 10 per cent of Minebea's shares. In addition, the Ministry of Finance concluded that as 10 per cent of Minebea's products were defence related, such as army pistols, industrial fasteners and aircraft bolts, it would postpone a decision. The 1980 law gave the government this discretion, and the 'decision-making process, normally completed within thirty days, was stretched out to four months' (Ishizumi, 1990). Meanwhile, Minebea placed shares with friendly shareholders and diluted Trafalgar's holding by issuing new bonds. In addition, it was argued by Trafalgar that the Ministry of Finance instructed Japanese securities firms not to co-operate with it in the take-over bid (Ames, 1986). This led Ames (1986) to conclude that 'administrative guidance is still very much alive in Japan'.

When summarising Japan's current approach towards inward investors, several writers stress its relative openness. For instance Booz, Allen and Hamilton (1987) observe: 'Japanese government restrictions no longer have any pervasive impact on direct investment decisions. Regulations still exist in selected industries, but they are no longer the primary barrier in most'. Turner (1987) argues similarly: 'in many areas, there is probably not a great deal more they can do to welcome foreign investors' (see also Watanabe's foreword, 'Japan is Now Truly an Open Market', in Ishizumi, 1990). Finally, in responding to the then French PM Edith Cresson's criticisms that Japan's market was closed, Mitsubishi's Chairman stated: 'I shouldn't say Mrs Cresson's attitude is obsolete, but she is clearly not aware of the current situation. What she refers to could have been the central focus five or ten years ago. I feel she should be brought up to date'.[8]

It does seem reasonable to conclude that direct investment in Japan is in some ways easier now than in the past. However, it is interesting that in a recent survey of investors by the American Chamber of Commerce in Japan, 31 per cent cited government regulations as a 'major factor' in inhibiting further investment, and a further 12 per cent as a 'minor factor' (American Chamber of Commerce in Japan, 1991). This hardly suggests a 'liberal' climate. Our view is that foreign investors still have to face potentially-significant hurdles. Japan has a flexible system which can be used restrictively where it is deemed necessary. Such flexibility was evident in the Minebea case. Such a view is consistent with past history and with the conclusion in United Nations (1988):

> the real test for the Japanese authorities will come when a genuinely established foreign company puts in an unwanted bid for a significant Japanese company. Legally there seem to be few barriers to such bids. Doubts, however, remain as to whether Japanese investors would yet be willing to sell equity control to a foreigner in such circumstances, and if they did, whether the Ministry of Finance would authorise the acquisition.

In such a case it would seem that the government would have public sympathy for action; a 1989 public survey indicated support for the protection of important businesses such as Nippon Steel, NTT, Toyota, Mitsui and Matsushita.[9]

What is crucial in understanding Japanese policy is that Japan has consistently pursued its own interests. It has not allowed itself to be dictated to by transnational corporations. Strategy in Japan has generally been Japanese strategy, rather than the strategy of transnationals. Japan has opened investment doors in response to outside pressure but when it has felt ready. Barriers have been eased once an industry was deemed strong enough to compete with foreign investment. Thus 'liberalisation' has in fact been a carefully-staged process. Moreover, as barriers have come down, the government has remained concerned about the dangers incoming transnationals could bring. This is seen very clearly from Wallace's (1982) comment that Japan's Fair Trade Commission has assumed investment monitoring functions, taking on a 'watchdog' role over incoming transnationals operating in Japan, to 'guard against any activity which would result in a competitive advantage over the domestic counterpart'. She goes on to note that the Commission has

> even taken the initiative, in keeping with the Japanese government practice of making and publishing periodic surveys on the activities of foreign-affiliated enterprises in Japan, to conduct its own study of potential problem areas caused by foreign-based multinationals in the Japanese economy.

Hence there is a sense in which there is no suggestion that Japanese policy has substantially changed since the 1960s.

FRANCE

Some features of French policy have similarities to those seen in Japan, for example: a trend towards more leeway for transnational corporations, outside pressure for change, alteration more apparent than real on a number of occasions, flexibility in policy and a concern over technology. Also like Japan, albeit less explicitly, France has shown an awareness of potential problems associated with transnationals' presence.

Before 1967, the formal position was that prior authorisation was required for inward and outward investments under complex exchange control regulations. The effect of this varied over time. For instance, in the mid-1960s the stance towards inward investment, especially from the US, became more restrictive; the

31

attitude was typified by the following statement from the Finance Ministry:

> All potential investments are scrutinised carefully to ensure that they contribute substantially to French technology or business know-how, or promote aid to important but expensive lines of research . . . we just object to anything that looks like speculation, a simple takeover, or an investment which France can perfectly well handle itself.[10]

The precise method used to block inward investment is unclear. One view is that it was simply by delay; although it was never admitted, 'it was widely reported that all applications for approval of new investment were blocked – simply by not being acted upon' (Gillespie, 1972). Torem and Craig (1968) state that outright rejection of investment proposals was very unusual and that instead pressure was put on applicants to voluntarily alter or withdraw applications regarded as 'unsuitable', although this does not seem to square with Manuali's claim that forty-seven out of 138 investment applications were denied from January to September 1965 (Torem and Craig, 1968). Yet whether the method was delay, or requesting applicants to withdraw, or outright rejection, inward investments were in fact blocked.

In 1967, the need for authorisation was replaced by a declaration procedure. This is discussed in particular by Torem and Craig (1968), a key source for much of our comment. The procedure was introduced under new legislation which provides a basis for policy up to the present day. As regards direct investments, for example, the change was seen as a liberalisation, because whereas before 1967 there had been a general requirement for prior authorisation, 'that which is not expressly forbidden is now permitted' and henceforth 'to block or delay an investment the government must assume the burden of intervening and expressing its dissatisfaction' (Torem and Craig, 1968). In practice, however, any liberalisation was more apparent than real.

Under the new procedure, foreign individuals and companies (and French companies under foreign control) had to submit a declaration to the Finance Ministry detailing any proposed direct investment. Virtually the same rules also applied to outward direct investment. In addition, non-residents had to declare an acquisition of a direct investment from another foreign individual or company. The same applied if a foreign corporation having a French subsidiary wished to merge with another foreign corporation. The last two requirements were an extension of the scope of investments subject to an approval procedure. In this sense, despite the acclaimed liberalisation, the law actually intensified control (Gillespie, 1972).

After receipt of the declaration, the Ministry had a period of two months in which it could request postponement, otherwise the investment went through automatically. This postponement could be permanent or temporary, to allow further examination or to allow the application to be modified. Once a final decision was made, if permanent postponement was not wanted the applicant was notified 'in a document that has all the attributes of an authorisation' (Torem and Craig, 1968). This 'authorisation letter' could also list conditions on the investment. In these situations follow-ups were provided to ensure fulfilment. The monitoring of transnationals' behaviour in this respect has carried on to the present day.

Accordingly, whilst the legislation was viewed as a liberalisation, in that prior to 1967 there was a general requirement for authorisation, it both widened the categories of investment subject to an approval procedure and in its administrative application continued with an authorisation process. Inward investments were scrutinised for their costs and benefits. True, outright rejections of investments were rare. Even for investments affecting the 'national interest', where the impact was so great that government approval was seen as crucial, the likely result was still ultimate approval. However, the point is that every proposed investment was considered, and in certain cases the disadvantages led to rejection.

The declaration procedure remained a cornerstone of French policy throughout the 1970s, although there were further changes. For instance, in 1971 inward investments from European Community countries were exempted from the procedure, in response to European Commission pressure. However, it is again interesting that this change was more apparent than real; exchange control regulations were applied to Community investors and hence French ability to keep a tight rein on transnationals was not affected (de Marsac, 1976).

In practice it seems that outward investment was encouraged in the 1970s and inward investment welcomed, yet the climate was not liberal (although again the OECD takes a different view[11]). Strict observance of the declaration procedure was insisted upon and worries over inward investment remained (Lea and Webley, 1973). For instance, there was concern that any single sector could be (or already had been) dominated by foreign interests. This can be seen in comments by Finance Minister D'Estaing.[12] Having described British investment in the food industry as 'excessive', he observed that

> concentrated investments in a single sector of the French economy are not desirable . . . we wish to see a more moderate development of investments and we will keep the technical means necessary to maintain such a development. There must be no ambiguity on this score.

Moreover, worries were translated into action; inward investments were blocked and modified (Bertin 1977; Behrman and Fischer, 1980).

Since 1980 there have been various changes and the French rein on transnationals has continued to become more relaxed. Among the alterations has been the introduction of a new procedure. In 1980 all outward and inward direct investments to and from other European Community countries were apparently exempted from any approval process. Henceforth the government only required prior notification of such investments; it appeared that the government only needed to be told of events. However, there was yet again a sting in the tail. The Finance Ministry had two months in which it could notify the firms that they fell within certain categories subject to a review procedure. These categories included investments relating to public order, health, security, defence materials; investments obstructing the application of French laws and regulations; and investments in sectors participating in the administration of public authority 'even occasionally'. Thus, although there appeared to be a relaxation for Community investments, there was still a screening process and the government could decide that investments fell into broadly-defined categories subject to review. Furthermore, inward investments from European Community countries by firms owned by non-Community companies were still subject to declaration (United Nations, 1985).

The notification procedure still remains a key aspect of French policy, although its details have changed since its introduction. More generally, by the early 1990s France had considerably relaxed its controls on inward and outward investment compared to earlier years. This is seen, for instance, in Table 3.1, which summarises the

Table 3.1 The French legislative position on inward direct investment as of June 1992

The meaning of direct investment

An inward direct investment covers:
(a) the purchase, creation, or expansion of a business in France;
(b) any operation leading to the holding by foreign residents of a 'controlling interest' in a French company. A 'controlling interest' is 20% of a firm's capital or voting rights if the company is listed on the Stock Exchange, or one-third of its capital or voting rights if the company is unlisted. A 'controlling interest' may also include any other form of control gained by the granting of loans, advances, warranties and so on.

European Community investments

In principle these are subject to prior *notification*. The Finance Minister has fifteen days to decide if they are subject to review. If nothing is said by the Minister, the investment proceeds automatically.

Non-European Community investments

These remain subject to prior *declaration*. The investment is deemed to have been approved if the authorities have not postponed (temporarily or indefinitely) the proposed investment within one month of the declaration being made. Investments under Fr10 m are subject to *notification*, similar to a European Community investment.

Exemptions

There are various exemptions from notification and declaration. In such cases a report generally has to be submitted to the government within twenty days following the investment. The exemptions include:
(a) greenfield investments;
(b) the expansion of an existing firm's activity;
(c) mergers and partial mergers between French companies under foreign control belonging to the same group.

Source: Adapted from a more detailed table in Bailey, Harte and Sugden (1994).

legislative position on inward direct investment at the time of writing. This position undoubtedly reflects a different welcome for overseas firms compared to the mid-1960s, for example.

Even with an increasingly relaxed attitude, however, the government has not had a hands-off approach. For example, some government officials have argued that it is because they have been firm with transnationals that they have succeeded in attracting Japanese investors.[13] Also interesting is DTI (1989) which notes that institutional advisers believed there is little French opposition to foreign bids '*so long* as the acquiror can indicate to the relevant authority that the investment will benefit France in terms of increased wealth and employment' (our emphasis). This is in line with Finance Minister Beregovoy's statement, prior to the blocking of the 3M (Minnesota Mining and Manufacturing Company) bid for Spontex in early 1989, that 'France should be open to foreign investments *when* these are economically profitable to the country; that is, *when* they are wealth creating'.[14] In other words, the government still has to be convinced of the benefits that would accrue from a foreign takeover. The DTI report concludes on this point that given the French government's concern to see that there is an 'industrial logic' to any takeover, 'the degree of uncertainty engendered by this may itself be seen as a formidable barrier by a would-be acquiror', and that 'even when management agrees to an offer [of a takeover], it is quite possible for there to be sufficient government interference to delay or prevent the success of the offer' (ibid.).

Several examples concerning particular firms illustrate government sensitivity to the transnationals' issue in the 1980s and 1990s. For instance, in 1988 there was an £88 m bid by the British publisher Pearson for the French newspaper *Les Echos*, whose owners agreed to the bid. The French Finance Ministry blocked the deal, claiming that Pearson – because it was 20.5 per cent owned by Rupert Murdoch (an Australian-born US citizen) – was not a European Community company and that rumours surrounding possible bids for Pearson meant that 'its capital is not stable' (DTI, 1989). The owners and staff of *Les Echos* publicly objected to the government ruling, and eventually the Finance Minister allowed a revised bid where Pearson acquired two-thirds of *Les Echos*, with purchase of the other third delayed for a year. The 1989 DTI report argued that the government had delayed the bid in an attempt to find a 'French solution'. A similar outcome was at issue in a case we have already mentioned, the 3M bid for Spontex. In September 1988, 3M announced that it had agreed to purchase Spontex. In an attempt to delay the deal and find a 'French solution', the government announced that the purchase would be referred to the Competition Council. Whilst the Council was considering the takeover, the French government gave 'indications' that it would prefer a 'French solution', and a counter bid was set up by a French consortium. In March 1989 the Competition Council cleared the takeover. However, the French government ignored this, announcing that it would block the 3M bid on the grounds that 3M/Spontex combined would have 76 per cent of the scouring goods market. With the foreign takeover blocked, the French bid could go ahead, and 'although the government officials insisted that the bid was blocked purely on competition grounds, many commentators were unconvinced' (DTI, 1989). In short, the government had used the Competition Council as a delaying tactic, and then ignored its advice anyway to ensure a 'French solution'! Even more recently there was an interesting case suggesting a concern over technology. In 1991 the newly-appointed Prime Minister, Edith Cresson, froze talks between the state-owned computer manufacturer Bull and the Japanese firm NEC. NEC wanted to swap its 15 per cent stake in Bull HN, a subsidiary, for just under 5 per cent in Groupe Bull itself, as part of a restructuring package designed to return Bull to profitability. Cresson asked Bull for more details on NEC's intentions and their likely impact. The government wanted to be certain 'that the long-term independence of Bull would be assured', a senior official stated.[15] The French government had to decide whether to trade off national independence in the computer sector for access to foreign assistance. Cresson finally concluded that there was no alternative; Japanese assistance was essential. Hence she reached a 'compromise' in the form of a promise from Bull that it would not allow NEC to gradually take control. In fact this was not strictly necessary, as legislation limits private firms to minority stakes in state-owned firms, with a condition that full government control is retained.[16]

Looking more generally at the French attitude towards trans-nationals over the last thirty or so years, one thing that stands out is that France has clearly not left everything to the market. It is true that the outright rejection rate for investments has been very low (Safarian, 1983) and that even where the impact of an investment has been so great that government consideration of the proposal was viewed as vital, the result was still likely to be ultimate approval. The crucial point, however, is that the government has made those decisions. While one might argue that the government has appeared to have had little impact, it is likely that their policies have influenced the shape and form of investment proposals. If an investment was authorised pre-1967, or was not postponed under the 1967 declaration procedure, or passed through the notification system in the 1980s, there was still some kind of screening process.

Our overall impression is that it would be wrong to simply characterise the French attitude as either obstructionist or liberal. Rather, France has taken an approach which has been astute and

37

inventive – illustrated by legislative changes with effects on policy more apparent than real; it has screened and considered individual initiatives; it has sometimes left transnationals to do as they wish and sometimes intervened in their activities; and all of this has been in an attempt to pursue French interests.

THE UNITED STATES[17]

In contrast to Japan and France, the United States has traditionally pursued an 'open door' policy towards foreign direct investment. It has also been at the forefront in pressing other countries to reduce their use of restrictions and incentives. Indeed, we have already seen this in our discussion of Japan. However, there have been concerns expressed by the government, Congress, organised labour and the public over various aspects of transnationals' activities. The nature of these concerns has changed over time as the US position in global investment flows has changed. In the 1960s and early 1970s the focus was on outward investment but it subsequently moved to inward investment. To some extent these concerns have been turned into actual policies, without thus far precipitating any fundamental change to the 'open-door' approach. They have also spawned a lively and interesting debate.

Consider for instance the United States' position on inward investment.[18] In the early 1970s, official Federal policy welcomed such investment for its perceived balance of payments and employment effects; in fact Lea and Webley (1973) labelled it the 'non-problem'. This changed in 1973, when inward investment surged to US $17.7 bn, a 24 per cent rise on the previous year. Congress therefore examined the 'open-door' approach and various bills were introduced with the aim of restricting transnationals (Gerowin, 1975). For example, the 1973 Dent-Gaydos Bill aimed to limit foreign firms to 5 per cent of the voting shares of a US public company.

As it turned out, Congress decided that a change in policy was not necessary. Nevertheless, Congressional hearings revealed a lack of detailed statistical information on the type and scale of inward investment. To rectify this, and more importantly to fend off more restrictive legislative proposals to which it was deeply opposed, the Ford administration seized on a 'moderate, one-time, information gathering proposal enacted to facilitate the formulation of an intelligent FDI policy' (ibid.). This was the Inouye-Culver Bill, later to become the Foreign Investment Study Act of 1974. The idea was to obtain information on foreign ownership by sector, owner, owner's home location, means of financing, net assets, cash flows and profit distribution (ibid.). This pattern, concern leading to bills being put before Congress and the administration agreeing to limited measures to thwart more ambitious proposals, has since been repeated on various occasions.

The Foreign Investment Study Act was not enough to stifle anxieties in the mid-1970s. Over 1974 and 1975 the Ford administration and the Treasury Department re-evaluated policy, concluding that no change was needed (Gerowin, 1975; US Committee on Government Operations, 1980). Nevertheless, various proposals came before Congress. These were attacked by the administration, stressing the economic loss that would result if foreign-based transnationals were discouraged from investing in the US. In further attempts to forestall restrictive legislation, however, the administration gave in to various measures in the mid- to late 1970s. These included the passing of the 1976 Foreign Investment Survey Act, which sought to conduct on-going surveys of direct inward and outward investment (US Committee on Government Operations, 1980). They also included the creation of the Committee on Foreign Investment in the United States (CFIUS).

CFIUS was set up in May 1975 by President Ford. This inter-agency committee includes permanent representatives from various government departments but, crucially it seems, is chaired by the Treasury representatives. CFIUS was charged with 'primary continuing responsibility within the Executive Branch for monitoring the impact of foreign investment in the United States, both direct and portfolio, and for co-ordinating the implementation of US policy on such investment' (reproduced in US Committee on Government Operations, 1980). In doing this, CFIUS was to: arrange for the preparation of analyses of trends and significant developments in foreign investment in the US; provide guidance on arrangements with foreign governments for advance consultations on prospective major foreign governmental investments in the United States; review investments in the US which, in the judgement of the Committee, might have major implications for US national interests; and consider proposals for new legislation or regulations relating to foreign investments as may appear necessary (ibid.).

If CFIUS decided that an investment has major implications for

39

the national interest, the CFIUS Chairman would inform the Economic Policy Group and the National Security Council asking them to agree to notify the foreign government involved in the investment. Whilst CFIUS did not have the power to block or alter a proposed investment, the Treasury was confident that in the case of investments by foreign governments, diplomatic pressure would be enough:

> it is almost inconceivable that a foreign government would persist in this country over the strong objections of the US government. Even if it were insensitive to the implications, it would realize that the US government could always take action after the fact.
>
> (US House of Representatives, 1978)

In addition, the Office of Foreign Investment in the United States (OFIUS) was created to support CFIUS. Since 1975 it has been given responsibility for monitoring and analysing the impact of inward investment. OFIUS was given a very broad remit. It was mandated to study a number of areas, comprising: the concentration and distribution of inward investment by industry, area and so on; the impact of inward investment on national security, energy, natural resources, agriculture, environment, real estate, employment, balance of payments and trade; the methods used for the inward investment, for example, whether by acquisition or greenfield, whether finance is domestic or foreign; and government laws and policies and how they affect inward investment. In addition, OFIUS was given responsibility for preparing reports and analyses for Congress, the public and itself, and for describing and analysing significant inward investment trends and transactions (see US Committee on Government Operations, 1980).

Hence on one level it might seem that CFIUS/OFIUS was an effective body looking at the entry of foreign transnationals into the US. This was the view of Canada's Foreign Investment Review Agency (FIRA) in 1982, in defending its own position. FIRA's belief was that not only had CFIUS reviewed a number of foreign investments over the years, it had also engaged in much more activity than it actually disclosed. However, Congress was highly critical in the late 1970s and early 1980s of government efforts in monitoring inward investment and its policy towards inward investment generally. CFIUS and OFIUS came in for particular criticism.

40

In 1980 the Congressional Committee on Government Operations reported on the adequacy of the government response to foreign investment (US Committee on Government Operations, 1980). Having noted that inward investment might have adverse effects on, for example, the balance of payments and competition, the report heavily criticised OFIUS for having done little. By 1980, it had prepared just five industry studies (four of which had yet to be published) and only two State studies. It had apparently failed to develop reliable quantitative techniques or models to measure more precisely the impact of inward investment, and was inadequate operationally. In addition, OFIUS had become engaged in promotional activity, which was not one of its mandated roles; the Invest-in-the-USA Bureau was responsible for this.

CFIUS came in for even harsher criticisms. It had allegedly met rarely and had done little (in contrast to FIRA's view). It had met only ten times in its first five years. Between mid-1976 and mid-1978 it did not meet at all. In May 1978 the State Department asked the Treasury to reconstitute CFIUS, because there had been significant developments, notably increased inward investment. The Treasury was apparently unperturbed. Treasury Secretary Carswell and Assistant Secretary Bergsten were more concerned that reconstituting CFIUS would be read by incoming transnationals as a change in policy and suggested an 'innocuous' public statement about the 'routine' nature of the meeting. This was allegedly typical of the Treasury's position; it was most bothered about foreign transnationals' perceptions and this dominated the way CFIUS operated. In fact CFIUS was seen as having been set up to enable the administration to keep its liberal position and as having played a central role in efforts to dissuade Congress from enacting new restrictions on foreign investment. A Treasury memo from Bergsten to Carswell cited by the Congressional Committee is particularly revealing: 'We have been able to reassure Congress that we could anticipate and deal effectively with any threats in this area, and at the same time maintain our basically liberal policy'. The Treasury's approach was seen as crucial to CFIUS's failure to function effectively and it was argued that the Treasury was particularly opposed to CFIUS becoming more active. The Committee on Government Operations concluded that the 'Treasury is extremely reluctant to have CFIUS review investments, irrespective of the implications to the national interest'. The fear, it seems, was that more frequent reviews would make CFIUS seem more like a screening agency.

The view of the Committee on Government Operations was that CFIUS had 'grossly neglected its responsibilities to the President, the Congress, and the public'.

Given this, the Committee called for a policy reassessment, arguing that:

> most other industrial countries manage foreign investment in a way that benefits their economies and minimises the harmful effect of such investment. There is no valid reason why the United States cannot manage its foreign investments with the same objectives.

It argued, for example, that the impact of inward investment had to be monitored and evaluated before a prudent policy could be formulated and implemented. The Committee endorsed a registration mechanism for investors; it was felt this would mean appropriate information would be disclosed and hence a suitable policy could be followed. The Treasury's line that this would bring retaliation from abroad and would reduce inward investment was rejected. In fact, Robock, in evidence to the Committee, had argued that some foreign transnationals might actually favour registration. He quoted a senior official from a French-based firm who had stated in most other countries they had found a door saying 'enter here to register', but they were confused when they could not find such a door in the US. More generally, in rejecting the Treasury's view that any restrictive legislation was undesirable, the Committee suggested that other countries engaged in such activity, and that this had not stopped US transnationals investing there. Restrictions, controls and performance requirements could be imposed in a way that did not discourage foreign investment, the Committee argued.

Despite its forceful criticisms and suggested alternatives, the Committee on Government Operations report did not yield substantive policy changes. In the ensuing few years, CFIUS continued in much the same way as before and Congress continued to be a focus for criticism. True, between 1980 and 1983 CFIUS reviewed twenty-five cases. One interpretation is that this increased activity may have been a response to Congressional prodding (Safarian, 1983). Whatever, Bale (1983) argues that it did not indicate a shift in the government's attitude.

Rumbling discontent was still being heard in the late 1980s, when the number of foreign takeovers led to queries. Foreigners were involved in 446 acquisitions in 1988, against 363 in 1987, with the

US $60.8 bn of funds committed by foreigners in 1988 accounting for 25 per cent of the total dollar value of all takeover activity in that year. Hostile takeovers were also becoming more common. For example, the five largest British investments in 1988 were all hostile (Ayres and Chubb, 1989). Debate was fuelled in particular by the US $2.6 bn Bridgestone (Japanese) acquisition of Firestone in 1988, which heightened Congressional and public concern. A survey reported in the *Wall Street Journal*[19] revealed overwhelming public support for tighter legislation on incoming transnationals, with 78 per cent in favour of a law limiting the extent of inward investment, and 40 per cent favouring an outright ban on any further inward investment (United Nations, 1988). Not surprisingly, therefore, in 1988 a number of amendments to the Omnibus Trade Bill were proposed relating to inward investment. Among these was the Exon-Florio Provision.

As in the 1970s, the administration reluctantly agreed to this measure to forestall other proposals calling for the disclosure of all foreign investments in the US.[20] Opposed to Exon and Florio's original proposals, the administration managed to weaken them to the point where it found them acceptable.

Under Exon-Florio, after it had been notified of a proposal by a foreign investor, CFIUS was given thirty days to decide whether to investigate, forty-five days to investigate and make its recommendations, and fifteen days for the President to announce his decision. The President was empowered to block a proposed acquisition, or to order divestment of a completed acquisition if there was 'credible evidence that the foreign interest exercising control might take action that threatened to impair national security' and if other laws could not be used to protect national security (Herzel and Shepro, 1990). In this the President had broad discretion. He only had to decide that there was 'credible evidence' that a foreign acquiror 'might take action' and his decision could not be over-turned by the courts (Davidow and Schott-Stevens, 1990). In addition, if notice was not filed then the time period did not start running and the government had an unlimited period to block the acquisition if it was felt necessary.

'National security' was broadly perceived by James Florio, co-sponsor of the bill; 'a strong economic base is as essential to national security as are weapons'.[21] Similarly, Ayres and Chubb (1989) note that Exon viewed national security as 'a broad, but not limitless, term', and that national security concerns could be raised by foreign acquisitions of US high technology firms not related to defence, communications or traditionally-sensitive industries such as energy. The breadth caused alarm amongst business; the only sectors implied as being safe were toys and games, food, hotels, restaurants and legal businesses.

The legislation also raised fears that it would be open to 'abuse' by US firms trying to fend off hostile takeovers. Knee (1989) pointed to Minorco's bids for Consolidated Gold Fields, arguing that Gold Fields managed to 'embroil' the US government in its defensive strategy by alleging that the takeover could increase US reliance on strategic minerals from South Africa (Minorco's largest shareholders were South African). This was seen as an example of the tendency for hostile takeover targets 'to attempt to use [Exon-Florio] for tactical or "defensive" purposes not related to true national security' (New York State Bar Report, 1989, in Knee, 1989). CFIUS reviewed the two separate Minorco bids and allowed them to proceed. Knee's point, though, is that it was not how many hostile bids triggered a forty-five day investigation, but that Exon-Florio could disrupt unwanted bids and could be used as a defensive weapon (Knee, 1989).

The administration tried to ease such fears by pointing to how the law was actually applied. Canner, Chairman of CFIUS, illustrated this; of the one hundred voluntary notifications in nearly a year of operation, all but five were approved in the thirty-day initial period. Of the five that did go to the forty-five-day investigation, three were approved by CFIUS, one was withdrawn, and only in one case was a negative verdict likely. This was Tokuyama Soda's proposed acquisition of General Ceramics, which made parts for nuclear warheads. In this case CFIUS made it clear it would oppose the acquisition, the bid was withdrawn and restructured to exclude the area of concern, and was then approved.[22] Despite the broadness of the legislation, it seems clear that the administration's attitude was that Exon-Florio was initiated, and was to be implemented, only as 'a last resort for protecting US security interests' (Davidow and Schott-Stevens, 1990).

By March 1990, notifications to CFIUS under Exon-Florio were running at around 350 a year, approximately half of all foreign acquisitions over US $1 m. Only seven investigations beyond the initial thirty-day period had been undertaken by CFIUS. Of these, two had been withdrawn, four had been approved by the President and only one was stopped. The latter came in February 1990, when President Bush ordered Catic (the Chinese National Aero-Technology Import and Export Corporation) to sell the US aircraft components manufacturer Mamco, which it had acquired at the end of 1989. The deal was blocked because Mamco made components for Boeing aircraft and CFIUS was concerned over earlier Catic attempts to gain military technology. Catic was given three months to dispose of Mamco. The administration stressed that this did not represent a change in US policy, and did not set a precedent on inward investment from China or elsewhere.[23]

Meanwhile, Congressional pressure for more stringent legislation has continued and there has been some support for this in government circles (Defense Science Board, 1990). A potential opportunity for change came with the October 1990 lapse of Exon-Florio. Democrats and Republicans tried to extend the scope of a renewed provision, and further bills have been introduced. For example, the Technology Preservation Bill was put before the House of Representatives in June 1991. It called for new criteria to block acquisitions which impair 'the industrial and technological base of the United States', and would have enabled the President to call for written assurances from an investor about its 'plans and intentions'.[24] The significant point about such bills is not whether they stood much chance of being passed – apparently most did not – but that they suggest a rising tide of concern.

As it was, in August 1991 Exon-Florio was made permanent and in December 1991 the Treasury issued its final regulations regarding implementation. These clarified Exon-Florio's application in various areas, for instance, making it clear that the review process cannot be used to give a target firm time to defend hostile bids. Most controversy, though, centred on Presidential powers over firms that do not submit notifications. This delayed publication of the regulations and eventually a compromise was adopted, government agencies being limited to a period of three years after an inward investment occurs to instigate a review.

Looking at the overall picture, inward investment flows into the US have caused considerable concern over the last twenty years. Whilst the administration has steadfastly opposed limits on the free flow of international investment – with limited exceptions on national security grounds – it has reluctantly agreed to a number of measures relating to inward investment to quell concern that government provisions were inadequate. These included information-gathering measures, the creation of CFIUS, and most recently

Exon-Florio. Nevertheless, both CFIUS and Exon-Florio have failed to satisfy many in Congress and outside that enough was being done.

What we have witnessed is a policy debate involving politicians in and around government. This debate seems to have gone in cycles: Congressional and public concern mounts, the administration reluctantly agrees to a limited measure to thwart more ambitious proposals, and then implements it in such a narrow manner, with support from the Treasury in particular, that concern soon mounts again that it was inadequate. This has happened with both CFIUS and Exon-Florio. At the time of writing this debate is ongoing and concern once more appears to be reaching a pitch. Recent history suggests it will be difficult for those pressing for more stringent controls to be successful; they will need to break out of the cycle. However, it is not inconceivable that this will happen sooner or later.

CONTRASTS WITH BRITAIN

In contemplating contrasts between Japan, France, the US and Britain, at this stage our concern is the general picture rather than specific details. This is not to deny that there are interesting comments to be made about the details and indeed to some extent we will return to these subsequently in the volume. Rather, in this chapter we are simply at an earlier stage in the argument about an appropriate transnationals strategy for Britain.

The first point to note is that countries' attitudes towards transnational corporations over recent years have clearly differed. Amongst the four countries we have considered, Japan and France are at one end of the spectrum, the United States and Britain at the other. The latter have both given transnationals an essentially free rein. The same cannot be said of either Japan or France, most obviously in the 1960s but also more recently. Of course this does not mean that Japan and France have chosen a better approach, but it does mean that Britain's attitude is questionable. Japan, for instance, is widely regarded as a dramatic success story in post-war development. We have not explored the precise contribution its transnationals strategy has made to that success, if indeed it has made any significant contribution at all. To explore such issues would take us far beyond the confines of a single volume. Nevertheless, a mere description of Japan's approach encourages us to ask questions of Britain's very different stance. In recognising this, it is also important to appreciate that our questions do not simply arise because of Japan's approach twenty or thirty years ago; they arise in light of our suggestion that Japanese strategy in the 1990s still leaves foreign investors facing potentially significant hurdles.

Moreover, a query over Britain's attitude also stems from events in the United States, even though we recognise that both of these countries have had an essentially identical policy. In Britain policy towards transnational corporations has received very little attention; not only has it been basically unchanged across governments, it has not been the subject of real dispute amongst politicians. In contrast, we have outlined a lively debate in the US. One interpretation of this is that Britain should take comfort. Although the US has had a long running debate, very little has changed in policy. Not only might this indicate a sound basis for the policy, but because Britain has taken the same stance it might suggest that Britain would be wasting its time opening discussion of the issue. However, another view is that the US debate suggests Britain's policy is perhaps inappropriate and should at least be reviewed. This is the view we take. We have recognised that it would be wrong to suggest that merely because Japan and France have taken a different stance Britain should necessarily make changes. Similarly, it would be wrong to argue that because the United States debate has in some sense essentially endorsed Britain's approach then that approach is necessarily appropriate. The main point is that the different stance towards transnational corporations in Japan and France, and the lively US debate, each mean that Britain's attitude is not beyond dispute. Hence the attitude should be questioned by those in and around British government.

It is also interesting to consider the views underlying these different experiences. In Chapter 2 we identified the broad explanation for Britain's approach as the belief that the country gains both from the presence of foreign-controlled firms and from allowing British transnationals to do as they please. The idea of benefiting from transnationals' activities is also a factor underlying the policies of Japan, France and the US, and alternatives raised in the US debate. Recall, for example, Pearl's (1972b) view of the Japanese 'facade of liberalisation' which began in 1967; in designing the changes, one issue was access to overseas firms' technology. Help with technological progress was also in issue when the French Prime Minister focused on NEC's involvement with Bull in 1991.

An implication of this is that to pursue or to advocate an alternative approach to Britain's is not necessarily to dispute that transnationals' presence can be beneficial. This is an important point to bear in mind. However, an interesting contrast with Britain is that the actual policies of Japan and France, and the debate in the US, reflect a greater willingness in these countries to consider and act against transnationals' alleged disadvantages. This has been illustrated time and again in the last three sections. The contrast over treatment of disadvantages is at the root of these countries' undeniably different experiences in recent history. (We recognise that it is also possible to identify particular instances in Britain where disadvantages have caused concern. Nevertheless, we suggest these instances are consistent with characterising British experience as typically different. Indeed, it is worth recording that one of the reasons we looked at Japan, France and the United States in such detail is that merely referring to specific illustrations can be deceptive.)

The contrast over treatment of disadvantages should again raise questions in Britain. This most obviously applies to those who believe that any disadvantages are so insignificant they are irrelevant – a view which Chapter 2 suggested was probably held by some in the Thatcher governments, at least – but it also applies more generally. For instance, we have pointed to the fear in Britain that the cost of a country making any attempt to significantly influence the activities of overseas transnationals is that the firms will take their investment elsewhere. Experience in Japan, France and the United States casts doubt over the rationality of this view. Japan and France have both received inward investment yet both have shunned the free rein approach. Indeed the section on France reported that some French government officials have argued that it is because they have been firm with transnationals that they have been successful in attracting Japanese investors. Moreover, the US debate is again interesting on this point. The fear seen in Britain is also seen in the US but there it has been challenged. Especially worth emphasising is the US Committee on Government Operations (1980) view that US firms had not been stopped from investing in other countries by restrictive legislation in those countries; the Committee argued that restrictions, controls and performance requirements could be imposed in a way that did not discourage foreign investment. If that is true for the US, then why not for Britain?

The final contrast we wish to focus upon concerns information. Chapter 2 observed that Britain's free rein for transnationals has not been based on good information about their activities. This issue has figured very prominently in the US debate and is the area where the government has been most willing to act. Especially relevant is the establishment of the Committee on Foreign Investment (CFIUS) and its associated Office on Foreign Investment (OFIUS). We have seen that, measured against the intentions and desires of Congress, these bodies have attracted substantial criticism. Nevertheless, they suggest another important question for those in and around British government: if even the United States – one of the most relaxed countries when it comes to worrying about transnationals – takes the information issue more seriously than Britain, is Britain making a mistake? Furthermore the relevance of this question and thus the further doubt over Britain's approach is reinforced by experience in Japan and France. Although our description for these countries did not explicitly focus on information to the same extent as our US discussion, this does not mean these countries take the issue lightly. On the contrary, an inherent feature of their tighter rein on transnationals is the belief that information on certain matters is essential. We have noted that both countries have screened investments. This has necessarily entailed the gathering of information. For instance, consider again the French declaration procedure, at the heart of which is a submission to the Finance Ministry detailing a proposed investment, and the French notification procedure, which at least implies knowledge of certain activities. The section on France also reported that there has been French monitoring after investments have taken place to ensure that any conditions have been met; compare this to Chapter 2's comments on the Chrysler takeover of Rootes, where it seems that the British government did not know whether Chrysler's undertakings were being fulfilled. As for Japan, recall, for example, Wallace's (1982) description of the Fair Trade Commission as a monitoring watch-dog. It seems that, in Japan, monitoring and a carefully-staged process of 'liberalisation' have gone hand in hand; by monitoring transnationals (both domestic and foreign) whilst implementing policies to develop domestic industries, the government has had the information it needed to decide when it was appropriate to make the economy more open.

CONCLUSION

Our task in this chapter was to explore attitudes towards transnational corporations in Japan, France and the United States, and to contrast these with Britain.

We suggested that Japanese policy over the last thirty or so years has responded to international pressures to open up to investment flows but that any alterations have been carefully planned, and have been influenced by an awareness of potential problems associated with transnationals' activities. Before 1967 Japan tightly controlled firms using the 1949 Foreign Exchange and Foreign Trade Control Law and the 1950 Foreign Investment Law. A series of so-called 'liberalisations' began in 1967, when various categories of industries were defined. Nevertheless, we characterised Japan as having a relatively tight rein on transnationals in the 1970s. Further changes were described for the 1980s but we argued that foreign investors are still faced with potentially significant hurdles, the concept of 'administrative guidance' being especially important in the 1990s.

France was also shown to have experienced a trend towards more leeway for transnationals. Before 1967, the formal position was that prior authorisation was required for investors under complex exchange control regulations. In 1967 a declaration procedure was introduced. We characterised this as a liberalisation more apparent than real. We also described further changes, for instance introduction of a notification procedure in 1980, and looked at various cases. We were left with the overall impression that it would be wrong to simply label the French stance as either obstructionist or liberal; we suggested that even though its attitude has become more relaxed, the French government still does not follow a hands-off approach.

A different picture was drawn for the United States, depicted as a country with an 'open-door' policy towards foreign direct investment but one where there has been an interesting debate. The latter was explored. We described a cycle: Congressional and public concern over inward investment mounts, the administration reluctantly agrees to a limited measure to thwart more ambitious proposals, and then implements it in such a narrow manner, with support from the Treasury in particular, that concern soon mounts again that it was inadequate. A lot of attention was given to the Committee on Foreign Investment, the Office of Foreign Investment and the Exon-Florio provision. Our conclusion was that more stringent controls on transnationals may be introduced in the future.

In contrasting recent Japanese, French and US experience with that in Britain, we focused on the general picture rather than specific details. It was argued that attitudes have clearly differed, Japan and France being at one end of the spectrum, the United States and Britain at the other. We suggested that this raises questions over Britain's stance. Moreover, this was reinforced by reference to the lively US debate. The discussion then turned to the views underlying different countries' experiences. It was noted that the idea of benefiting from transnationals' activities is a factor underlying the policies of Britain, Japan, France and the United States, and alternatives raised in the US debate. However, it was also noted that the actual policies of Japan and France, and the debate in the US, reflect a greater willingness in these countries to act against transnationals' alleged disadvantages. We suggested that this contrast should raise questions in Britain. For instance, it casts doubt on the fear that a country making any attempt to influence significantly the activities of overseas transnationals will receive none of their investment. The final contrast focused upon information about transnationals' activities and raised a further question: if even the United States – one of the most relaxed countries when it comes to worrying about transnationals – takes the information issue more seriously than Britain, is Britain making a mistake?

NOTES

1 We have provided further, more detailed information and analysis elsewhere: see Bailey, Harte and Sugden (1992c) on Japan, (1991a) on France, (1992d) on the US and (1994) on all three countries (as well as Britain and Germany).

2 It is also interesting to look at Behrman (1970). He quotes a director of the Fiji Bank arguing in 1967 that

the time for licensing [foreign firm's technology] is running out. US companies are becoming increasingly reluctant to part with technology without some equity interest – some insist on control – in the Japanese companies that will be using the patents and the techniques. Clearly, Japan may have to start acceding to the demands if the needed technology is to be obtained.

3 Quoted in US Senate (1975).

4 Pearl (1972b) also argued that 'the leaders of Japanese business and government remain unconvinced that free capital flows will be ultimately beneficial to them'.

5 Government was not all-powerful; see for instance Johnson's (1982) discussion of liberalisation in the car industry.

6 *The Times*, 26 April 1973.

7 *The Times*, 9 June 1972; 10 June 1972.

8 *Financial Times*, 31 May 1991.

9 *Financial Times*, 8 December 1989.

10 Quoted in Graham (1982).

11 According to OECD (1979), 'foreign direct investment in France is not normally restricted and, in practice the regime is liberal'.

12 *The Times*, 8 November 1972.

13 See *Financial Times*, 10 November 1986; 25 March 1987.

14 *Financial Times*, 22 March 1989, our emphasis.

15 See *Financial Times*, 24 April 1991; 18 May 1991; 25 May 1991.

16 *Financial Times*, 15 June 1991; 16 June 1991.

17 In looking at the United States our focus will be national (rather than state) policy.

18 Concerns over outward investment are discussed in Bailey, Harte and Sugden (1994), for instance.

19 *Wall Street Journal*, 8 March 1988.

20 *Financial Times*, 28 March 1988.

21 *Financial Times*, 28 March 1988.

22 *Financial Times*, 15 September 1989.

23 *Financial Times*, 3 February 1990.

24 *The Economist*, 29 June 1991.

4

A MONITORING STRATEGY

This chapter is a turning point in the analysis. Until now our prime concern has been with various approaches already pursued or suggested in different countries and not directly with the strategy we advocate for Britain. Building on the foundations of Chapters 1–3, we will now propose and begin to explore a strategy of monitoring transnational corporations.

The first section will briefly recap two especially important points that emerged in the previous discussion. In addition, the section will identify a third point that we suggest also needs to be heeded in designing a future strategy. Bearing this in mind, the second section will outline our monitoring approach. We will propose the creation of a British Centre on Transnational Corporations. This would collect information on transnationals' performance and impact, prepare accounts and use these to influence economic policy and attitudes of and towards transnationals. The third section will discuss various significant attributes of the approach, including the benefit it can offer a country. We will argue that the idea is a logical development from previous initiatives. This concern with experience will be pursued in the fourth section, emphasising that the proposal is unique and drawing distinctions from Canada's Foreign Investment Review Agency. The fifth section will consider some operational details of the envisaged Centre, including a cost estimate. The Conclusion will indicate ways that the proposal will be explored in subsequent chapters.

BACKGROUND CONSIDERATIONS

A point that was made very clear in our earlier analysis is that both Britain's recent attitude towards transnational corporations and the reasons for this attitude are open to question. Chapter 2 suggested that Britain has given both domestic and overseas transnationals an essentially free rein over the last thirty years. The broad explanation for this attitude was put in terms of alleged benefit to the country and particular reference was made to the believed advantage of free markets and the fear of discouraging investors. However, we identified disagreement and raised doubts about this under-lying reasoning. The alleged association of transnationals with deindustrialisation, divide and rule tactics, and the arguably super-ficial contribution of inward investors to employment and the balance of trade were all mentioned. Moreover, Chapter 3 noted significant contrasts with Japan, France and the United States. The stance towards transnationals in these three countries was described and then used to raise queries about Britain's approach. Without denying that the idea of benefiting from transnationals' presence may have some appeal, it was argued that the actual policies of Japan and France, and the debate in the US, reflect a greater willingness in these countries to act against transnationals' alleged disadvantages (thereby echoing the assertion in Chapter 1 that there is widespread agreement that there may be some disadvantages to transnationals' presence). It was also suggested that this greater willingness to act seriously questioned the fear that a country making any attempt to control transnationals will receive none of their investment. A conclusion we draw from all of this is that Britain's attitude towards transnationals needs to be re-examined.

Nevertheless, there is a further point which should be recognised and which has not been emphasised thus far: the reasons for Britain's attitude, though open to question, none the less impose real constraints on the relatively immediate policy options. More specifically, our impression is that belief in the advantage of free markets and the fear of discouraging investors are very real factors influencing many policy-makers and need to be kept uppermost in mind when contemplating a future strategy. If we are to design a new strategy which appeals to today's policy-makers it is important to address these factors; whilst our earlier comments will hopefully cause policy-makers to doubt their approach, they are unlikely to overcome many people's belief in free markets and/or their fear of driving investors elsewhere. In short, we need to design a (second best[1]) strategy which directly addresses these beliefs. Indeed it is partly because these beliefs seem to be so entrenched that this entire volume is intended to advocate a particular strategy via a series of steps designed to maximise appeal and acceptance amongst policy-makers reluctant to question and change their current attitude and, moreover, a strategy which is minimalist in the sense of being the least that can be done to significantly move Britain in a suitable direction.

A third point to emphasise is that Britain has lacked appropriate information on which to base its policy and, compared to Japan, France and the United States, has failed to take the information issue seriously. This is again something which was made very clear in our earlier analysis. Chapter 2 pointed to the inadequate information on British and overseas transnationals, for instance, referring to the absence of any systematic, effective monitoring of inward investment in Britain. Stark contrasts with Japan, France and the US were noted in Chapter 3, which ended with a pertinent question: if even the United States – one of the most relaxed countries when it comes to worrying about transnationals – takes the information issue more seriously than Britain, is Britain making a mistake?

Particularly bearing in mind these three points – namely: that Britain's attitude towards transnationals needs to be re-examined; that Britain has lacked appropriate information on which to base its policy and has failed to take the information issue seriously; that there is a real belief amongst many British policy-makers in the benefits of free markets and/or the strong likelihood of discouraging investors – we are now in a position to outline a new approach.

OUTLINE OF A STRATEGY

We suggest that a worthwhile alternative is to establish a British Centre on Transnational Corporations. This would collect information on transnationals' performance and impact, prepare accounts and use these to influence economic policy and attitudes of and towards transnational corporations.[2] This approach would deal immediately with the three points raised in the last section. It is simple, potentially of significant direct benefit, and it would be the start of an evolutionary process of policy development which would allow a government to feel its way forward at its own pace, without trying to move too quickly too soon. These attributes should become clear as we proceed.

What we have in mind is a Centre that has the ability to collect information on issues that are deemed to be important. We will discuss the identification of these issues in Chapter 5. Resource constraints would prevent the continuous observation of every aspect of every transnational, but it would be appropriate to continuously monitor especially important issues in a set of larger corporations and randomly[3] monitor other areas and other firms. It is envisaged that the Centre would process information by compiling 'economic and social accounts' of particular transnationals. These would be formal accounts which would go beyond traditional accounting concerns to encompass the wider economic and social consequences of transnationals' activities. For instance, they could report effects on employment quality and quantity, competition, regional development and technological progress. The Centre would then analyse the accounts very broadly; the impact of transnationals would be explicitly highlighted and policy possibilities discussed. By doing all of this a British Centre on Transnational Corporations would prove to be a valuable new[4] initiative.

SIGNIFICANT ATTRIBUTES

The value that should be attached to a Centre compiling and analysing economic and social accounts is in some way analogous to the value that equity investors attach to the preparation of conventional financial statements for particular firms and then to investment analysts discussing these accounts. In other words, we are proposing that society bases the pursuit of its interests on a systematic approach with similarities to that used by equity investors as a foundation for their pursuit of private interests.

More particularly, any future policy-makers hampered by fear that investors will be pushed elsewhere would at worst have little to lose by creating a Centre but at best a lot to gain. Creating a Centre need not imply reduced efforts to market Britain to potential investors and would be consistent with offering assistance to attract certain firms, if this is what a government wanted. Furthermore, by its terms of reference a monitoring body could be required to explore immediately its own impact on potential investors;[5] economic and social accounts could be compiled and analysed with any fear paramount. On the one hand, if it reveals that the fear is indeed justified and in fact outweighs all of its offsetting benefits, the monitoring body could be instantly disbanded without any significant loss in investment. At least government policy would then have a solid foundation, unlike in the past. On the other hand, should the fear prove groundless, a government might have set itself on a more suitable policy direction. For similar reasons, policy-makers with a strong belief in free markets would at worst have little to lose by establishing a Centre but at best would have a lot to gain.[6]

The potential benefit would essentially originate from three areas. Firstly, generalising an argument just made, the monitoring strategy would provide a pool of knowledge which might enable the formulation of coherent, detailed and successful strategies in the future. We have already indicated in Chapter 2 that British govern-ments have lacked good quality information; recall, for instance, Hodges's (1974) view that there was ignorance about drawbacks to inward investors' presence in the 1960s and that there was generally inadequate information to formulate a co-ordinated policy. Such ignorance, which has typified all of recent history, is surely unacceptable; it leads to errors of omission and commission in the design of policy. A Centre's accounts and analysis would attempt to rectify this defect. Precisely what the future strategies would be is obviously something unknown at this point in time.

A second and related source of benefit is that a Centre's analysis would provide a permanent catalyst and focal point for broad discussion of strategy options. The idea is for a Centre to discuss policy possibilities; this is included in its analysis of accounts function. It might thereby lead to more detailed and complete strategies in the future. Again, the form future strategies would take is unclear. Part of the Centre's aim would be to explore possibilities in the context of the accounts it prepares. The possibilities might include something similar to strategies pursued in Japan. Perhaps they would entail initiatives closer to the French approach. Possibly a detailed strategy for bargaining with investors, as advocated in Sugden (1990b). Whatever, a crucial point is that the Centre would be a stimulant, contributing to and activating discussion, potentially leading to something which goes beyond mere collation and analysis of information. Thus not only would creating a Centre be a coherent and systematic approach to the transnationals issue in itself, by its very nature it might spawn other strategies in the future. Moreover, it would be part of an on-going process; it would institutionalise concern with transnationals in a permanent body. This matters, for example, if it is felt that there is a potential downside associated with transnationals that will not go away and will not remain static. Establishing an appropriate monitoring body can ensure that a strategy for approaching transnationals remains prominently on the policy agenda.

Third, the information a Centre would provide might have significant direct effects because it might beneficially influence transnationals' behaviour. The reason is that transnationals arguably trade on ignorance, see, for instance, GLC's (1985) report of German-made cars being bought as British and more generally Sugden's (1990b) view that its image is an Achilles' heel for a transnational. Our argument is very simple: by dispelling ignorance the information a Centre provides might influence consumers' perceptions of a firm, thereby affecting the firm's sales and therefore causing the firm to alter its activities. For example, suppose a firm has monopoly power in Britain because it is seen as a domestic producer yet it has in fact run down British activity in favour of production overseas. The firm may be induced to regenerate British production by consumers being made aware of its deindustrialisation strategy.

What is emerging from all of this discussion is that a notable characteristic of our proposal is its inherent flexibility; it not only leaves all future options open, it actually facilitates and encourages their consideration. Hence, for example, it accommodates policy-makers whose attitude towards transnationals is likely to change over time.

Moreover, an even more notable characteristic is that the necessary and sufficient conditions for accepting that monitoring is worthwhile are extremely weak. Accordingly, policy-makers with very different attitudes towards transnational corporations could find monitoring acceptable. It is necessary and sufficient merely to accept that, in an economy: (a) transnationals are important actors; (b) there may be scope to significantly influence their impact in the interests of society. Monitoring is worthwhile if it is felt that transnationals only have important positive benefits and that these may be made significantly more beneficial. It is sufficient but not necessary to believe that transnationals have important advantages and disadvantages, that the disadvantages may be substantial and that it is a reasonable possibility that these disadvantages can be significantly mitigated. It is not necessary to believe that transnationals are the big baddies of the modern world. Nor is it necessary to believe that they can undoubtedly be influenced to yield better effects. We have already suggested in Chapter 1 that (a) is the case for Britain and (b) is a clear implication of Chapters 2 and 3.

A further attribute of our proposal stems from our earlier discussion of contrasts between Japan, France, the United States and Britain. We suggested that each of these countries, except Britain, has taken the information issue very seriously. For instance, we argued that an inherent feature of the tighter rein on trans-nationals in Japan and France is the belief that information on certain matters is essential. What this means is that the creation of a British Centre on Transnational Corporations can be seen and presented as following in the footsteps of Japan, France and the US. Thus although it would be making a significant break from the past and be doing something extremely important, it would hardly be doing anything particularly radical. It is a logical development from events elsewhere. This might appeal to policy-makers who, for one reason or another, are wary of changing Britain's recent approach.

A UNIQUE APPROACH

Having established that creation of a British Centre builds on the experience of other countries, it should be recognised that we are proposing something which is not precisely the same as initiatives advocated or pursued elsewhere. As far as we are aware, no country has done what we are suggesting. Although others have 'monitored', in some sense, this has at least tended to be part of something more, for example, some form of screening process.[7] For instance, out-ward investment has been screened and thus in some sense 'monitored' in France, Greece, Ireland, Italy, Portugal, Spain, Norway, Sweden, Japan and Australia (OECD, 1979; Globerman, 1986). This volume is unambiguously not advocating screening of transnationals' activities. Moreover, whilst there is little public knowledge of how countries have gathered and processed information on transnationals, our ideas about systematically preparing and analysing economic and social accounts seem to be novel.

There is little or nothing to be gained from labouring these points by examining every country's policies. Nevertheless, a common reaction to our suggestions is the argument that a very similar approach was adopted by the Canadian government when they introduced the Foreign Investment Review Agency (FIRA), yet this has since been replaced as unsuitable. Thus it is argued that our suggestions have already been discredited in practice. This argument warrants a response. Accordingly we will now outline aspects of Canadian policy and then distinguish our proposals.

Growing concern over the degree of foreign ownership in the Canadian economy prompted the Gray Report in 1972. This criticised the performance of foreign transnationals operating in Canada, and recommended the establishment of a Foreign Investment Review Agency to try to improve the net benefits from inward investment (Safarian, 1983). The Foreign Investment Review Act established FIRA in 1973 at the federal level, to screen foreign investment applications. FIRA was wide-ranging, applying to all greenfield investments and any proposed acquisition of Canadian firms with assets over C $250,000 or gross revenues over C $300,000 (United Nations, 1978). Expansion of an existing foreign-owned firm was not reviewed unless it was into a new area of business (Safarian, 1983). However, a change of foreign parent did necessitate review. In assessing investments, attention was paid to the criteria listed in Table 4.1.

Table 4.1 Criteria for assessment of investments, and for subsequent 'monitoring', under Canada's Foreign Investment Review Act

The effect of the investment on the level and nature of economic activity, including the effect on:
  Employment;
  Resource processing;
  The use of parts, components and services produced in Canada;
  Exports from Canada.

The degree and significance of participation by Canadians in the Canadian business and in any industry in Canada of which it forms a part.

The effect of investment on:
  Productivity;
  Industrial efficiency;
  Technological development;
  Product innovation;
  Product variety.

The effect of the investment on competition within any industry or industries in Canada.

The compatibility of the investment with national industrial, economic and cultural policies.

Source: Safarian (1983).

The review procedure aimed to ensure 'significant benefits' for Canada, and incoming firms could be required to make undertakings relating to the criteria. After investment had taken place, the 'monitoring' process generally continued for five years.[8] In the few cases where undertakings were not met they were renegotiated by FIRA, which also had the power to take legal action against transnationals refusing to comply with the terms and conditions of their investment.[9]

The annual rejection rate for proposed investments ranged from a high in the teens to a low well under 10 per cent.[10] Such figures were seized on by both those in favour of a strong policy and those against. The former argued that FIRA was too soft – 'more like a lapdog than a watchdog' (Fry, 1983) – whilst the latter argued that foreign investors were deterred because of the 'secretive, arbitrary nature of the review process' (Fry, 1983). The critics of FIRA prevailed and the coming to power of a Conservative government in 1984 marked a distinct shift in policy. FIRA was replaced in 1985 with the Investment Canada Act establishing a new agency, Investment Canada, specifically to encourage and facilitate investment in the country. This prompted Prime Minister Mulroney to announce that 'our message is clear here and around the world . . . Canada is open for business again' (quoted in Raby, 1990).

Put alongside our earlier comments about the envisaged British Centre on Transnational Corporations, this description of FIRA's activities suggests two very different initiatives. FIRA was essentially an agency for screening inward investment applications and for negotiating investment conditions. The British Centre on Transnationals would not screen investments and would not negotiate conditions; in this sense it would do less than FIRA attempted. Rather, the Centre would collect information on the performance and impact of British and overseas firms, prepare and then analyse economic and social accounts. The idea is simply to provide an information base, to discuss strategy possibilities and to dispel ignorance. This focus is very different to that of FIRA. In short, it is wrong to argue that our proposals amount to establishing a FIRA-like institution for Britain. Furthermore, if the real argument in raising the FIRA example is to suggest that it deterred investors and a British Centre would do the same, we can at least repeat that the Centre's remit could include immediate exploration of its own impact on potential investors.

OPERATIONAL DETAILS

Although the proposed Centre is very different to FIRA, a lesson from Canadian experience for the operational details of our envisaged policy is that a government should clearly specify the Centre's aims and remit. We mentioned earlier that FIRA was criticised for its allegedly secret and arbitrary review process, apparently deterring investors. More generally, it seems that investors value clarity and simplicity in policy design. Without denying that there may sometimes be advantages for a government in leaving some uncertainty – for instance the French have arguably benefited from a policy towards transnationals that has been flexible because it has been secretive and vague – there is no merit in deterring investors by designing unclear, complex policies without good reason. In our case, there is nothing to gain from government failure to unambiguously specify the aims and remit of the Centre. Indeed, this is effectively one reason why we have taken the trouble to distinguish the Centre from FIRA!

Turning to other operational details, it is difficult to be too precise, for instance, because a strategy for approaching transnationals would have to fit into a wider industrial policy, consideration of which goes far beyond this volume. Nevertheless, various points are worth discussion.

We have in mind a Centre that prepares accounts by bringing together information currently in the public domain and, where necessary, by obtaining further information from firms themselves. We would like to see firms co-operating with the Centre, although this might not happen. In fact it is not inconceivable that some firms' response to the envisaged monitoring approach might be very obstructionist, and as a consequence preventing the Centre from functioning effectively. In this case there would be a need for subsequent initiatives to improve the information flow, although the obstruction could be itself revealing about transnationals' activities. This illustrates the general point that the Centre would need to learn from its experience.

In collecting and processing information there is a need to be systematic, coherent and consistent. In a sense this should go without saying yet the latter contrasts with experience in Britain. An aspect of British industrial policy has been to give firms regional aid and, to a limited extent, government departments have gathered information on use of the aid. This review process has been criticised by the National Audit Office (1988), suggesting inconsistency in the standards to which different government departments have done different aspects of the job. None the less, Bachtler (1990) suggests Britain has been broadly in line with other countries; he argues that it has been less stringent than some but that this is reasonable given the relatively lower amounts of aid on offer. Bachtler's view also has a useful implication for the British Centre on Transnationals: the idea should not be to monitor at all costs, rather to monitor to the point where the marginal cost of doing so equals the marginal benefit. This is particularly important to bear in mind when considering the Centre's preparation of economic and social accounts. The nature of these accounts and the difficulties in their preparation – issues discussed in subsequent chapters – means that a Centre would have to be conscious of drawing a line, beyond which attempts to collect and process information would not yield net benefits.

The general aim of the Centre would be to provide publicly available accounts and analysis. We recognise that there may be problems of confidentiality over firm specific information in certain circumstances and the Centre would need to work out procedures and mechanisms for maintaining confidentiality, where appropriate. However, the general objective should be openness. Three of the reasons underlying this view are as follows.[11] Firstly, we have argued that one of the Centre's explicit purposes would be to dispel public ignorance. This necessarily requires public access to its accounts and analysis. Secondly, we have argued that another of the Centre's significant attributes would be for it to provide a permanent catalyst and focal point for broad discussion of strategy options. Again, this stimulatory, proactive function necessarily requires openness. Thirdly, unless the Centre is a transparent organisation producing publicly-available accounts and analysis there is a very real danger of its capture by transnational corporations. When preparing accounts the Centre would attempt to co-operate with transnationals, which would provide it with information. This would give the firms ample opportunity to essentially takeover the Centre and turn it into an instrument serving their purposes. Openness is one way of trying to prevent this happening.

Another operational aspect of the Centre concerns its relationship to government departments and ministers. We envisage a distinct public agency directly responsible to the Cabinet Minister for Trade and Industry. A close relationship with the Minister is vital, bearing in mind the thrust of this volume, namely, that a strategy for approaching transnationals is an important aspect of government industrial policy. Even so, because the Centre is designed to be a catalyst and stimulant in discussing strategy options, it is important that views expressed in its analysis are not seen as necessarily those of the Minister. The Centre would need a degree of freedom to prompt and promote discussion. Thus it would need to be created as responsible to, yet not a mouthpiece of, the Minister. As for its relationship with the Department of Trade and Industry, the Centre could participate in the Department's activities at appropriate points but there would be no gain from actually bringing it within the Department. The Centre would be carrying out the sort of function easily handled by a separate public agency and, at least in terms of the Department's current organisation, to put the Centre within the Department would run a severe risk of its becoming entangled in a Whitehall, Civil Service bureaucracy. Moreover, it would also run a risk of the Centre being diverted into other Departmental concerns and hence losing sight of its aims and objectives.

In line with this, we envisage a dynamic agency that is not civil servant-dominated. The idea is to staff the Centre with a core of experts from various disciplines and assorted backgrounds. These experts would bring different but relevant perspectives to bear on the Centre's tasks. They would be drawn from the worlds of business, academia and the Civil Service. The experts would include technologists, management scientists, lawyers, as well as economists and accountants.

As for the Centre's size, it is impossible to be categoric if only because our unique proposal means that the Centre would need to learn and adapt from its experience. Having recognised this, however, if the Centre is to have a telling impact it must monitor a significant number of firms. We suggest that a reasonable target would be to prepare economic and social accounts for seventy-five transnationals each year. Judging from the data we presented in Chapter 1 – where, for instance, it was reported that a mere forty-five leading UK transnationals accounted for roughly one-quarter of total UK manufacturing employment in the early 1980s – a target sample of seventy-five would suffice, at least to begin with; it would be enough firms to ensure the Centre focused on a significant segment of the British economy. The seventy-five would be chosen to encompass both British and overseas firms, reflecting the concern with transnationals and not firms from particular countries. Fifty of the transnationals would be continuously monitored over several years, at least. They would be amongst the largest firms.[12] The continuous monitoring would enable a profile and analysis to be built up over time, and implies limited resources being focused on those firms likely – because of their relative size – to have an especially significant impact, a priori. The other twenty-five firms would be randomly chosen each year. The seventy-five firm target would not be suitable for the Centre's first year of operation, given the learning process that would have to occur; perhaps it would be sensible to build up to the target over, say, three years. Based on our experience in attempting to prepare an economic and social account for Glaxo, and on the observation that it seems private sector investment analysts tend to assign one specialist to each industrial sector they are concerned with, we tentatively suggest that the preparation and analysis of seventy-five accounts would require a core staff of fifty to seventy-five experts. The latter would also need computing, administrative and secretarial support.

The cost of this would probably be £7–10 million per annum. This figure is based on comparison with Britain's Monopolies and Mergers Commission and Office of Electricity Regulation (OFFER). In 1991–2 the Commission had an annual budget of £6.16 million. Its staff numbered approximately thirty-three Commissioners, some of whom were part-time, and one hundred others, including accountants, economists, lawyers and secretaries. Over the same period, OFFER had a total staff of approximately 220 and a budget of £10 million. To put our estimated cost in perspective, Brech and Sharp (1984) estimate that government tax reliefs and expenditures to the benefit of merely foreign-controlled transnationals in the year 1981–2 amounted to £1,500 million. This suggests that even £10 million for a Centre monitoring both British and foreign firms is a relatively small amount.

CONCLUSION

We have proposed the establishment of a British Centre on Trans-national Corporations. It has been suggested that this simple strategy is potentially of significant direct benefit and would allow a government to proceed at its own pace. We began to explore this strategy; the intention is to do so in greater detail over the next four chapters.

Chapters 5 and 6 will consider, in general, the nature of the information the Centre should collect and the form of accounts it should prepare. Chapter 5 will maintain this volume's broad aim of drawing from experience. It will identify issues that have concerned governments in France, Japan and the United States over the performance and impact of transnationals. We will suggest that these issues might be of interest to the proposed British Centre. Given this, Chapter 6 will analyse the form of accounts that the Centre should prepare. As indicated earlier and as will be explored in considerable detail, we reject the sole use of traditional historic cost (or even current cost) accounts, such as those currently filed by some subsidiaries of transnational corporations with the Registrar of Companies. Instead, the preparation of economic and social accounts is advocated. This will be followed in Chapter 7 by a detailed case study; the proposed accounting method will be explored by examining Glaxo, a transnational widely hailed as very successful in recent years. We are not in a position to mimic what a Centre could do and accordingly that will not be the aim. However, the chapter will give some indication of what can and cannot be reported using currently available public information on Glaxo. The significance of our tentative attempt to prepare an economic and social account of a transnational corporation will then be discussed in Chapter 8.

NOTES

1 When examining policy options, there are two basic choices. One is to pursue a first best solution. This would be an ideal strategy from the viewpoint of a particular criteria, for example, Pareto efficient allocation. The other is to design what might be called a second best strategy, something which takes account of the overall economic, social and political environment. We are focusing on the latter. In doing so, we are not advocating that anything be sacrificed in terms of theoretical rigour or the quality of analysis more generally. We are merely extending the analysis beyond relatively abstract considerations.

2 Some may believe that establishing a Centre is doomed to failure from the outset, because of secrecy problems in gathering information and so on. This reveals the power they believe transnationals wield and, if anything, puts a greater premium on Britain's need to design a new approach to such firms.

3 Chick (1990) discusses random investigation of monopoly abuse by firms.

4 Concern with information is not a new policy idea for Britain, see for instance Labour Party (1977), calling for 'substantial new legislative requirements on disclosure of information by . . . British and foreign-owned multinationals' as part of a much wider package, Wilms-Wright (1977), and Hood and Young (1981) on the attraction and regulation of inward investors. However, we believe our analysis is different in various respects. For instance, in so far as we are aware, no others have given the same emphasis to systematic information gathering and

processing as the start of an evolutionary process of policy development, and no others have proposed the continuous, wide-ranging compilation and analysis of economic and social accounts that we envisage. As regards a concern with information in other countries, this is discussed subsequently in the text.

5 Clearly the assessment of the impact of introducing a Centre would be a complicated matter, both technically and politically. For example, transnationals could suggest that decisions to postpone or redirect investment were due to the conditions created by the Centre, even if this was not the case.

6 Likewise, the same would be true for those fearing British transnationals would suffer from retaliation by other countries if Britain established a Centre; the Centre's terms of reference could accommodate such worries.

7 The United Nations has produced a manual (primarily for developing countries) on 'monitoring' transnationals, covering the need to 'monitor' and sources of information, United Nations (1991).

8 Personal communication from John Knubley, Director of Research at Investment Canada, 18 December 1991.

9 Ibid.

10 Personal communication from John Knubley, 8 November 1991.

11 A fourth, more controversial reason, is that social efficiency necessitates democracy, an argument explored in general by Cowling and Sugden (1993b) and one which, in the context of this volume, requires that a monitoring body provides public accounts and analysis.

12 The firms might not be the largest, bearing in mind (1) the aim of covering both British and overseas transnationals, and (2) the desirability of covering a range of sectors.

5

ISSUES OF CONCERN

We have suggested that a British Centre on Transnational Corporations should collect information on transnationals' performance and impact. More specifically it should collect information on issues that are deemed to be important, should continuously monitor as regards especially important issues and should randomly monitor as regards others. To operationalise this idea it is necessary both to identify the issues about which information could be collected, and to determine their separation into especially important and other concerns. It is necessary to identify the Centre's agenda of concerns and to prioritise items on this agenda. These problems are the focus of this chapter.

To illustrate the sorts of issues that would be on the agenda and to form a starting point for more detailed discussion, it is both useful and interesting to look at other countries' concerns. In the spirit of our earlier analysis, this is not to say that these issues must preoccupy a British monitoring body; it is merely to say that some are likely to be relevant and that all warrant consideration, in order to determine the relative importance (or lack thereof) in the British case.

With this in mind, and again in keeping with our earlier analysis, we have accordingly attempted to identify the main issues that have concerned France, Japan and the United States over recent years. The results will be presented in the first section. The specific focus on these three countries is useful for the same reason that it is useful more generally when considering a British strategy for approaching transnationals; experience in the mature economies of France, Japan and the US – countries which British policy-makers are likely to see as, for example, direct competitors in international markets – may be seen as especially relevant to Britain. The first section will present and discuss a matrix of concerns in the three countries. It will include detailed consideration of how the matrix was derived. It will be left to the second section to concentrate on how these issues might be relevant for the Centre and how they can be classified, reflecting different priorities. As will be seen, the issues cover a wide range of economic and social matters; the range leads us to suggest that a Centre would need to construct economic and social accounts of the impact and importance of individual transnationals.

CONCERNS IN FRANCE, JAPAN AND THE US

The starting point for our research was the English language literature on government policies and attitudes towards trans-nationals (e.g., Dicken, 1986; Gillespie, 1972; OECD, 1979, 1987; Safarian, 1983; US Senate, 1975). Although a number of prominent studies had been prepared in the past dealing with the position in different countries over shorter periods of time, there was little by way of specific country studies over longer periods.

Our project sought, in the first instance, to review policies and practices over the last thirty years in three industrialised countries, France, Japan and the USA. A paper was prepared which reviewed developments in each country in chronological order, divided into specific time periods (often based on changes in government or specific industrial policy changes). These papers formed the basis for Chapter 3. They covered policy instruments and government action, in addition to what was stated or could be inferred to be of concern to governments. The reviews also incorporated specific examples of transnational corporation-government relationships, particularly in respect of (attempted) takeovers and plant closures. Both inward and outward investment were reviewed. Each of the papers prepared was discussed at length by the researchers and circulated widely as research papers for comment (Bailey, Harte and Sugden 1991b, 1992a and 1992b). Specific papers, dealing largely with inward investment, were also published (Bailey, Harte and Sugden 1991a, 1992c and 1992d).

The research reports were then used to identify specific issues of concern to governments of the three countries over the last thirty years. At this stage we simply sought to prepare a list of matters of concern, such as balance of payments, employment and impact on the exchequer. In some respects this was a very basic form of

69

content analysis (Kassarjian, 1977), where emphasis was on identifying issues and broad concerns, rather than some attempt to measure in quantitative terms either significance or frequency.

The next stage was to make sense of the long list of issues, to summarise it in some way and to exclude, where possible, any duplication of points. This was done in the first place by preparing a summary of issues of concern drawn from literature on monitoring transnational corporations (e.g. Labour Party, 1977; Safarian, 1983; Globerman, 1986; Sugden, 1990a) and our research papers referred to above. This resulted in a very broad categorisation of matters under four headings; financial (specific transnational details alone), financial (transnational details relative to some wider scale), other economic issues and non-economic issues. Specific detailed issues were listed in subgroups under the four main headings. We then took this analysis and our discussions, and proposed a more detailed categorisation drawing more on our specific country studies than previously. This was the first draft of our issues framework.

The next stage involved using the issues framework to review the country studies and record the instances of interest. This was tried, leading, after some further discussion involving all three researchers, to a final list of seventeen issues as seen in Tables 5.1 and 5.2. This agreed classification was then used once again to record the relevant details contained in our three country studies. Using the three research papers we identified situations where concern was expressed by government, recording them under their relevant time period within the overall thirty years, producing three matrices. The matrices were prepared by one researcher and checked thoroughly by another. This led to lengthy discussions and some changes before we agreed the details contained in Tables 5.1 and 5.2. The individual country matrices are presented together in summarised form in Table 5.1 with the further details of specific matters of concern outlined in Table 5.2.

The neatness of Table 5.1 hides a number of complexities, which will already have been clear to the reader from our previous account of its preparation. First this is clearly a summary, and so involves considerable loss of information. Table 5.2 presents the necessary background data, although the specific detailed matrix for each country, based on Table 5.2, is presented in Bailey, Harte and Sugden (1994). In addition, the table cannot reveal the extent to which the emphasis under specific headings may have changed over

Table 5.1 French, Japanese and US Government concerns regarding transnational corporations, 1963–93

Issues	FRANCE				JAPAN				UNITED STATES			
	1963–5	1966/7–80	1980–8	1988–93	Pre-1967	1967–73	1973–80	1980–93	Pre-80	1973–	1980–8	1988–93
1 Ownership and control	X	X	X	X	X	X	X	X		X	X	X
2 Competition	X	X	X	X	X	X	X	X		X	X	X
3 Research and development/technology	X	X	X	X	X	X	X	X	X	X	X	X
4 Productivity and efficiency						X						
5 Impact on Exchequer	X									X	X	X
6 Employment and industrial relations	X	X	X	X	X	X			X	X	X	X
7 Balance of payments (inc. repatriation of profits)	X	X	X	X	X	X	X	X	X	X	X	X
8 National 'competitive' position	X			X	X		X	X				
9 Compliance/co-operation with wider economic and industrial policy	X	X	X	X	X	X	X	X				
10 Regional impact/development policies	X	X	X	X		X		X	X			
11 Use of national/local components and resources	X			X	X		X			X	X	X
12 'Basics'				X	X			X	X	X	X	
13 'Fairness'	X	X	X	X	X	X			X	X	X	X
14 'Cultural issues'				X	X	X						
15 Openness, accountability and information						X		X	X	X	X	X
16 Environmental impact						X						
17 Miscellaneous	X	X	X		X	X	X		X	X	X	X

Key: X indicates an issue of concern to the government.

Table 5.2 Analysis of the issues of concern

1 *Ownership and control*

Concern regarding takeovers
Changes in ownership
The structure of the enterprise
Local participation as shareholders
Local management/directors
Importing managerial techniques
Concern to protect key sectors (not technological)
Loss of decision-making powers

2 *Competitive implications*

Concentration/market share/industrial structure
Marketing: Pricing
               Marketing policies/strategies
               Distributional impact
'Pressure' on small- and medium-sized local businesses
Concern over licensing/technical agreements, e.g. restrictions on price
Not access to the most 'lucrative' (highly profitable) sectors
Level of concentration of foreign ownership in the industry
Prevention of a competitive challenge in a particular sector

3 *Research and development/technology*

Concern to protect key sectors
R&D/technological processes the firm can bring or take abroad
   ('technological impact')
Ownership/transfer of technology and dependence
Product innovation/variety/quality
Training
'Accelerating modernisation'
Concern that the most profitable or advanced production activity
   would be saved for the foreign parent
Whether encourages or discourages national research

4 *Impact on productivity/'efficiency'*

Value added
Division of value added
Desire to export low productivity activity

5 *Impact on the Exchequer*

Taxation: Income and Corporation
Transfer pricing
Whether the target firm had received government funds (in the case of
   an inward acquisition)

6 *Employment and industrial relations*

Rate of 'exploitation'
Conditions of work and life
Job quality
Job security

Table 5.2 Continued

Employment prospects (number)
Equality of opportunity and treatment
Impact on industrial relations/trade unions
Competition for scarce labour

7 *Balance of payments/international trade*
Currency stability (including financing)
Currency convertibility
Size of capital outflows/concern over repatriation of profits
Balance of payments
   – impact on imports
   – impact on exports – new export markets
                         – strengthen trade links

8 *Impact on national 'competitive position'*

9 *Compliance/co-operation with wider industrial and economic policy*
Whether 'indifferent to national interest'
Impact on the 'smooth running' of the economy, or its rehabilitation
Maintenance of 'order' in native firms/must not adversely affect
   domestic firms
Supplementing domestic investment activity
Scale relative to national investment levels
Compliance with monetary policy
Economic independence
Contribute to 'self-support and sound development' of the economy
Inflationary impact
Impact on national income

10 *Regional impact/development policies*
Treatment of local/regional community
Location of investment – fits with regional policy
                         – regional policy impact
Subcontracting
Impact of sudden divestment

11 *Use of national/local components and resource processing*
Concern that investments use local resources and components
Concern that raw materials are not exported
Concern to secure raw materials from abroad
Energy

12 *'Basic'*
Involving, for example, national security, public order, health and safety

13 *'Fairness'*
Not acceptable if 'unfair'
Not free from fraud, duress or 'undue influence'
Ethical

Table 5.2 Continued

Bribery
Not 'speculation'

14 *'Cultural issues'*
'Local way' of doing things

15 *Openness/accountability/information*
Disclosure of international activity
Information gathering
Openness in conducting takeover

16 *Environmental impact*

17 *Miscellaneous*
Political involvement/donations
To/from which country
From a foreign government
Whether had 'harmful' political consequences

Source: Bailey, Harte and Sugden (1994).

time or differed between countries. For example, Japan's concern with technology has changed from initially allowing only licensing agreements to later encouraging inward investment to link up with domestic research and development activity (Bailey, Harte and Sugden, 1992a). Similarly, in France there was a change from concern with inward investment as a whole to concerns with acquisitions only, and in some cases only when the investment was greater than a certain sum (Bailey, Harte and Sugden, 1991b).

Some changes may also have been more cosmetic than real. The concentration of research in this area on what governments say rather than do makes this a real danger. There appears to be very little research which compares actions with intentions. There is also the problem of quite contradictory matters appearing under the same heading. For example, Competition covers the desire to attract investment in order to stimulate local economic activity as well as the fear of the impact of incoming transnationals on local business (a particular concern of Japan's).

Terminology was also a problem. The same concern may have been expressed differently between countries and over time meanings may have changed. One example of such problems of terminology concerned the matter of technology, where in Japan and France initial concerns to protect local business seem to have given way to a desire to work with and obtain the benefits from incoming foreign firms. We should also note the fact that two of the three countries are not English speaking, and so there may be limitations of our classification due to translation.

We should also acknowledge that for some time periods we worked on less information than others. Since much of our literature is secondary, particularly in the case of France and Japan, this problem is probably inevitable. For example, we have somewhat less detail for France in the period 1980–8 and Japan for 1973–80. As a result we could either deal only with what we discovered or we could examine the periods before and after to look for details of any changes in concerns. We chose to do the latter. In the absence of contradictory detail we have assumed continuity of concerns.

Another problem arose from the issue of single cases. Although much of our evidence of interest comes from documented secondary sources, which draw on specific government statements, there are also the individual cases of government actions. We have treated actions as indicative of concerns, even where only in response to a single case or corporation.

In contrast there are instances of expressed concerns where there may not have been government action. There are also cases where there may have been further criteria which were not made public (for example, see Gillespie, 1972, reporting on the position in France in the 1960s). The tables also fail to reflect the relative importance of matters to governments. This is partly a result of the limited research on the activities of governments, in contrast to the reviews of their stated interests, as well as the undoubted difficulty of attributing significance to statements and actions in the political arena.

Although we have outlined our detailed approach, emphasising its arbitrariness and our attempts to control or audit, alternative matrices could and would be prepared by other researchers. Yet this should not be a matter of too great concern to us here, since it is the overall impression of the tables rather than every specific detail which is of most concern. The tables should therefore not be taken too literally. They are intended to give the reader a general impression of matters of concern to the three governments over the last thirty years.

ANALYSIS OF THE ISSUES OF CONCERN

Despite the acknowledged limitations of our tables the seventeen heading analysis of issues of concern is sufficient for our purposes here. Our intention is to illustrate the extent to which matters such as these have been of concern to the three countries and various governments over the last thirty years. We do not intend that this list be seen as our suggestion for use by the British government in setting up a Centre, but rather that this is an indication of the concerns in comparable countries, and so might at least be of interest to a British Centre on Transnational Corporations. Clearly a British Centre would wish to set its own agenda of concerns, reflecting current government policies and community interests. We suggest, however, that Tables 5.1 and 5.2 could contribute to the discussion of the agenda. At the very least, the importance of these issues for arguably influential rivals suggests that each should be considered for inclusion on the British agenda.

It is also not our intention to restrict the range of issues the Centre might focus upon; it is certainly conceivable that Table 5.1 omits area(s) that would be considered (especially) important for the British Centre on Transnational Corporations. In saying this we are conscious that the set of significant issues would change over time. A Centre would need sufficient flexibility to accommodate these changes, and indeed to do so by learning from its own experience.

This point is also relevant to the priority a Centre should give to each issue of concern. We have already suggested that it is important for a Centre to have priorities. It is also important for these to be determined in a way that accommodates changes over time, rather than to have a standard approach where all issues are examined in respect of each monitored transnational at all points in time.

To achieve this categorisation, we suggest that items on the Centre's agenda be analysed under three headings: core, political and random issues. The proposal is that core and political issues would be the especially important concerns relevant to each case of monitoring by the Centre on Transnationals at a point in time. The random issues would comprise the menu from which the Centre would randomly choose areas to focus upon in each case.

The idea of core issues is that they are concerns of central importance and for issues that would prove to be especially relevant in the British context as the Centre's work progressed. These would be issues that continually arise whenever governments and researchers contemplate the performance and impact of transnational corporations. Focusing solely on the concerns in Table 5.1, for instance, the core issues are those which appear frequently and which are widespread. By definition, core issues would be relatively constant over time but not fixed; new issues might eventually emerge and existing items be relegated to lesser significance. In contrast, there is likely to be greater fluidity over political issues. These are currently important for political reasons but are not established concerns, although they might become so in the future. It is impossible for us to identify these issues for Britain; the political agenda would be essentially determined by politicians, and we are not politicians.[1] As for so-called random issues, these are important yet residual concerns. Using our matrix, for instance, they are the issues in Table 5.1 not classified to the core or political agenda. More generally, random items would change over time as new issues emerged and once important issues become less relevant. This is also the part of the Centre's agenda likely to be most immediately influenced by its own experience; we envisage a Centre identifying new issues as it operates and putting these initially on the random agenda, from which they might eventually move to, say, core concerns.

Drawing these points together, and again emphasising that we are providing a starting point for more detailed discussion, applying our suggested classification to Table 5.1 produces the following agenda[2] for a British Centre on Transnational Corporations;

Core issues
  Ownership and control
  Competition
  Research and development/technology
  Employment and industrial relations
  Balance of payments
  'Basics'

Political issues
  Compliance/co-operation with wider economic/industrial policy
  Regional impact/development process
  Environmental impact

Random issues
  Productivity and efficiency
  Impact on the Exchequer
  National 'competitive' position
  Use of national/local components and resources
  'Fairness'

'Cultural issues'
Openness, accountability and information
Miscellaneous

CONCLUSION

This chapter has begun more detailed exploration of our suggestion that a British Centre for Transnational Corporations should collect information on the performance and impact of transnationals. We have attempted to identify the main issues that have concerned France, Japan and the United States as regards transnationals over recent years. The aim has been to illustrate but not constrain the sorts of issues that would be on the agenda for a British Centre, and hence to provide a starting point for more detailed discussion. We have also considered the prioritisation of concerns, suggesting a flexible division into core, political and random issues, and commenting on how these might vary over time.

Emphasising the overall picture more than the detail, one of the points standing out in the chapter is that a Centre would be concerned with wide-ranging issues. This is revealed very clearly from the matrix in Table 5.1. Although only illustrative, the matrix implies that the Centre would be occupied by a broad range of economic and social matters. Given that we see the Centre as concerned with society's interests, this range should not be surprising. As will be seen in the following chapter, however, it raises questions regarding the accountability of transnational corporations, and in particular doubts as to the adequacy of corporate annual reports and accounts for monitoring purposes.

NOTES

1 To illustrate the point, however, looking solely at the concerns of Table 5.1, our guess is that the political agenda for Britain at the moment would include impact on the Exchequer. For the purposes of this analysis we have included only those matters which are currently of importance but are not established concerns, taking matters which are of importance in terms of the three countries towards the end of our period.
2 As the Centre gains in experience, we envisage the agenda might vary across sectors and firms.

6

THE FORM OF ACCOUNT

In previous chapters we have concentrated on building a case for the monitoring of transnational corporations, and have examined practices in other western industrialised countries, identifying a wide range of interests and concerns regarding the performance and impact of transnationals. This chapter and the following two will look more closely at the work of our proposed British Centre on Transnationals. We will discuss in greater detail the nature of the information which a Centre will need to collect in order to fulfil its function.

Our discussion of the information needed by the Centre can be seen as an accounting problem, since what is sought is information to enable the preparation of an account of the impact and performance of individual transnational corporations. Thus although accounting, and in particular external financial reporting, is often seen to be concerned with the operations of capital markets, the subject is more generally seen as seeking 'to provide information which is potentially useful for making economic decisions and which, if provided, will enhance social welfare' (American Accounting Association, 1975). This suggests that it can be appropriate to other groups in society, who may be seeking to achieve their objectives, rather than simply those participating in capital markets (Cooper and Sherer, 1984).

This chapter will begin by briefly considering the financial accountability of transnationals in Britain at the present time. Although we have suggested that the primary purpose of external corporate accounting reports is generally seen to be as an aid to the efficient operation of the capital markets (e.g., Dearing Committee, 1988; FASB, 1978; ASB, 1991) and in particular institutional investors and analysts, the dominant actors in today's markets, we will draw a parallel between this emphasis and the work of the proposed Centre. Despite the fact that we identify different objectives for the Centre compared to those of institutional investors, and recognise that this is significant in determining what information should be collected, we will also suggest that there is considerable similarity in the process of monitoring conducted by both. In particular we will suggest that the Centre, like institutional investors, should construct its own account of the performance and impact of transnational corporations, in line with its specific objectives and concerns.

Given the kind of wider economic and social concerns which will be important to the Centre, perhaps similar to those identified in Chapter 5, we describe the preparation of this account of the impact and performance of transnationals as the preparation of an 'economic and social account'. We liken this task to the preparation of social accounts or social audits, and so spend the remainder of the chapter discussing the practice of social accounting/auditing, its meaning, problems, limitations and what it has to offer a transnationals monitoring unit.

THE FINANCIAL ACCOUNTABILITY OF TRANSNATIONAL CORPORATIONS

The primary accountability of transnationals' economic activity is to shareholders, actual and potential. In Britain, as in most industrialised market economies, this is governed largely by the law (primarily the 1985 Companies Act as amended by the 1989 Companies Act), the accounting profession (in its contribution to the Financial Reporting Council and the Accounting Standards Board) and the Stock Exchange. In practice it is widely recognised that the most important users of accounting reports are the institutional investors who dominate the markets, such as insurance companies and pension funds, and analysts.

In general relatively little has changed this century regarding the nature of such financial accountability. Although the degree of detail provided has increased enormously (particularly with the requirements to produce a profit and loss account and consolidated financial statements) and there is now greater regulation, partly due to increased business complexity and sophistication, the historic cost accounting model remains the foundation (see Lee, 1979, for details of changes in one company's reporting during this century).

Table 6.1 Typical contents of a transnational's annual report and accounts

Financial facts summary
Chairman's statement
Chief Executive's review of activities
Report of the directors
Annual accounts
Consolidated profit and loss account
Consolidated balance sheet
Consolidated source and application of funds statement
Holding company balance sheet
Notes on the accounts
Report of the auditors
Statistical review
Principal subsidiary and associated undertakings
General information
Financial calendar

This model, based on the accounting equation (assets − liabilities = capital) produces two main financial statements, the balance sheet and the profit and loss account.

In Britain the annual report and accounts is the primary means of accountability for the economic performance of transnational corporations. It is likely to contain the various sections shown in Table 6.1.

The report is dominated by the financial accounting information, in particular the two main financial statements; the profit and loss account, which matches the costs and revenues for the year in order to calculate profit; and the balance sheet (the accounting equation), a statement of the financial position which presents the assets, liabilities and capital of the business at the year end. A third statement, the Funds Statement or Cash Flow Statement is also presented showing the changes in working capital or liquid assets respectively during the year. These statements are prepared using a modified historic cost accounting system.

This traditional historic cost accounting model relies substantially on market exchanges which are generally considered objective and free from bias, although there are serious doubts as to how useful accounting practice based on historic costs can be to the demands of the market system (e.g., Whittington, 1984; Lee and Tweedie, 1977, 1981).

Of more importance for our purposes is the fact that current accounting practice reports on only a subset of all economic exchange transactions (Tinker, 1985). The traditional view is that external financial accounting statements should report only those costs and revenues that are internal to an organisation (Solomons, 1991) in order to measure and communicate economic information which will be relevant to decision-makers. As a consequence traditional accounting excludes a wide variety of economic exchange transactions where there is no market price. Only externalities which result in some financial impact on the firm (i.e., which must be internalised) will be recorded. Other activities, for which there may be an economic or social consequence (such as environmental impact) will remain unreported, unless there is a market exchange involving the firm.

In the final sections of this chapter we consider a form of accounting, social accounting, which attempts to record the wider economic and social impact and performance of organisations. Before this we will review the main criticisms of the traditional accounting report, and consider its contribution to the work of institutional investors and analysts. In particular we will illustrate the subjectivity and partiality of the traditional accounting model. We will argue that accounts are socially-constructed phenomena, and that the Centre's likely interest in a wider economic and social picture of transnationals' performance and impact requires us to consider the alternative social accounting model. However, our first task is to summarise the main criticisms of the historic cost accounting model in order to illustrate how unsuitable it would be as a basis for monitoring transnational corporations.

CRITICISMS OF TRADITIONAL ACCOUNTING

Traditional financial accounting reports based on historic cost accounting are criticised on numerous grounds. The most frequently expressed concern the inherent flexibility and subjectivity of such an apparently objective historic model. For example, despite the largely historic nature of current practice some subjective judgement ('considerable discretion' – Boothman Committee, 1975), looking into the future, is needed in order to allocate costs such as depreciation of fixed assets, or in deciding whether to carry costs forward or write off now, e.g., research and development expenditure. Similarly, the prudence concept requires one to look to the future and estimate asset and liability values when preparing accounts so as not to overvalue assets and undervalue liabilities.

Related to this and arising from its implied definition of capital, income (profit) includes only gains which have been realised in cash or near cash form. Thus increases in asset values are not, in general, recognised in profit until the asset is disposed of.

Historic cost accounts are also said to be riddled with opportunities to choose from a range of different ways of accounting for costs in particular (Thomas, 1969; Griffiths, 1986). Problems arise because it is preferred to allow choice of method in allocating costs. For example, when depreciating fixed assets not only must you estimate the life of the asset and its expected scrap or disposal value, but in addition you need to choose a method by which to allocate the net cost over the life of the asset. Each method will likely produce a different pattern of charges (thus affecting annual profit) and different asset values in the balance sheet at the end of each year. Like the judgement of asset life and scrap value the choice of method will be that of management, subject to audit.

Historic cost accounting can also be criticised for failing to reflect all benefits of current actions in a period's financial statements. Future benefits, which may arise from current actions, are generally ignored although sometimes they can be used to justify a policy of deferring costs. However, the problems of justifying the deferral of costs (the need to be reasonably certain of future benefits) means that often important intangible assets (such as skills, brands and market dominance) are omitted from the balance sheet. Recently, however, we have seen determined efforts to incorporate some intangibles, such as brands and goodwill on corporate balance sheets (Power, 1990; Barwise et al., 1989). Such attempts raise questions as to the nature and purpose of external accounting, since some advocates of the inclusion of brands and other intangibles seem most concerned to reflect a closer approximation of the economic value of the organisation or its individual assets in financial statements (Kransdorff, 1991), rather than simply provide information which may enable this to be done.

All of these problems are made worse by the failure of historic cost accounting to reflect changing prices in the economy, thus often involving, in its balance sheet in particular, an aggregation of asset and liability values in pounds from different dates, and hence different values, few of which will be current. As a consequence of these criticisms it is difficult to disagree with the view that accounting practice and corporate balance sheets in particular are a 'hotchpotch of costs, valuation and adjusted figures which indicate neither the worth of an entity as a whole nor the separate worth of its individual components' (McMonnies, 1988).

Other criticisms of traditional accounting highlight failure to reflect new managerial concerns with quality, productivity, innovation and the quality of the work-force (e.g., Kaplan, 1984), contrast private sector reporting with developments in public sector accounting such as value for money (e.g., McSweeney, 1986), or note concern regarding the absence of reporting on the environmental impact of business (e.g., Gray, 1990a). Yet the emphasis in accounting practice, as illustrated by the annual report and accounts, remains largely the same as it was at the turn of the century.

In many respects the direction of change in financial accounting practice appears to be more concerned with refining a picture of so-called economic reality (e.g., McMonnies, 1988), and continues to be explored very much within the neo-classical or marginalist economic paradigm (Tinker, 1985). Thus the major debates in professional accounting in recent years have centred on the nature and purpose of corporate reporting and in particular the measurement of asset values, capital and income (McMonnies, 1988; Solomons, 1989), with little attention being paid to market imperfections or aberrations, particularly in the analysis of transnational and monopoly business (Tinker, 1980). Although transnational and international accounting are suggested to offer opportunities for radical and dramatic changes in accounting (Tinker, Merino and Neimark, 1982), there are few signs that scholars or practitioners are interested.

This pursuit of economic reality and the search for a conceptual framework of accounting, specifying objectives and characteristics, both reflect a common-sense reasoning which assumes the existence of a definite reality, and in particular that this economic reality exists independently of accounting practices (Hines, 1991a). Reality, specifically economic and not social, is out there just waiting to be accounted for. The major role of accounting is to communicate economic reality (Hines, 1989). Thus one prominent author feels able to liken accountants to journalists and messengers (Solomons, 1991). External financial reporting is seen as an attempt to faithfully reproduce the economic reality which is thought to exist 'objectively, inter-subjectively, concretely and independently' of financial accounting practices (Hines, 1991a). An alternative view would suggest that conceptual frameworks, and financial accounting in general, can be seen as forms of worlding, which begin with certain assumptions about the world, may seek to legitimate a particular view of the world or set of structures and relations, and suggest that there is a single objective reality (ibid.). They may account for a reality, but not the reality, since reality is seen to be socially constructed.

Hines's criticisms draw on the view (attributed to Poggi, 1965) that any way of seeing is a way of not seeing. In other words that there are in theory, and there can be in practice, different pictures of reality, and that therefore there can be different accounts of reality. Whereas for some the task of accountants and accounting is to provide information as free from bias as possible and as useful as possible (Solomons, 1991), and that accounting information should be value-free, others have argued that accountants typically construct reality in limited and one-sided ways (e.g., Morgan, 1988). Whilst accountants might see themselves as objective appraisers of reality (Morgan, 1988), and therefore offering the true picture, accounts can be seen as socially-produced phenomena with no natural or true meaning (Hines, 1991a following Silverman, 1975). This latter view suggests that meaning is not corresponding but situation specific (it relies on who is asking for an account and from what perspective it should be prepared) (Hines, 1991a).

In relation to our focus on concerns regarding the performance and impact of transnationals, this recognition of constructing reality would seem to suggest that the economic and social account to be prepared by the Centre could, and should, change according to the government in power and its concerns. And that a single form of accounting, as seen in the traditional corporate annual report or as envisaged by a revised annual report which may result from such conceptual framework deliberations, will not be suitable. To use the traditional corporate annual report as the basis for the monitoring of transnationals, rather than to acknowledge this as an alternative objective of reporting (to the present objective of facilitating the operation of capital markets), would allow the nature of extant accounting practices to dominate the interests underlying the desire to monitor. The tail would be wagging the dog.

Our earlier review of the interests of France, Japan and the USA over the last thirty years, indicates a wide range of matters most of which are excluded from corporate annual reporting. In general traditional accounting reports tell one less about the impact of a transnational corporation than about the financial performance as it affects controllers of capital and their investment. In respect of our identified issues of concern it is unlikely that one would find details of corporate structure, pricing and marketing policies, training, productivity, transfer pricing, job quality, exploitation, imports and exports, spending in local economies, consumption of resources, political involvement and environmental impact etc.

Accounting can be seen as a language which like any other names, bounds and separates (Hines, 1991b), and in this respect the real significance of traditional accounting, for our purposes, is as much in what it denies (Lehman and Tinker, 1987). Thus in relation to the practice of financial accounting, social costs are seen as values (to be excluded) whereas market costs are fact, and so can be accounted for (Hines, 1991a). Facts are related to reality and are the basis of accounting, whereas values are not and so are excluded from what is accounted for. Hines illustrates this by reference to the exclusion of references to alienation, poverty, pollution and unemployment etc. from accounting reports (Hines, 1991a). In our case we have technology, productivity, employment and use of natural resources etc. as matters unlikely to feature in the traditional accounting reports of transnational corporations.

Thus the apparently objective and precise economic calculations of accounting reports, whether prepared for internal use or for external reporting, give prominence to certain matters whilst ignoring others, and can constrain the basis on which action can be based (Hopwood, 1986). It is suggested that the apparent objectivity of financial accounting and the rationality of the financial system as a whole, is a safeguard for the dominant economic system and interests, whilst suggesting that it is in some sense apolitical rather than biased to particular social interests (Cripps *et al.*, 1981). Yet clearly the lesson from our discussion of the pursuit of economic reality and of a conceptual framework by the accounting profession and its academic researchers, is that all accountings, including that prepared by the Centre, are subjectively determined, and therefore prone to being constructed in order to further particular social interests.

However, whereas most accounting research appears to ignore the possibility that the economy is dominated by large, transnational corporations often operating in oligopolistic or monopolistic markets (Cooper and Sherer, 1984) and consequently fails to reflect general social and human consequences as well as the wider strategic impact of such organisations (Morgan, 1988), our discussion and proposal will seek to recognise this.

THE USE OF CORPORATE REPORTS BY INSTITUTIONAL INVESTORS AND ANALYSTS

Before turning our attention to social accounting, and in particular the lessons that may be learned from previous practice, we consider the use of corporate reports by institutional investors and analysts. Our concern here is to draw a parallel with the work of the British Centre on Transnational Corporations. We see the Centre's monitoring task involving the construction of an alternative account in a manner similar to the work of investors and analysts. We will suggest that both obtain information in order to prepare or construct an alternative account of the performance of transnationals.

Perhaps not surprisingly there are relatively few studies of institutional investors' and analysts' use of accounting reports on which to draw.[1] Studies of the use of accounting reports have largely concentrated on the effects of accounting information particularly on share prices (Beaver, 1981). Such research concentrates on the aggregate impact of disclosures on share prices rather than focusing on individual actors and their use and understanding. This emphasis on the market's reaction has been criticised, partly as a result of doubts regarding market efficiency, but also because information should not be seen as an absolute commodity, rather one which can be interpreted in different ways according to one's objectives (Hines, 1982). This is illustrated to some extent by the contrasting approaches to investment appraisal revealed in Arnold and Moizer (1984).

Although there are relatively few studies to draw on, and in some cases there must be doubts as to the extent to which we can rely on the results, it is worth looking at the contribution of corporate annual reports as a source of information for institutional investors and analysts.[2] Hines (1982) produced a table which, amongst other things, detailed sources of information revealed to be of importance

Table 6.2 Percentage of respondents ranking the annual report/financial statements as their most important source of information, and ranking as a source

Study	%	Ranking
Anderson (1979)	38.6	2
Baker and Haslem (1973)	7.9	5
Chang and Most (1977)	46.8	1
Chenhall and Juchau (1977)	30.0	1

in different studies. Table 6.2 uses some of that information drawn from studies of general shareholder use of information, to show the percentage of respondents rating the annual report or financial statements as the most important source, and its ranking with other sources.

Two other studies reported on whether stockbrokers and institutional shareholders found annual reports critical to their investment decision-making. These revealed that 60.8 per cent (Clift, 1973) and 16.7 per cent (Mason, 1971) of investing institutions and 33.3 per cent of stockbrokers (Mason, 1971) found them to be so. Rankings of the importance of annual reports relative to other sources of information were first, fifth and second respectively. Although these studies reveal a mix of responses, there is some indication of accounting reports making an important contribution. Yet more importantly it is clear that accounting information is only one of a wide range of sources of information.

Two more recent qualitative research studies have also shown the apparent importance of the corporate annual report yet, as with previous studies, confirm the use of other sources of information. It would seem that the company's account of its performance is not sufficient alone. Day (1986) suggests that the corporate annual report is vital to analysts. Her research indicated that the report was sometimes read at leisure, being used as something of a reference document. It appears to be analysed in detail, being broken down before building up (constructing) forecasts (Day, 1986). Gniewosz (1990) confirms this importance, finding that the annual report is the most heavily-consulted source. He documents its use in checking against forecasts, in establishing whether a trend exists, as an information base (reference) with which to explain results, as a confirming document and as a stimulus in identifying questions (Gniewosz, 1990). Information from annual reports is seen as incremental rather than revolutionary. However, it is not the only important source of information.

These studies are significant for our purposes because they appear to show the corporate annual report as one of a number of sources of information, albeit an important one. For example, Day's study reveals other sources including industry statistics, preliminary figures, previous accounts, company contact, the retail price index, share price data, newspapers, Extel Cards, the interim statement, rights issue documents, Textline, Datastream and Companies House (Day, 1986). The suggestion is that analysts and institutional investors have to gather information from various sources in order to construct their own account of the (past and expected) performance of the investment opportunity.

This construction of an account appears to be analogous to the proposed work of the Centre on Transnationals, which is expected to collect information from a wide variety of sources in order to construct economic and social accounts of the impact and performance of transnational corporations.

SOCIAL ACCOUNTING

Our earlier review, in Chapter 5, indicated a wide variety of issues of concern in other western industrialised countries. Clearly this is a social construction, since it is based on our research, our interpretation of what is relevant and our writing up of these findings. Accepting this, our tables illustrate that governments have been concerned with a wide variety of what to traditional accounting are wider economic and social matters not normally accounted for. Such concern with the wider economic and social aspects of business performance has, in accounting, most often been reflected in calls for social accounting or social auditing (Geddes, 1992). Our intention here is not to suggest that transnational corporations should prepare social accounts for the benefit of the Centre, but that the Centre should prepare economic and social accounts of the performance and impact of such firms. For this reason we see value in identifying problems and any lessons from the social accounting literature.

A social accounting approach to the monitoring of transnationals would concentrate on their wider social and economic impact attempting to reflect the social, economic and political context in which they operate (Cooper and Sherer, 1984).[3] Thus whereas traditionally accounting has concerned itself with an organisation's own financial performance, reflecting its links with the outside world and its internal transactions, a social accounting would seek to incorporate an examination of the impact of the organisation on outside parties. This may mean a concern, not only with what it has done, but also with what it has failed to do (e.g., maintain investment in plant).

Clearly this begs a number of questions: is social accounting concerned with the voluntary preparation of a report by organisations (the type of thing which is often seen as largely a public relations exercise due to the absence of critical data) (Estes, 1976) or reports required by legislation; is it reports prepared for internal or external use; or are social accounts those reports prepared by external organisations whether or not appointed by management; must a social account be audited; are social accounts quantitative or qualitative or both; if quantitative are they financial or non-financial?

In discussing the practice of social accounting we draw on all of these types, since we do not seek to specify in too detailed a manner what we see as the work of the Centre. However, our discussion will make it clear that we see specific problems with particular forms, especially the in-house and unaudited type and those models so favoured by accountants which concentrate almost solely in representing social and economic matters in financial terms.

DISCUSSION OF SOCIAL ACCOUNTING

Social accounting is often seen as an attempt to redress the concentration of traditional accounting on market transactions. The most recent calls for such a form of accounting have arisen from concern with the environmental impact of firms (Gray, 1992). The following discussion concentrates on a number of issues raised in debates of social accounting and accounting generally. Each of the matters raised is considered of significance to the setting up of a British Centre on Transnationals, and in particular the question of collecting information to be used to assess the impact and performance of transnationals.

Our discussion begins with the question of externalities, before going on to consider the limitations of calculative approaches and in particular financial social accountings. We then address the difficulty of choosing appropriate measures of impact and performance, before developing our discussion to consider the scope of such accounting. We conclude with comment on the absence of a generally-agreed theoretical framework, noting some further problems not considered in detail here.

Externalities

Concern with social or environmental impact is frequently seen in terms of the need to recognise externalities, a matter at the heart of social accounting (Estes, 1976; Ramanathan, 1976). Externalities are the wider economic and social consequences of actions which are not reflected in market prices. Thus where production or consumption has an impact on another producer, consumer, employee or the community an externality may exist. In neo-classical market economics externalities are not reflected in market prices and so are not normally accounted for or considered in decision-making. In some cases legislation may be passed or taxes are levied to deal with externalities (e.g., Pearce *et al.*, 1989).

Some critics operating from a positivist emphasis on contracts and markets as mechanisms of control have identified problems with the definition and the measurement of externalities, suggesting that control of any adverse consequences of business actions should not be the remit of accounting but of regulators and legislators (Benston, 1982). Similarly, a radical critique has suggested that a major weakness is the ambiguity of the concept of an externality. For Tinker (1985) an externality is a subjective and arbitrary concept derived from marginalist economics. The source of the ambiguity is in deciding and valuing the consequence, since alternatives are either pre-given or subjectively determined by economic agents rather than specified by the theory itself (Tinker, 1985). For example, Tinker uses the case of a corporation which is subject to claims from employees as a result of asbestos-related illness. Does an externality exist only if the firm loses a legal case, and if so is the value of the externality equal to the damages awarded? To do so accepts our society's institutions, reasoning and valuations at face value, rather than drawing on a specific social theory.

This radical criticism is supported by doubts that a form of accounting can emerge which is critical of current structures (such as transnational corporations) from a society dominated by interest groups and distorted communication (Puxty, 1986). Social accounting, like conventional accounting, is seen to be steeped in the conditions of the social system from which it emerges, and rather than it offering some hope for change, things can only improve through changes in the structures of society (Puxty, 1986).

Fortunately we do not suggest social accounting as some wonder solution to the problems of examining the impact and performance of transnationals. What we propose here is that governments, and in particular the British government, should take the practical step of setting up a transnationals Centre, in part in order to be better informed about transnationals' performance and impact. In deciding what information to collect, we suggest that there may be some value in examining the social accounting literature (and in particular the work of critics). We describe the work of the Centre as involving the preparation of economic and social accounts, but above all we consider this to be accounting, rather than just social accounting. We see this as an accounting which is preferable to the traditional accounting solution which ignores the wider consequences of corporate activity.

Calculations

Accounting practice, as discussed above, has developed and encouraged a numerical and specifically financial view of reality, which we are suggesting is partial and fails to capture the complexity of the economic and the social (Morgan, 1988). It has been stressed that all calculations create an apparently impartial authority which appears to be factual (Hopwood, 1986), where what is seen as real is what is capable of being calculated, and what is not capable of calculation is seen to have only a subjective existence (Gorz, 1989). Recent environmental concerns and green thinking suggest, in contrast, a need to emphasise qualitative objectives of social progress, rather than quantitative (Steward, 1989), and it is suggested that quantifying our environment must inevitably further alienate people from nature (Hines, 1991b). Yet we need to recognise that calculation gives a precise status to phenomena which would otherwise remain descriptive, and likely be treated less seriously (Hopwood, 1986). Though quantitative measures are necessarily partial they can be practically useful, provided their limitations are well understood (Boddington *et al.*, 1986).

A Centre's economic and social accounting would be no different if it were to take a calculative form, whether in financial or non-financial terms. Similarly, the earlier criticism that accounts cannot be passive or neutral, that they allow institutions to define themselves, and be defined by others (Tinker and Neimark, 1988), would be as applicable to the accounting of the Centre. Preparation of economic and social accounts would be a means of defining the Centre and of redefining, for policy-making and public perception, what is considered to be important about the performance and impact of transnationals. Any strategy for their control which recognises potential conflict of interest between the community and transnational corporations must involve construction of an alternative account to that which corporations themselves propose primarily for the capital markets.

Financial focus

Often the focus of social audits appears to have been on the financial rather than attempting to reflect performance or impact by a mixture of financial and non-financial measures. Gray, Owen and Maunders (1987) devote more space to academic accounting proposals for financial social accountings than non-financial, and reviews of such accountings for plant closures revealed greater emphasis on the financial than non-financial aspects (Anell, 1985; Harte and Owen, 1987). In one review the alternative to traditional accounting which is considered is broadly cost-benefit analysis (Anell, 1985), seen from an overall societal perspective (impact on the economy), while another study concentrates on reports whose financial focus was largely to highlight the cost to the Exchequer of unemployment in terms of the incremental costs (benefits etc.) and lost revenues (taxes etc.) (Harte and Owen, 1987).

Such financial approaches to social accounting (e.g., Estes, 1976; Linowes, 1972; Dilley and Weygandt, 1973) generally attempt to convert the performance of organisations into financial costs and benefits in order to incorporate the social dimension into the traditional financial account. The perspective taken is often that of the firm, rather than the community or society, and there is apparently most concern to reflect the social performance for the benefit of controllers of capital. As Gray *et al.* (1987) point out, these attempts ignore the struggles of welfare economics to convert social factors into financial figures (Bauer, 1973) and mean that information is actually lost due to the artificial conversion into financial figures (Dierkes and Preston, 1977). A contrast to this approach is offered by what might be described as community audits, where the focus is on a a specific local community, examining the impact of sometimes unspecified events (e.g., a plant closure) on the condition of the community (e.g., Dunston Community Workshop, 1983; Miller, 1981).

The financial approach also raises the question of the appropriateness of market prices for such accounting. In some situations the problem stems, not only from the fact that such prices are marginal, but also the imperfection of the relevant market and the politically-determined nature of many costs. As well as the general influence of government policy (or lack of) on interest rates, inflation, etc. government may determine relevant factors such as grants, subsidies, benefits and taxes. This was particularly well illustrated in a number of social audits of plant closures in the 1980s, when government policies of reducing income taxes and social security benefits resulted in plant closure social audits recording a lower financial cost than would previously have been the case (Harte and Owen, 1987).

Appropriate measures

Breugel (1989) has stressed the importance of developing processes of evaluation which embody alternative concepts of efficiency, and express appropriate needs and values. However, despite the variety of social auditing practice there has been relatively little attempt to evaluate the appropriateness of many measures. The emphasis, rightly in our view, appears to have been primarily on experiment rather than evaluation. Clearly, as we have seen, there will be problems of subjectivity (both in selection and in measurement) as there is in traditional accounting. In contrast to the traditional model which excludes so much economic and social activity and so may somehow appear less subjective in selection, and which has a single measuring unit (and so may appear less subjective in measurement), a social accounting approach seems to be more so. Yet clearly this is in part an appearance arising from its seeking to cover more in a variety of different ways.

All models of accounting are subjective at least in their choice of focus. In particular the likely inclusion of multipliers, to reflect the wider consequences, will lead to numerous problems of how to calculate and where to get information. Input-output tables, when available are frequently long out of date, are prepared on a regional or national basis and comprise average figures. They are also quite inappropriate in monopoly or monopsony situations. Some would argue that knowledge of externalities is not needed (Peasnell, 1974), and that such matters are best dealt with by macroeconomic measures such as taxes (Pearce *et al.*, 1989). Yet information on the extent of a problem and the contributing parties at the micro-economic level would seem relevant, particularly where one is taking decisions which involve choice between firms (whether as an investor or as a government monitoring home and overseas firms).

Experts

The preparation of accounts even in this alternative form can encourage the development of new experts (Hopwood, 1986).

Although we do not explore this matter in detail here, we should recognise the dangers of such regulation being captured, in the generally-accepted economics sense, by transnationals. This illustrates the concern expressed by some about accounting and social accounting being controlled by powerful interests in society (Puxty, 1986). The whole idea of a government-sponsored monitoring unit would be of concern to many who would doubt the potential for such an arm of the capitalist state to act other than in the interests of capital (Miliband, 1984). This problem is illustrated by the US government's actions in giving control of CFIUS (Committee on Foreign Investment in the United States) to the Treasury, probably the arm of government most closely associated with the economic system (see Chapter 3). Alternatively, a Centre set up within a particular government department might find itself 'ring fenced' and unable to obtain information and co-operation from other departments.

The involvement of the accounting profession or any other body of experts sanctioned by the state in the development of social accounting can be seen as a potential threat to the development of an accounting more sensitive to the interests of those affected by transnationals. Whereas some commentators see a potential role for accountants, largely in light of the importance of information systems and control, though not necessarily only accountants (see Gray, 1990b; Adams, 1992; Carey, 1992; Ing, 1992), others seem to be so critical of what accountants have already been involved in, and call for social audits which are socially and politically open, responsive and democratic (Geddes, 1992). For some any technology incorporates a set of values, interests and a set of biases, and is likely to construct rather than serve demands (Power, 1991). Experts mean dependency and loss of power (Hopwood, 1986). The danger of the accounting profession's involvement stems from its bias to calculation and in particular financial calculation (Power, 1991), ('the technicians of money' – Geddes, 1992), as well as the fact that the most influential firms in the accounting profession are themselves transnational organisations and have close links with transnational corporations. This was a matter of concern to one group proposing a monitoring unit who felt that 'accountants wield so much power that they cannot be left as they are' (Labour Party, 1977: 77), particularly given their own transnational status and the links they have with transnational corporations, their main clients.

Scope

We have previously raised questions about the breadth of focus (how wide do you look for the ripple effect) for social accounting. We now raise the matter of the geographic scope of social accounting. We have already referred to Tinker's (1985) criticism of the definition of externalities. However, given our pragmatic policy-making emphasis we have produced from our detailed review of events in other western countries a summary of matters of concern. To this extent we are suggesting that a monitoring Centre could begin its work by focusing on the issues identified here. This follows Gray et al.'s (1987) suggestion that social reports (here the collection of information by a Centre) be prepared from a statement of objectives, whilst recognising that all things are connected and that complete understanding is impossible (Gray, 1992). We should recognise the impossibility of identifying and measuring all social and economic effects (Gray et al., 1987).

The question of geographic scope is crucial for a Centre. Later, in Chapter 9, we suggest that one should counter the transnational power of such corporations in a manner which builds alliances and regional/international governmental co-operation. However, in terms of the collection of information by a British Centre, it does seem important to recognise the transnationality of such firms. This means knowing about global strategy and details of performance and impact elsewhere in the group, not just in Britain. A central feature of transnationalism concerns the flexibility of such firms to relocate at relatively short notice and to play off countries and plants against each other. In many ways this contrasts with the focus of some social audit practice. Closure audits prepared by local authorities appear to have taken little account of what was happening elsewhere in the corporation (Harte and Owen, 1987). Similarly, company social audits prepared by Social Audit (e.g., Social Audit, 1976) have generally looked at the group as a whole with little attempt to examine relationships between plants, and with the centre. Clearly a British Centre on Transnational Corporations would seek to focus on such connections.

Absence of a theoretical framework

The debate concerning the practice of social accounting has indicated an absence of any clear theoretical framework (Gray et al., 1987).

Although there are indications that a multiplicity of interest groups are recognised, and that there are competing interests on many occasions (Social Audit, 1973, 1974 and 1976), there are few clear, consistent statements of the intention of such reporting. Consequently, not surprisingly, the scope and objectives appear to vary from situation to situation. Thus for our purposes, where our intention is quite specifically identified (to monitor transnationals), we should be wary of the extent to which lessons can be learned from social accounting which has been developed and debated with other interests and intentions in mind. Consistent with our earlier discussion of traditional conceptual frameworks it seems more appropriate for a Centre to define its objectives and the desirable characteristics it seeks from accounting reports, rather than be concerned with other frameworks.

Other problems

In practice there are numerous other problems concerning matters such as the lack of additivity, because of the mix of financial and various non-financial measures and access to information. Obtaining information from transnationals could be their opportunity to continue to dictate the agenda and focus, offering a legitimacy in a manner similar to their disclosure of information to trade unions (Ogden and Bougen, 1985), and also consistent with the way in which codes of conduct for transnationals appear to have become documents offering legitimacy to such organisations (Hamilton, 1984). Thus in general social accounting may legitimate corporate activity (Puxty, 1986) due to the capture by transnationals or their agents, as a result of their controlling the flow of information.

CONCLUSION

In view of the discussions above, our advocacy of the Centre's collection of information in order to prepare an economic and social account, much of which is likely to be numerical, is therefore cautious (Hopwood, 1986). The Centre would be guided by politicians and their objectives and concerns. The danger of being controlled by either accountants and other experts, or transnationals, illustrates that such accounting calculation can be both politically-enabling or restrictive (Hopwood, 1986). We do not suggest that the work of the Centre would be easy, particularly in its attempts to decide what would be useful information and how to collect it. We have already referred to the problems of gaining co-operation from other government departments. Yet the search for perfect measures should not halt the flow of information (Medawar, 1976). One should not accept that in the absence of an ideal solution there is no problem (Gray, 1990a). We see value in the use of subjective and imprecise indicators which offer an improvement on the current limited corporate reporting (Schreuder and Ramanathan, 1984), and go some way to accounting for the economic and social matters likely to be of interest to a Centre. The more we include the less important is what we exclude (Cherns, 1978). In this respect a monitoring Centre which is set up as a result of identified concerns with the impact of transnationals has as its objective the preparation and telling of a different story from that contained in the transnational's own story, the annual corporate report, and goes some way to rectifying the transnational corporations' censoring in their own corporate reporting (Tinker and Neimark, 1988).

The focus here has been on the collection of information for monitoring. We suggest that traditional accounting reports are insufficient alone for the monitoring, and consistent with the expression of wider concerns a unit would have to collect appropriate social and economic information. Several lessons drawing on the debates concerning social accounting have been emphasised. In particular we have cautioned against seeking perfect measures, stressed the limitations of quantitative measures and in particular too narrow a financial focus, and warned of the dangers of capture by accountants or transnational corporations themselves. The intention here has not been to propose a particular form of accounting which could be imposed on transnationals, rather we have attempted to examine the implications for a Centre with a wide variety of economic and social interests. Our intention here was neither to lay down what a monitoring Centre should be concerned with, nor what information it should collect in order to monitor, but to begin to explore some of the problems it would have obtaining useful information.

We know that transnational corporations are significant agencies having substantial economic and social impacts. Our suggestion is that a government-sponsored Centre on Transnationals should attempt to assess this and contribute to industrial policy. In the following chapter we focus on a particular transnational corporation,

Glaxo, and begin to construct an economic and social account of its performance and impact using publicly-available information. In doing so we also draw on specific examples of social accounting practice.

NOTES

1 This is due in part to the influence of positive economics, and concentration on the so-called facts of economic life, in accounting research (Cooper and Sherer, 1984).
2 See Arnold and Moizer's (1984) criticisms of questionnaire studies.
3 The literature on social accounting uses various terms to describe practice. Gray *et al.* (1987) provide a detailed discussion of the relationships between social responsibilities, social accountability and social reporting, and the differences between social reporting, social accounting and social auditing. Parker (1986) also explores the various terms used. For our purposes such detailed separation of types of social accounting are not so important. We follow Puxty's (1986) view that concern with the multiplicity of terms is more an indication of the paucity of debate. We will define social accounting in very general terms as the preparation and reporting of the economic and social impact and performance of an organisation.

7

TOWARDS AN ECONOMIC AND SOCIAL ACCOUNT

A case study

Before turning to examine our chosen transnational, Glaxo, we will explain the purpose of this chapter, discuss what we see as the work of the proposed British Centre on Transnational Corporations, comment on our choice of Glaxo, briefly describe Glaxo's business, and then summarise our approach in exploring the economic and social account.

BACKGROUND

Purpose of the case study

This case study explores the work of the proposed Centre in greater depth by examining a transnational corporation, Glaxo, in terms of the issues of concern identified in Chapter 5 and publicly-available information. We are not attempting, here or elsewhere in this text, to say precisely what the Centre should do, what it should focus on or how it should carry out its tasks. Rather we are conducting this case study, and the subsequent discussion and analysis in Chapter 8, in order to identify further relevant matters to our overall proposal for a monitoring Centre. Our intention is to tentatively prepare an economic and social account but not an account the Centre could prepare; we will begin to collect information which a Centre might find useful in preparing its account.

We stated in the previous chapter that what we believe should guide the Centre should be its own aims and objectives and those of its political overseers. We do not expect that the Centre should restrict itself to collecting only publicly-available information. Thus our case study differs not only in terms of the issues it focuses on, but also in its restriction to publicly-available information. In addition we did not attempt to gain the co-operation of the chosen transnational corporation, Glaxo. This had the obvious consequence for us of involving the collection and use of less material. As three academics with limited resources it was not realistic to request co-operation from Glaxo, since this would certainly have involved us in further time and funds.

If Glaxo had been willing to co-operate (and there must be some doubt about this) there may have been a danger in our being flooded with information. Clearly restrictions are placed on what publicly-quoted companies can disclose to individual parties, since financial markets are supposed to operate on the basis of all parties having the same information. Any discussion we might have had with Glaxo would have been subject to such conditions, because of our potential to act in the market. Direct contact with a transnational would also have raised further problems regarding the extent to which we could have relied on any information obtained, and would have made our case study much more like the work of the proposed Centre. We do not think that three academics with a limited range of accounting, economics and business experience (not to mention legal, international, environmental and industrial relations background) can begin to seriously act like the Centre. We assume that a monitoring Centre's greater resources would mean its being able to collect more information, perhaps in direct negotiation with transnationals. Earlier, in Chapter 6, we commented on the danger of regulatory capture. We were well aware of the dangers of our own capture. For these reasons we did not seek the co-operation of Glaxo.

We did attempt, at one stage, to extend our analysis beyond publicly-available information by investigating the collection of information on transnationals by government departments. Since we envisage a Centre being related to a government department in some way it seemed worth exploring the potential for co-operation with other departments. Although we did not expect the departments to provide us with information on Glaxo, we did hope to get some indication of what kind of data is collected at present. Our experience was that most government departments have no single source of details of requests to corporations for information, and that our enquiries could not be dealt with in a reasonable time, if at all by some departments. In addition our restriction to publicly-available information enables us to test the view expressed in the previous chapter as regards the appropriateness of such information, and in particular annual corporate reports, for monitoring. In fact, as we will see, the case study confirms the significance of accounting information to public discussion of Glaxo, and how the basic data of the corporate annual report contributes substantially to the creation of further sources often offering little new information.

Finally, we are not seeking to set detailed objectives for the Centre. We do not wish to restrict the range of issues the Centre could look at. Different issues will be of varying significance at different times and in respect of different firms. While such an approach may be said to be too uncertain, it appears that some countries, particularly France, Canada and Japan have used similar uncertainty in their favour (Bailey, Harte and Sugden, 1991a). Instead we are seeking to draw on the interests identified by governments in Japan, France and the United States over the last thirty years, as an illustration of what the Centre could focus on, and considering the extent to which publicly-available information matches such concerns. What this enables us to do is comment on the suitability of publicly-available information, and therefore the likely need to gain the co-operation of transnationals. In addition it will allow us to develop our comments on the problems likely to be faced by a Centre in attempting to construct its economic and social accounts of the impact and performance of transnationals.

The Centre's work

A purpose of the British Centre on Transnationals is, we believe, to provide information on the impact and performance of transnational corporations in line with government industrial policy objectives. This monitoring of transnationals (involving the collection and analysis of information) would be intended as primarily proactive, for example, concentrating on identifying what positive beneficial contributions transnationals can make to the goals of the British government and community. Suggesting a more positive contribution by transnationals will, in some cases, involve assessing opportunities where there is no current impact, while in others it will be a matter of assessing adverse impact in order to be specific about what could be changed and to what extent. Thus our focus has to be on the overall performance and impact of transnationals in line with the community's interests. One important clarification is worth noting at this stage, in case our emphasis is interpreted as rather nationalistic. We hope that the British community's interests, and therefore the concerns of the Centre, would extend to interest in how other communities are treated by transnationals. We do not equate Britain's interests solely with the financial wealth of its citizens, particularly where this is created at the expense of other less powerful communities.

Why Glaxo?

Glaxo was chosen for a number of reasons. Firstly, by selecting a firm which is still widely seen as a British transnational we have emphasised that the work of the Centre should not be restricted to foreign firms but to transnationals, both foreign and British. Secondly, when seeking a corporation on which to base a case study we decided to focus on a firm which was expanding and generally perceived to be doing well in conventional market economic terms, based on financial wealth or growth. We also sought to choose a firm which was highly thought of rather than one which is or has been widely criticised, such as one from a declining industry faced with closures and disinvestment. We wanted this case and the work of the proposed Centre to be seen more in terms of identifying opportunities, rather than dealing with problems as, for example, in the wake of disinvestment decisions. Other analysis has stressed the importance of industrial policy creating and backing winners (see especially Cowling, 1987). The intention was to select a transnational firm which was expanding, yet one which still involved change and restructuring. Glaxo emerged from a review of recent company studies of the so called 'best corporations' (e.g., *The Economist*, 9 September, 1989; *The Sunday Times*, 4 November 1990; *The Economist*, 26 January 1991; *The Mail on Sunday*, 5 May 1991). It appealed to us as a suitable case study not only because of its spectacular growth ('the major corporate success story of the 80s') but also for its high ranking on various other criteria (e.g., financial soundness, quality of products and services, quality of marketing and capacity to innovate). It also offered interesting possibilities as an increasingly important member of a significant industrial sector, pharmaceuticals, with a multidimensional relationship with the State. For example, in addition to the usual legal requirement imposed by the State (in health and safety, product and other matters), the tax relationship, and Glaxo's likely receipt of

State financial assistance, we also see the State as a significant customer, as defender of the company and the sector as a whole (particularly as regards patents) and as a beneficiary of Glaxo's trading and investment overseas.

In practice Glaxo has offered us much of what we might have seen in examining a traditional manufacturing corporation, apart from their problems of closure, but in addition has raised matters such as patents, research and development (due to the importance of ethical drugs), location of corporate headquarters and health and safety, which reflect more contemporary concerns with industry.

On the other hand Glaxo is not a perfect choice. It is after all a British transnational, and so may be less likely to offer us a chance to discuss overseas operations and the possibilities of attracting other parts of a transnational to Britain, given its substantial presence here already. However, as we mentioned above, the selection of Glaxo confirms that our interest is in transnational corporations not in overseas or foreign firms with interests in Britain. Although the choice of Glaxo, or any other transnational registered in Britain, does not raise the specific problems of dealing with a foreign transnational with headquarters overseas, we still encountered problems obtaining information on many of the issues raised in our review.

Glaxo

Glaxo describes its activities as follows; 'Glaxo is an international group of companies, which conducts research into and develops, manufactures and markets ethical pharmaceuticals around the world' (Glaxo Holdings plc, 1991, Report of the Directors).

The Glaxo group comprises a large number of subsidiary and associate companies, located around the world. The main primary production facilities are at Ulverston, Annan and Montrose in Britain and Singapore, with secondary production (involving diluting, mixing, packing and preparing active ingredients) at Barnard Castle and Ware in Britain and in Italy and the USA.

The group's main product is Zantac, an anti-ulcerant which is the world's best selling drug and accounted for 48 per cent of the corporation's sales in 1990/91. Other important products include Ventolin (a respiratory medicine), Fortum (a systemic antibiotic), Zofran (an anti-emesis drug), Serevent (an anti-asthmatic drug) and Imigran (for the treatment of migraine).

Approach

The period covered by our review was the financial year ended 30 June 1991. However, in view of the practice of reviewing any relevant and material matters which occur after the balance sheet date before signing the accounts, we have extended our search and incorporation of data to 19 September 1991 the date on which the 1990/91 accounts were signed. We have also looked at the periods just before and after these dates, occasionally drawing on matters of interest in our discussion.

Probably the most significant source of publicly-available information was Glaxo's annual report and accounts. Other sources included other Glaxo publications, brokers' reports and media reports, including those in trade journals.

The contents of Glaxo's annual report and accounts are listed below in Table 7.1 in some detail so as to give an indication of the sorts of matters covered, and because substantial reference is made in the remainder of this chapter to its subject matter.

Our review of the publicly-available information is presented below. Although we identify numerous problems and matters of interest as we go along, we reserve our main discussion of the overall significance of these issues for Chapter 8. However, in reading this chapter it may be of particular value to note the number of occasions on which we comment on the fact that there is very little information available in respect of individual companies in the Glaxo group or in respect of Glaxo's operations in individual countries. For example, there seems, at the moment, to be no obvious, straightforward way of obtaining information on a specific transnational subsidiary resident overseas, other than through local sources. This problem of disaggregation is balanced by our recognition of the difficulties of providing reliable segmented data for a group such as Glaxo. We are particularly concerned to emphasise the extent to which disaggregated details may have to be subjectively constructed in many cases. This problem will be discussed under a number of different headings below and in general in Chapter 8.

Finally we should repeat what we are not attempting. This chapter is not trying to provide the definitive Glaxo economic and social account. Nor are we trying to prepare an analysis in the way of a Centre on Transnationals. We are trying to explore what the Centre might do in order to be able to identify some of the

Table 7.1 The contents of the 1990/91 Glaxo annual report and accounts

page:	
1	Statement of corporate purpose
2	Financial facts; a summary of mainly financial highlights, e.g., turnover, profits, assets (1990 and 1991)
3	Geographical analysis of turnover (1990 and 1991)
3	Therapeutic analysis of turnover (1990 and 1991)
3	Capital expenditure; analysed according to manufacturing, research and development and other (1990 and 1991)
4–7	Chairman's Statement; a discussion of the financial results referring to sales, margins, profits, investment, management of funds, product performance, sales in particular markets, new products, research and development, organisational structure, community links, Board matters and appreciation of staff
8–21	Chief Executive's Review of Activities; discussion of overall performance, successful drugs, comments on the world pharmaceuticals industry, leading national markets in terms of estimated sales, Glaxo's sales growth compared to the market as a whole, leading pharmaceuticals markets by country and Glaxo's share, discussion of new products and established products, mention of patent challenges, discussion of sales by geographical region (Europe, North America and the Rest of the World), research and development (research programmes, development programmes, world wide research and development manpower (sic)), manufacturing operations, capital expenditure, environmental protection, and Glaxo in the community
22–3	The Board of Glaxo Holdings plc; photographs, names and personal details, responsibilities and for non-executive directors relevant current and former positions
24–6	Report of the Directors; brief details of activities, dividend details, political contributions, share options and capital issued, details of substantial shareholders, director changes, directors' interests including details of shareholdings and changes, comments on employee involvement, share option details, employment policy including comments on the position of disabled people, auditors' reappointment, and details of the annual general meeting
27–45	Annual Accounts; consolidated profit and loss account, consolidated balance sheet, consolidated source and application of funds statement, company balance sheet, notes to the accounts (on the basis of consolidated accounts, accounting policies, segment information, details of operating costs less other income, remuneration of directors and employees, investment income less interest payable, taxation, extraordinary items, profit for the financial year-holding company, earnings per share, dividends, tangible fixed assets, fixed asset investments, stocks, debtors,

Table 7.1 Continued

page:	
	current assets investments, creditors, net liquid funds, provisions for liabilities and charges, share capital, reserves, convertible bonds, contingent liabilities, commitments, other statutory information), report of the auditors
46–7	Consolidated profit and loss account and balance sheet in US dollars
48–9	Reconciliation to US accounting principles
49–53	Statistical review; e.g., sales, profits, research and development expenditure, share statistics, assets, return on capital employed, employees (all for the last twenty years); therapeutic analysis of turnover and associated undertakings' profits and asset details (both for the last ten years)
55–7	Principal subsidiary and associated undertakings; name, country, chairman, managing director, activity and shareholding
58–60	General Information; analysis of ordinary shareholdings, details of share option schemes, share and stock issues and capital gains tax details, administration of ordinary shares, administration of American ADRs, sub-division of share capital, filing of statements in USA and Japan, availability of the EC Code of Conduct Report, trade marks, addresses for correspondence, a financial calendar

Source: Glaxo Holdings plc, *Annual Report and Accounts*, 1991.

problems likely to be faced when setting up and operating a monitoring body. We are concentrating on information problems here, and in particular are able to comment on the usefulness of publicly-available information.

It may also seem odd to stress that the following account of Glaxo's impact and performance is not particularly meaningful and is necessarily partial. Although we have chosen to focus on Glaxo, the selection is relatively unimportant. We needed to choose a real transnational corporation for our discussion, and Glaxo was appealing in the many respects to which we have already referred. Some of our comments which follow may be construed as critical. This is only our intention in order to identify the sorts of issues that might interest a Centre, however, it is not our intention to be critical of Glaxo *per se*. Glaxo is an example here, and our comments on the absence of information could almost certainly have applied to most other transnational corporations. In fact Glaxo appears in many respects to disclose more detail than is legally required and probably more than many transnationals, despite its suggested reputation for secrecy (Cowe, 1987).

The remainder of this chapter is concerned with a discussion of information collected in relation to matters raised in the issues framework of Chapter 5, and is organised according to our core, political and random proposal. Whenever possible our discussion has been arranged after the more detailed concerns identified. In discussing what information might be seen to be relevant in respect of an issue we have, on a number of occasions, tried to contrast what has been found with suggestions from the social accounting literature. We have used a relatively small number of actual social audit reports to illustrate, including some prepared by companies to report on their own performance (Atlantic Richfield, 1980; Dow Chemicals, 1984), and others prepared by Social Audit, the leading independent exponents of the practice to date (Gray, Owen and Maunders, 1987). Much of the information is presented in tables which appear at the appropriate point in the chapter after our concluding comment.

CORE ISSUES

In Chapter 5 we suggested that a Centre should identify those issues of central importance and monitor all relevant transnationals in this respect. For the purposes of illustration we have defined core as those issues which our review reveals were most frequently expressed as concerns and which were widespread. We assume that continued recurrence can be taken as some indication of importance. The core issues identified from Table 5.1 in Chapter 5 are ownership and control, competition, research and development/technology, employment and industrial relations, balance of payments and basics. We consider each of these in turn.

Ownership and control

In many respects one could argue that a focus on individuals or groups when discussing ownership and control ignores any pressure to act in a manner consistent with a market-based economic rationale. In other words, that ownership and control is relatively unimportant given the rules and expectations of the market system. Yet there do seem to be good grounds for a monitoring unit looking closely at the matter of ownership and control, not least because of the way that governments may be able to bring pressure to bear. A monitoring Centre should recognise the possibility of different organisational cultures and strategies for achieving the aforementioned economic rationale, and so may seek to identify where the power lies in order to understand and negotiate.

Our review of government concerns revealed interest in takeovers (of local businesses) and changes in ownership, the structure of the overall enterprise, the extent of local participation as shareholders, the role of local management and directors, importing of managerial techniques and a concern to protect key sectors. To some extent our chosen case study, Glaxo, precludes some of this interest since its investment activity and expansion appears not to take the form of takeovers (at the present time). Later under other headings we will address the extent to which Glaxo's expansion may still affect local business. For the moment we will consider what is known about owners and controllers of the Glaxo group. Our discussion considers shareholdings, the board of directors and the group's structure (the last of these perhaps indicating the degree of decentralisation and therefore relating to control).

Shareholdings

Some information on shareholdings is produced in the Glaxo annual report. Table 7.2 presents an analysis of shareholdings according to

Table 7.2 Analysis of ordinary shareholdings in Glaxo, at 30 June 1991

	Number of accounts	Ordinary shares
Holding of:		
Up to 1,000 shares	48,672	22,322,040
1,001 to 5,000 shares	26,210	60,308,019
5,001 to 100,000 shares	10,887	173,115,686
100,001 to 1,000,000 shares	725	217,486,053
Over 1,000,000 shares	165	1,026,369,954
	86,659	1,499,601,752
Held by:		
Nominee Companies	13,902	940,519,119
Investment and Trust Companies	2,115	71,000,426
Insurance Companies	1,055	187,562,059
Individuals and other corporate bodies	69,587	300,520,148
	86,659	1,499,601,752

Source: Glaxo Holdings plc, *Annual Report and Accounts*, 1991.

Table 7.3 Size and value of average shareholdings in Glaxo

	Average holding[a]	Value[b]
		£
Holding of:		
Up to 1,000 shares	459	6,247
1,001 to 5,000 shares	2,301	31,317
5,001 to 100,000 shares	15,901	216,413
100,001 to 1,000,000 shares	299,981	4,082,741
Over 1,000,000 shares	6,220,418	84,659,888
Held by:		
Nominee Companies	67,654	920,771
Investment and Trust Companies	33,570	456,888
Insurance Companies	177,784	2,419,640
Individuals and other corporate bodies	4,319	58,782

Source: Extel Financial Ltd and Glaxo Holdings plc, *Annual Report and Accounts*, 1991.
Notes
a Based on number of shareholders and total ordinary shares per Table 7.2.
b Based on average holding multiplied by share price of 1361p as at 19 September 1991 (prior to the bonus issue of October 1991).

size. Table 7.3 reveals the significance of large shareholdings by calculating average shareholding sizes for each category reported in Table 7.2 and computing a financial value based on a share price of 1361p, being the price on 19 September 1991. Of particular note is the average size and value of the largest shareholdings. Table 7.2 indicates that 165 accounts hold over 1,000,000 shares. Their total holding of 1,026,369,954 represents 68 per cent of Glaxo's ordinary shares. Unfortunately, because Glaxo's shares are quoted on the New York Stock Exchange as American Depository Receipts (ADR's) it appears that the 334,217,224 ordinary shares (22.28 per cent) held this way by BNY (Nominees) Ltd is recorded in one block rather than according to ultimate ownership. If we remove this shareholding the shareholdings of over 1,000,000 shares number 164, with total ordinary shares of 692,152,730 (being 1,026,369,954 − 334,217,224). This means an average shareholding among those holding over 1,000,000 shares, of 4,220,443 shares. There is also a chance that some of the American Depository Receipts are held in large numbers by a small number of investors. That information is not available in the annual report or any of the other sources we consulted.

Clearly the size of the American shareholdings (up to 26 per cent according to Glaxo's interim results declared in February 1992) is

Table 7.4 Glaxo directors' shareholdings and options at 30 June 1991

Shares		
	Total directors' holdings of ordinary shares	150,214
	Total ordinary shares issued by Glaxo	1,499,601,752
	Directors' shareholdings as a percentage of the total	0.01%
Options		
	Total share options in issue	35,177,809
	Total directors' holdings of options	2,102,974
	Total other holdings of options	33,074,835
	Directors' holdings of options as a percentage of the total	6.0%
Ratio of directors' holdings of options to holdings of shares		14:1

Source: Glaxo Holdings plc, *Annual Report and Accounts*, 1991.

a matter of some potential significance, particularly as the proportion has increased considerably in recent years (16.8 per cent in 1983, falling to 8.2 per cent in 1986 and rising back up to 14.23 per cent in 1990). One source of information regarding share ownership would be the Glaxo share register, which can be inspected at the company's registrars. This may reveal a number of the largest shareholders, though in this case (and as is often the case) a large percentage of the shares are held in the name of nominee companies (63 per cent), who may either be unlikely to reveal the true owners, or who represent some kind of collective ownership on behalf of a number of funds or organisations.

According to the annual report Prudential Portfolio Managers are the largest shareholders with a holding of 63,527,470 (being 4.23 per cent, 4.39 per cent in 1990). This is likely to be significantly larger than any other shareholding since no other is disclosed and there is a legal requirement to disclose all holdings in excess of 3 per cent (Section 199(2), Companies Act, 1985). The extent to which Prudential's shareholding allows it to control or influence the activities of Glaxo is an empirical question which cannot be answered here. In fact Prudential's interest has only recently become visible, following the reduction in the cut-off to 3 per cent from a previous 5 per cent.

Glaxo's annual report also shows other indications of the importance of the US stock market to capital ownership. For example, the presentation of a consolidated Profit and Loss Account and Balance

Sheet in US dollars and the reconciliation to US accounting principles (which reduces profits available to shareholders by £71 million, but increases owners equity by £119 million).

Very brief details of share option schemes are included in the annual report's Report of the Directors. No details are provided of the extent to which employees own shares in the holding company, except in the case of directors. Table 7.4 summarises directors' shareholdings and options at 30 June 1991. Clearly these holdings

Table 7.5 Principal subsidiary and associated undertakings – where Glaxo shareholdings are less than 100%

Company	% Shareholding	Country	Activity
Cascan GmbH & Co KG	50	Germany	Marketing
Glaxo S.U.S.T.A.S.	87	Turkey	Production and marketing
Glaxo ABI S.A.E.	69	Egypt	Production and marketing
Glaxo Bangladesh Ltd	70	Bangladesh	Production and marketing
Nippon Glaxo Ltd	50	Japan	Production and marketing
Glaxo-Sankyo Co. Ltd	(note)	Japan	Marketing
Glaxo Laboratories (Pakistan) Ltd	70	Pakistan	Production and marketing
Glaxo Ceylon Ltd	78	Sri Lanka	Production and marketing
Glaxo Taiwan Ltd	90	Taiwan	Production and marketing
Glaxo (Thailand) Ltd	97	Thailand	Marketing
Glaxo-Vidhyasom Ltd	97	Thailand	Production
Chong qing Glaxo Pharmaceuticals Ltd	50	China	Production and marketing
Glaxo India Ltd	40	India	Production and marketing
Glaxo Korea Co. Ltd	50	S. Korea	Production and marketing
Glaxo Nigeria plc	40	Nigeria	Production and marketing

Source: Glaxo Holdings plc, *Annual Report and Accounts*, 1991.
Note: Nippon Glaxo Ltd holds 50% of the ordinary capital of Glaxo-Sankyo Co. Ltd, which results in the Glaxo Group having an indirect interest of 25%.

are quite insignificant proportions of the total shares issued. No similar information is provided for other employees, either in Britain or overseas. Although such information would perhaps be of interest, particularly a contrast between the position of other employees and that of directors, such shareholdings are almost certainly going to be in the holding company, not in one of the subsidiary or associate companies in which an employee works. In other words, employee shareholdings will not be an indication of participation in the local business, where there might be some scope for influence and opportunity to counter centralised decisions. Of all the principal subsidiaries and associated undertakings listed in the annual report (69 and 4 respectively) only those shown in Table 7.5 are not wholly owned by Glaxo. No details are provided to explain who owns the remaining interests in these companies. As a consequence little can be said about the potential for local community participation or control since little is known about the formal or informal involvement.

The Board

Details of the group Board of Directors are included in the annual report, including photographs, age, position, date of appointment and responsibilities. These reveal appointees with a political background including Sir Geoffrey Howe MP and Mrs A. A. L. Armstrong (former US Ambassador to Britain) as well as the recent appointment of a Japanese member. Very little information is given on the composition of subsidiary or associate company boards. The Chairman and Managing Director is noted for each principal subsidiary and associated undertaking in the annual report. Further details of subsidiary and associate boards would presumably be available in documents registered with each country's respective registrar of companies (where these exist).

Structure

Although details of directors provided in the annual report include positions held by executive directors, background of non-executive directors, reference to the forming of a Group Audit Committee and the reorganisation of the Appeals and Senior Emoluments Committees, relatively little information is given on the structure of the Glaxo group. This seems particularly important in the context of the policy of delegation and decentralisation referred to in the Chairman's statement. Specific details of group structure are probably best drawn from the Chief Executive's Review of Activities which discusses products, geographical sales, research and development, manufacturing and capital expenditure.

A second source of limited information is the list of principal subsidiaries and associate companies, where activities (such as production, marketing and finance) are specified. This is discussed further in the section below on balance of payments/international trade. Yet despite this detail, and the possibility that it provides more information than some other British groups, we are left without a clear picture of the flows of activity in the group and how this is managed. Greater evidence of decentralisation is needed than general statements, and the enduring feeling is that Glaxo, even in its expansion and spread of operations, may remain a relatively-centralised group. The implication for governments seeing Glaxo invest within their borders is that local management freedom and power may be extremely limited.

Although information has been limited, this first section has raised several questions about control by Glaxo of subsidiaries, and we have seen the increasing significance of the United States financial markets. The greatest concern for a British Centre on Transnationals is likely to be one of whether these are indications of a possible shift of corporate headquarters to the USA, an event which would lead to Glaxo's operations in Britain becoming those of a foreign transnational, and whether there is a general shift of operations to other parts of the world, whether due to proximity to markets or lower costs and/or higher subsidies. Lynn (1991) suggests that the Chairman has already raised this possibility with the Board. Certainly there are indications that Glaxo is at least less of a British transnational than once was the case. Some of these matters will be explored in later sections.

Competition

Government concerns with the competitive implications of transnational corporations have stressed marketing, pricing and distributional policies, the impact on local, especially small and medium-sized, businesses, the impact of licensing and technical agreements and generally the effect on industrial structure, concentration and market share, where there is special concern that transnationals might target 'lucrative' (highly profitable) sectors.

Information on such matters is rarely conveyed in a company's annual report, although sometimes details can be obtained which are relevant to forming some impression. However, on the whole, possibly because of desires for commercial confidentiality, little detail is normally given on pricing, profitability and marketing. Yet our impression is that there is a great deal more discussion of Glaxo's pricing than is the case in respect of many other businesses. This may be due to the relatively small number of products of great importance or to the state being a major customer, as well as the effective sanctioned monopoly of patents, with the consequent public interest.

Our discussion of the competitive implications begins with consideration of the general absence of forecast data, before moving on to discuss the problems of obtaining information on specific parts of a group of companies. The remainder of the section considers the importance of patents and marketing before concluding with discussion of market share and the complex relationship Glaxo has with government.

Forecasting

Our review of information available on Glaxo reveals three main sources of relevance here. The annual report is generally a historical document, which concentrates on reporting past performance but does to a limited extent discuss prospects, though normally without incorporating any specific detailed forecasts. The Glaxo annual report does contain discussion of current and new products, and of research and development, each looking to the future to varying degrees. Further comment on products and developments is reported in trade journals, largely based on Glaxo's press releases one can assume, while stockbrokers' reports take this a stage further and often attempt to forecast future performance as a whole or of specific products. Such forecasts concentrate on expected financial returns by assessing the technical strengths of products, expected markets, forecast sales and returns. Our search revealed a number of examples where analysts were willing to estimate future sales of new products. Often these were couched in very broad ranges. For example, in one case the range of the forecast was two-thirds of the lowest figure estimated. In another case the forecast was thought likely to be between two and five times greater than was stated. Obviously matters such as location, productivity etc. will be relevant in constructing such estimates, however these are not normally referred to in great detail. Stockbrokers' reports concentrate on the forecasting of sales and expected profits. There is therefore no clear picture of where the production takes place and how this has changed over the years, despite the likelihood that this is significant to important issues of currency management, investment and taxation (Parker, 1984).

The principal situation in which public-quoted companies may publish financial forecasts arises when raising share capital. A prospectus is issued which may contain both historic and forecast information. In general, however, annual forecasts are not published by firms. This can easily be seen as a matter of some inconsistency. The annual report is a document presented to shareholders for their approval at the company's AGM. Specific approval must be given to dividends, and so in consequence is needed for retention of profits (since dividends are that part of profits distributed). Such retention is in fact the raising of capital, yet no prospectus or forecast is needed. This seems to be approved by Glaxo's Chairman, who has expressed opposition to the ideas of including forecast information in annual reports (*Accountancy*, June 1992).

Some years ago a proposal for the publication of forecast information was contained in an influential discussion document coming from the accounting profession (Boothman Committee, 1975). This suggested the presentation of a Statement of Future Prospects, disclosing:

(a) future profit levels;
(b) future employment levels and prospects; and
(c) future investment levels,

along with a note of major assumptions.

Similar suggestions have also been made more recently by the Research Committee of The Institute of Chartered Accountants of Scotland (McMonnies, 1988). They suggest that information used by management should where possible be made available to shareholders (their concern was less with desires for public accountability than the Boothman Committee, preferring to concentrate on measures to improve the efficient operations of capital markets). Their proposals include a narrative statement of the organisation's objectives, a three-year financial plan highlighting major projects, and a statement of future cash flows (McMonnies, 1988).

However, even such reporting, although possibly useful to a Centre seeking to anticipate transnationals' activity, is unlikely to be so helpful because of the level of aggregation and disclosure in reporting. We turn now to the problem of disaggregation.

The problem of disaggregation

This raises a significant matter regarding the availability and need for information likely to be faced by a transnationals Centre. If we assume that a Centre would be interested in the performance and impact of parts of a transnational group as well as the whole, then the Centre must be aware of problems of disaggregation. It is already evident that the main source of information on a company, the annual report, together with a number of the other sources, concentrates in general on the Glaxo group, an aggregation of the holding company, subsidiaries and associates. Similarly media reports and brokers' reports concentrate generally on the group. Sometimes details relevant to particular subsidiaries are published, but this is relatively rare. And anyway it can be very difficult to disentangle a part of the whole. Prices of internal trade flows (transfer pricing) are often constructed by management, as are certain cost allocations (see Thomas, 1969, 1974; Gray, 1981). As a consequence one must treat information regarding the performance of a part of the group with care, bearing in mind that it is constructed. Largely for this reason we have not analysed the financial statements of Glaxo's British subsidiaries. This point also applies to situations of disaggregation, where the whole picture for the group is divided into segments based on, for example, geographical location, line of business, degrees of risk, etc. As we will see such segmented data can be important in trying to assess aspects of a group's performance, yet serious questions as to its reliability can be asked.

Segmental data

In Glaxo's annual report we are presented with segment information of varying quality. Although there is more detailed discussion of geographical segments in the Chief Executive's Review of Activities, the segmented accounting data presented in the annual accounts is extremely limited, though in compliance with professional, legal and Stock Exchange requirements (see Table 7.6). By dividing

Table 7.6 Segment information (geographical analysis) for Glaxo

	Europe		North America		Rest of World		Total	
	1991 (£m)	1990 (£m)	1991 (£m)	1990 (£m)	1991 (£m)	1990 (£m)	1991 (£m)	1990 (£m) (restated)
Turnover:								
Turnover by location of customer:								
External turnover	1,481	1,338	1,359	1,316	557	525	3,397	3,179
Turnover by location of subsidiary:								
Total turnover	2,041	1,819	1,358	1,314	836	702	4,235	3,835
Inter-segment turnover	(505)	(426)	(3)	(3)	(330)	(227)	(838)	(656)
External turnover	1,536	1,393	1,355	1,311	506	475	3,397	3,179
Profit on ordinary activities before taxation:								
Segment trading profit by location of subsidiary	430	445	367	375	307	220	1,104	1,040
Investment income less interest payable							179	142
Profit on ordinary activities before taxation							1,283	1,182
Net assets:								
Segment net operating assets by location of subsidiary	1,374	1,082	513	412	273	184	2,160	1,678
Net liquid funds							1,212	1,127
Net assets							3,372	2,805

Source: Glaxo Holdings plc, *Annual Report and Accounts*, 1991.

Table 7.7 Profit margin and return on capital employed of Glaxo

	Europe		North America		Rest of World	
	1991 (%)	1990 (%)	1991 (%)	1990 (%)	1991 (%)	1990 (%)
Profit margins	28	32	27	29	61	46
Return on capital employed	31	41	72	91	112	120

Source: Based on figures from Glaxo Holdings plc, *Annual Report and Accounts*, 1991.

Table 7.8 Geographical analysis of turnover of Glaxo

	1991 (£m)	1990 (£m) (restated)	Change (%)
UK	385	337	+14
Europe (excluding UK)	1,096	1,001	+9
North America	1,359	1,316	+3
Latin America	95	77	+23
Africa and Middle East	79	64	+23
Southern Asia and Far East	298	298	0
Australasia	85	86	−1

Source: Glaxo Holdings plc, *Annual Report and Accounts*, 1991.

Table 7.9 Therapeutic analysis of turnover of Glaxo

	1991 (£m)	1990 (£m) (restated)	Change (%)
Anti-ulcerants	1,606	1,551	+4
Respiratory	775	723	+7
Systemic antibiotics	608	560	+9
Cardiovascular	43	50	−14
Dermatologicals	128	126	+2
Anti-emesis	78	2	++
Other	159	167	−5

Source: Glaxo Holdings plc, *Annual Report and Accounts*, 1991.

the world into three sections (Europe, North America and the Rest of the World) we receive no profit details regarding any single country, never mind any particular company in the group. Yet even this limited information is of interest and raises some questions. As Table 7.7 shows, profit margins and returns on capital employed vary across the three segments. One's attention is drawn to the significantly higher profit margins and returns in the Rest of the World compared to the position in North America and Europe. The further information on turnover, both by continent and on a therapeutic basis (see Tables 7.8 and 7.9) is not extended to profitability. Thus comment and disclosure is generally restricted to turnover details with little or no comment on marketing, pricing or profitability. Further details of turnover in particular countries are included in the Chairman's Statement. We discuss this in more detail below in the section dealing with compliance/co-operation with wider industrial economic policy, presenting an attempt to reconcile the details to the overall total which indicates the importance of the US market (37 per cent of turnover).

Patents

Before turning to discuss the matters of marketing and pricing, it is worth commenting on the important matter of patents. Although patents are related to research, and so are discussed briefly in that section, some understanding is needed here in order to consider competition.

The ethical drug industry survives by patenting its inventions, enabling inventors to have protection from competition by replication. Unlike generic drugs which are not sheltered from competition in this way, ethical drugs, when patented, entitle the holder to a period of protection, although this does not necessarily guarantee absence of competition. Patent law is, therefore, seen as protection and an incentive for pharmaceutical companies to invest in the necessary research to develop new and better products. In turn it affords companies and investors an opportunity for higher returns for a certain period.

The creation of such protection and potential for substantial rewards for research is an important contributor to the performance of drug companies, yet Glaxo's annual report makes surprisingly little reference to patents. This contrasts somewhat with the approach of brokers who are not only very concerned about patent registrations, but also expiries and challenges. For example, one broker's report refers to major patent expiry dates in its analysis of the financial prospects for Glaxo, identifying specific products and major market patent expiry dates (see Table 7.10). Similar details appear in Glaxo's 20F statement lodged with the Securities and Exchange Commission (SEC) in the USA.

In addition, during the period we cover, our search of trade

Table 7.10 Major patent expiry dates of Glaxo products

Product	United States	United Kingdom
Ranitidine	1995/2002	1997/2001
Salbutamol/Albuterol	1989	1987
Ceftazidime	1999	1999/2000
Beclomethasone dipropionate (aerosol formulations)	1994	1993
Cefuroxime	1993	1994
Labetalol	1994	1987
Cefuroxime axetil	2000	2005
Ondansetron	2004	2005
Fluticasone propionate	1999	2001
Sumatriptan	2008	2005

Source: Morgan Stanley, *Glaxo: A Tale of Two Headaches and Two Blockbusters*, 16 August 1991 (original source: Glaxo).

journals and newspapers revealed Glaxo's commencement of patent infringement proceedings in the USA in respect of Zantac, its best-selling drug, against Genpharm (*Financial Times*, 9 April 1991; *European Chemical News*, 15 April 1991) and the Canadian arm of the small Tabatznik group (*Business Week*, 29 April 1991). In addition we also traced reports of Smithkline Beecham's suit over allegations that Glaxo's Zofran infringes the former's patent rights in the USA (*Financial Times*, 1 May 1991; *European Chemical Business News*, 6 May 1991; and *Scrip*, 8–10 May 1991). A report in the *Financial Times* (10 April 1991) also outlined difficulties Glaxo appeared to be having in Canada as a result of the Canadian Government's attempts to force pharmaceuticals companies to licence generic versions before expiry of the original patents.

Brief mention of a challenge to the Zantac patent is included in the annual report, in the Chief Executive's Review of Activities, and a note to the accounts on contingent liabilities refers to the adequacy of provisions for claims concerning intellectual property (and product liability), without specifying either the amount of such provisions or any details as to products or cases. Further detail is provided in the 20F report filed with the SEC, in respect of both patent and product liability disputes.

Marketing

A further important influence on the performance of pharmaceuticals companies is marketing. It is often said that success in the drugs industry is as much a matter of marketing as research and productive efficiency, and that some drug companies, such as Glaxo, are market driven rather than research led ('The company clearly holds science subordinate to marketing: making money is more important than making medicines' – Lynn, 1991).

In general there is concern that marketing is driven by profit rather than health concerns, and that pharmaceuticals firms can persuade customers that some useless drugs are beneficial, or may make unfounded claims, or may be directed towards getting doctors to prescribe (Health Action International, 1992). Whereas the traditional view is that marketing concerns finding out what the customer wants, Lynn (1991) suggests that in the pharmaceuticals industry it is more likely that the researchers find out what the customer needs and the marketing is to ensure that the drug is consumed.

In a similar vein Cowe (1993) reminds us that cures are actually bad news for the drugs industry, since treatment is the money-spinner, with most research and development being the latter, and a development which is more akin to marketing. As with patents, however, Glaxo makes little or no comment on its marketing policies and infrastructure. We know little of its marketing costs. Little is known despite the likely importance and influence this has on sales. Brand names are said to provide market protection where doctors are induced by advertising (Abel-Smith, 1976). Information based on specific therapeutics and in relation to specific geographical markets would be of most importance, covering not only direct advertising but also other promotional activities. This seems to be particularly relevant given the frequent emphasis in the discussion of Glaxo's performance on research and development expenditure, which may actually be less than marketing costs.

One broker's report calculates selling and marketing expenditure as a percentage of sales, but in doing so seems to draw on data in the annual report incorrectly, by assuming all 'other operating charges' are selling and marketing costs. This is unlikely, since this figure will include administration costs etc., and salesforce salaries will actually be included in staff costs, a separate figure. During the year the media reported Glaxo's total salesforce as approximately 10,000 (*The Economist*, 6 April 1991; *Daily Telegraph*, 17 June 1991) and Glaxo's 20F statement reported a US salesforce of 2,346. One broker's report provides numbers of salesforce (see Table 7.11). Such detail might at first seem quite unnecessary for our

Table 7.11 Growth in Glaxo's pharmaceuticals salesforce

Year	Approx number of employees
1981	2,000
1982	2,100
1983	2,100
1984	3,400
1985	4,000
1986	5,000
1987	6,000
1988	8,000
1989	9,000
1990	10,000
1991	11,500
1992 expected	12,000
1993 expected	12,100
1994 expected	12,200
1995 expected	12,300

Source: County Natwest, *Glaxo Research and Development Update*, 4 December 1991.

purpose. However, concern with the marketing practices of drug companies in general, and the actions of 'detail men' (the salesforce), particularly in developing countries (Abel-Smith, 1976; Silverman, 1976) suggests that salesforce numbers may be of some interest in contributing to our understanding of marketing practices, particularly if segmented on a national basis.

Whilst, as we will see, considerable detail is given of research and development (including annual expenditure), marketing is barely accounted for by Glaxo. This may be acceptable to some who would wish to protect a firm's competitive position, yet seems to ignore its central importance to performance and therefore impact (Tucker, 1984), as well as a variety of criticisms raised of the industry (see Medawar, 1984; Braithwaite, 1984; Silverman, 1976; Tucker, 1984). For example, during our period media reports referred to criticism of Glaxo's use of a press release to publicise a product (as ethical drug companies are not allowed to advertise directly to the public) (*Financial Times* (North American edition), 12 September 1991), the American Food and Drugs Administration (FDA)'s scrutiny of videos distributed by a number of drug companies including Glaxo, to news agencies, describing their products, which could be seen as a form of advertising (*New York Times*, 22 August 1991), and concerns about the practice of Post

123

Marketing Surveillance (PMS), where pharmaceuticals companies may be seen to be recruiting patients (*Observer*, 10 March 1991) (the Association of the British Pharmaceutical Industry cleared Glaxo of allegations made by a competitor Astra that the promotional aspects of a PMS study for Serevent outweighed the medical ones (*Scrip*, 4 October 1991)).

Other more general criticisms of marketing behaviour in the pharmaceuticals industry suggest that drug companies may have much to account for. During our period *The Economist* (6 April 1991) published a highly-critical piece questioning promotions disguised as educational and fact-finding, the offering of gifts to doctors, and bad-mouthing rivals (specifically referring here to concerns with Glaxo). The prime concern expressed was that drug companies may be sufficiently strong and powerful to create demand, with heavy investment appearing to attempt to distort customer expectations. In this respect it is sometimes argued that supply leads demand due to the formidable power of transnational pharmaceuticals companies, not necessarily just because of the lack of competition, but also because of the industry's role as an educator (Tucker, 1984). In particular concern has been expressed at the increasing practice of testing competitor's products.

In general there appears to be sufficient reason to accept the importance of marketing in the performance and impact of drug companies to suggest the need for improved disclosure. Our search for further information revealed details of advertising spend (£110 m in 1990 and 1991) in the 20F report to the SEC. More generally, in many respects it is surprising that the importance of marketing has not been recognised in some way by Glaxo, even if only to detail a code of practice or indicate its intention to operate in a manner consistent with an industry code. Thus although Glaxopharm, a major subsidiary in the group, is reported to have a five-year plan which includes performance targets including to have no complaints upheld under the ABPI marketing code (*Scrip*, 12 June 1991), there is little reference to such issues in Glaxo's annual report or elsewhere. Glaxopharm's intention suggests that complaints may have been upheld in the past, though none are reported in the 1990/91 annual report.

In general little is mentioned about customer satisfaction or dissatisfaction, and there is little direct indication of the role of consumers in influencing research and development, although our wider search revealed Glaxo's clinical testing, post-marketing surveillance and an interest in pharmacoeconomics and quality of life.

On the matter of markets few details are provided of reasons for changes in turnover, despite the therapeutic analysis of sales (in Table 7.9). In a discussion of the impact of exchange rate changes on sterling in the annual report the Chairman points out that if average exchange rates for 1990/91 had remained as in 1989/90, turnover would have increased by 16 per cent rather than 7 per cent, and profit by 12 per cent rather than 5 per cent. On Zantac, Glaxo's most important product, he informs us that, if one ignores exchange rates, sales rose by 12 per cent. However, the most detailed picture of volume, price and currency effects on overall sales growth comes from a brokers' report. Table 7.12 presents such detail over the last five years, where the source is quoted as company data. Not surprisingly this deals with the group as a whole not the individual companies making up the group or the therapeutic subsectors. Given the importance of exchange rates, the world-wide scope of operations and the various pressures on prices it is difficult to see how analysts can construct their forecasts without a more detailed matrix of national and therapeutic sales and costs. Similar problems would be faced by a Centre wishing to understand or even guess at likely managerial policy.

Concentration and market share

Despite having only 3.5 per cent of the world pharmaceuticals market at the end of 1990, and so being the second largest drugs company in the world, it is clear that a better measure of size and significance requires us to address the particular subsectors of the market. With patent protection, a strategy targeting particular

Table 7.12 Reported sales growth of Glaxo

| | Price/volume/exchange rate effects since 1987 (%) | | | | | | | | |
| | 1991 | | 1990 | | 1989 | | 1988 | | 1987 |
	H2	H1	H2	H1	H2	H1	H2	H1	Yr
Volume	14	12	15	14	14	17	21	17	20
Price	1	2	2	5	4	4	3	3	6
Currency	−8	−11	−6	12	7	0	−6	−14	1
Reported growth	7	3	11	31	25	21	18	6	27

Source: Morgan Stanley, *Glaxo-Maintaining Momentum*, 14 February 1992 (original source: Glaxo).

Table 7.13 Therapeutic analysis of Glaxo group pharmaceuticals and food turnover

	1991 (£m)	1990 (£m)	1989 (£m)	1988 (£m)	1987 (£m)	1986 (£m)	1985 (£m)	1984 (£m)	1983 (£m)	1982 (£m)
Anti-ulcerants	1,606	1,551	1,291	989	829	606	432	248	97	37
Respiratory	775	723	585	457	362	287	255	217	179	148
Systemic antibiotics	608	560	396	299	226	181	112	95	94	91
Cardiovascular	43	50	46	48	46	36	33	19	22	12
Dermatologicals	128	126	101	96	86	77	74	70	66	67
Anti-emesis	78	2	–	–	–	–	–	–	–	–
Other pharmaceuticals	149	155	138	138	149	174	154	130	158	149
Animal health	2	4	5	25	30	26	37	48	48	40
Foods	8	8	8	7	13	42	64	65	93	95
	3,397	3,179	2,570	2,059	1,741	1,429	1,161	892	757	639

Source: Glaxo Holdings plc, Annual Report and Accounts, 1991.

subsectors can be sufficient to enable Merck, Glaxo and other pharmaceuticals companies to become among the largest transnational corporations in the world. In the case of Glaxo, as we saw earlier, the sale of one drug, the anti-ulcerant Zantac, accounted for 48 per cent of annual sales. There is, however, no indication of the attributable contribution or profit. It is necessary, therefore, to go beyond total pharmaceuticals market share to look at subsectors in order to assess the significance of such firms. Glaxo provides data to enable one to do this on a global basis (see Table 7.8), including a ten-year therapeutic analysis of turnover (see Table 7.13). However, national data is provided by Glaxo in total terms, not according to therapeutic category (see Table 7.14).

One matter which receives little attention in the annual report is agreements with other drug companies. Our search of other sources did not reveal any new agreements during the period 1 July 1990 to 19 September 1991, although soon after that date agreements were signed with Sankyo (*Pharma Japan*, 14 October 1991), Sandoz (*Chemical Week*, 23 October 1991) and most surprisingly Merck (*Scrip*, 26 February 1992). These illustrate examples of concerns expressed regarding the multinational pharmaceuticals firms that they may be tending to compete less and co-operate more, with increasing joint multinational marketing operations and licensing agreements (Tucker, 1984).

In addition to the support of patents, market share may be maintained by quality of product, pricing policy, non-market buying power or advertising persuasion. In the pharmaceuticals

Table 7.14 Leading pharmaceutical markets and Glaxo product shares

	Calendar years	
	1989 (%)	*1990* (%)
United States	5.4	5.7
Japan	1.6	1.6
Germany	2.6	2.6
France	2.7	2.8
Italy	12.7	13.5
Spain	2.7	2.8
Canada	5.4	5.2
Brazil	1.6	1.7
South Korea	1.2	1.2
Rest of the World	3.0	3.1

Source: Glaxo Holdings plc, *Annual Report and Accounts*, 1991.

industry, as in any other, it may well be a combination of these factors. Little is known about the first two as discussed above, and the influence of government and other agencies will be discussed in the following subsection. Both product quality and price have been matters of concern to critics of the pharmaceuticals industry over the years. Studies have shown price differences between countries (e.g., Abel-Smith, 1976; Gereffi, 1983; Tucker, 1984), as well as indications of price-fixing. Tucker (1984) refers to the collusion in the US drugs industry in the 1950s, when five of America's largest drug companies are said to have built their industrial empire on international price-fixing and keeping new wonder drugs beyond the reach of the world's population (see also Braithwaite, 1984). Similarly, drug indications have been seen to differ from country to country, sometimes apparently with potentially serious consequences (see Silverman, 1976; Medawar, 1984; Silverman, Lee and Lydecker, 1982).

Government

Governments' relationship with the pharmaceuticals industry is complex. In many countries government expenditure on health and welfare, like many other aspects of public spending, is under severe pressure and there are attempts to control spending on pharmaceuticals. In Glaxo's case a number of governments are attempting to control prices of established and new products. The Chief Executive's review of activities in the annual report deals to some extent with national markets, but makes few comments on these government pressures. He refers to legislation requiring increased discounts to the Medicaid programme in the USA, Canada's 'inadequate patent protection' (arising from that government's attempts to encourage generic manufacture), Japan's attempts to reduce spending on drugs and the Indian subcontinent's inadequate patent protection. But such comments are relatively unspecific.

They also fail to inform us of other matters, such as the Indian Government's 'massive' fine levied on Glaxo India (an associate company) (other companies were fined, although not as much as Glaxo) for overpricing betamethasone (*Chemical Weekly*, 31 July 1990), Glaxo's court case seeking to contest the legality of the Indian Government's demand for payment of US $38.4 millions into the Drug Equalisation Account (*Scrip*, 14 September 1990; *Chemical Weekly*, 13 November 1990), pressure on Glaxo to reduce the price of Marevan in New Zealand, where the British equivalent was said to be 80 per cent cheaper (*Scrip*, 9 October 1991), German, Italian and American attempts to reduce costs (*Sunday Telegraph*, 15 September 1991), and Dutch refusal to reimburse Imigran in oral form (*Scrip*, 18 September 1991).

Research and development/technology

The importance of research and development in the pharmaceuticals industry can be seen in discussions of pricing and in the existence of patent legislation. Proportionately a higher percentage of costs is spent on research and development in the case of ethical drugs than in most other industries. This is reflected in the annual report of Glaxo where there appears to be greater discussion of the subject than in many other corporate annual reports. Our review of government interests in this area revealed a concern to attract high technology, research-based industries and particular interest in product innovation, variety or quality. The impact of such industry in encouraging or discouraging national research and concern to protect key sectors showed a recognition of the opportunities and threats which can result, and in particular that the most profitable or advanced production could be kept for the foreign parent. Other interests included the need to attract specific industries in order to accelerate modernisation, and a desire to see training of indigenous workers as a result.

As with many other aspects of governments' interests, it is not clear how a monitoring Centre can obtain specific information to answer particular concerns, however, there is some indication of performance or impact disclosed which will be of interest. As mentioned above, Glaxo's reporting of progress on research and development appears to be more detailed than that of many other firms. The Chief Executive's review of activities offers both an overview of the world pharmaceuticals industry and of Glaxo's established products and research and development. In this section we discuss research and development/technology under the headings of staffing, the research and development programme, financial data, patents, product liability, product quality and training.

Staffing

The Chief Executive's Review discusses research then development programmes, referring to the division of research responsibilities

129

(elsewhere we are informed of the substantial investment in new facilities in the USA) between Europe (particularly Britain) and the USA. A pie-chart of world-wide R&D staff shows that 61 per cent are located in the UK, 15 per cent in the USA and 24 per cent in the rest of the world. Total research staffing amounts to 6,521 being 18 per cent of total employees. For Britain the concern may be that research is gradually shifting overseas, in particular to the USA. One report mentioned management concern over the quality of research staff available in Britain (*Daily Telegraph*, 22 October 1990). Yet Table 7.15 shows that although there has been a decline in the percentage of total research staff located in Britain, the absolute numbers have increased 45 per cent over the last three years.

Table 7.15 World-wide R&D staffing of Glaxo

	1991	1990	1989	1988
Britain	3,959 (61%)	3,529 (62%)	3,187 (63%)	2,722 (66%)
United States	947 (15%)	740 (13%)	641 (13%)	521 (13%)
Italy	334 (5%)	353 (6%)	329 (7%)	294 (7%)
Japan	220 (3%)	210 (4%)	173 (3%)	143 (3%)
France	211 (3%)	185 (3%)	133 (3%)	121 (3%)
Switzerland	143 (2%)	134 (2%)	129 (3%)	103 (2%)
Germany	116 (2%)	68 (1%)	N/F (–)	N/F (–)
Canada	89 (1%)	70 (1%)	64 (1%)	49 (1%)
Spain	64 (1%)	54 (1%)	38 (1%)	N/F (–)
Rest of the world	438 (7%)	379 (7%)	343 (7%)	175 (4%)
Total	6,521	5,722	5,037	4,128

Source: Glaxo Holdings plc, *Annual Report and Accounts*, 1991.
Notes:
N/F = no figure
No details are available in the annual reports prior to 1988

Research and development programme

Similar detailed discussion of research programmes, product approvals, etc. are reported in stockbrokers' reports and in the trade and financial media. In some respects the brokers' reports set events in context, with some comparing Glaxo's performance in relation to the industry as a whole or to particular competitors. One report identifies stages in the research and development process as discovery, exploratory development and full development. We present two tables from an analyst's report. One on exploratory development drugs identifies projects, drug class, indication and estimates sales potential (see Table 7.16). The other on full development drugs, notes product, indication, comments (such as significance, competition, etc.) and this time sales estimates (see Table 7.17). A slightly different classification is offered by another broker in a later report. Here a three-way classification is based on exploratory development, full development and emerging (see Table 7.18 for meaning and investment context comments).

Details of specific projects are then provided along with comments on technical significance, market potential (a qualitative assessment) and sometimes comments on the competition (see Table 7.19). This data and accompanying discussion is then followed by some comment on the next product cycle. For Glaxo it is apparent that the strategy is one of compensating for the relative decline of the best-selling Zantac, by developing alternative drugs such as Zofran, an anti-emetic drug which had received marketing approval in forty-eight countries since its launch in March 1990 (details from the Chief Executive's Review of Activities). Although such data and forecasts are of interest they fail to address the fundamental question of location of production, so likely to be relevant to a Centre.

Financial data

Specific financial accounting data provided in the annual report includes expenditure charged against profits (£475 m), capital expenditure in respect of research and development (£236 m), some detail on where (in which country) expenditure has been incurred, and inclusion of annual expenditure for the twenty years of the statistical review. Table 7.20 presents an analysis of growth of Glaxo's spending on research and development relative to group

Table 7.16 Exploratory development drugs of Glaxo

Project	Drug class	Indication	Sales potential (£m)
Infectious diseases			
GR 63116	Parenteral Cephalosporin	Antibacterial	135
GR 103665	Reverse transcriptase inhibitor	AIDS	90
GR 95168	DNA Polymerase inhibitor	Herpes	150
Cardiovascular			
GR 53992	Calcium channel blocker	Hypertension	75
Central Nervous System			
GR 68755	CNS indications 5HT₃ blocker	Anxiety	145
GR 85548	5HT₁ blocker effective against depression	Migraine	90

Cancer			
GR 63178	Mitoquidone analogue	Solid tumour anti-cancer	85
Metabolic			
GR 95030	HMG Co A Reductase inhibitor Cholesterol lowering	Lipid lowering in atheroma	90
Squalene Synthase inhibitors	Cholesterol control Atheroma regression	Lipid lowering in atheroma	120
Respiratory			
GR 63411	Bronchodilator, anti-inflammatory	Asthma and associated respiratory disease	100
	Lipoxygenase inhibitors	Asthma and associated respiratory disease	250
Gastro-intestinal			
GR 63799	Anti-ulcer prostanoid	Gastric ulceration	75
Total			1,405

Source: Morgan Stanley, Glaxo: *A Tale of Two Headaches and Two Blockbusters*, 16 August 1991.

Table 7.17 Full development drugs of Glaxo

Product	Indication	Comments	Sales estimates (£m)
Fluticasone propionate	Tropical allergies Asthma	Will face severe competition; to be filed end 1990	50
Lacidipine	Cardiovascular	Likely to gain small share in a huge market	70
Ondansetron (Zofran)	Post-operative emesis	Major indication	400
Ranitidine bismuth citrate	Anti-ulcer and related acid disease	Important in the protection of Zantac	350
GR 109714 3TC	AIDS	A long way behind Wellcome's Retrovir	70
Total			940

Source: Morgan Stanley, *Glaxo: A Tale of Two Headaches and Two Blockbusters*, 16 August 1991.

Table 7.18 Classification of new drugs stage of development

Classification	Meaning	Investment context
Emerging	Pivotal clinical trials completed. Major regulatory filing have, or are about to be made. May already have some market approvals	*Very important* – can be discounted into shareprice and incorporated into near-term earnings models
Full development	Pivotal clinical trials underway	*Important* – likely to come to the market within two to five years. Can be partially discounted into shareprice and longer-term earnings models
Exploratory development	Animal work and acute toxicological work largely completed. Preliminary human studies underway	*Not important* – high chance of failure through toxicology, efficacy, manufacturing or bioavailability. Should not be discounted into shareprice

Source: County Natwest, *Glaxo Research and Development Update*, 4 December 1991.

Table 7.19 Glaxo's 1990 Research and Development pipeline status

Status	Project	Drug	Comment
Emerging	Anti-emetic in cancer therapy	ondansetron (Zofran)	For use in prevention of nausea and vomiting associated with cancer drugs and radiotherapy. Highly effective and lacking in major side effects of other drugs.
	Anti-asthma	salmeterol (Serevent)	Very long-acting bronchodilator. Targeted as a prophylactic in asthma, particularly useful in preventing nocturnal asthma
	Migraine	sumatriptan (Imigran)	Highly effective yet free from serious side-effects of other migraine drugs
	Anti-inflammatory	fluctisone (Flixonase, Cutivate)	Potent steroid in inhaler form for asthma, and topical form for skin complaints
Full development	Anti-emetic in post-operative nausea and vomiting	ondansetron (Zofran)	A debilitating and unpleasant condition brought on by inhalation anaesthetics. Large potential market.
	Anxiety	ondansetron	Early work shows promise of good efficacy and no sign of rebound anxiety on stopping treatment, in contrast to diazepam (Valium). Some very early work started in schizophrenia, drug dependence and memory disorders
	Depression	fluparoxan	Hope for rapid onset of action and lack of serious side-effects compared to existing therapies
	Anti-clotting	vapiprost (GR 32191)	A thromboxane antagonist to prevent blood clotting [Under review]
	Injectable antibiotic	GR 69153	Broad spectrum antibiotic primarily for hospital use (Licensed from Mochida) [Under review]
Exploratory development	CNS disorders	GR 68755	A 5–HT$_3$ antagonist being explored in conditions such as schizophrenia and anxiety
	HIV disease	GR 109714	Anti-AIDS drug – same type as Wellcome's Retrovir
	Anti-asthma	GR 63411	Profile similar to salmeterol
	Hypolipidaemic	GR 105155	Novel mechanism to reduce cholesterol levels
	Anti-cancer	GR 63178	Targeted at solid tumours
	Anti-ulcer	GR 63799	Cytoprotective agent

Table 7.19 Continued

Status	Project	Drug	Comment
	Anti-viral	GR 95618	Anti-herpes drug – same class as Wellcome's Zovirax
	Hypolipidaemic	GR 95030	Designed to lower elevated cholesterol levels – same class as Merck's Mevacor
	Analgesic	GI 87084	Opioid injectable
	Migraine	GR 85548	Same class of drug as sumatriptan
	Anti-diabetic	GR 79236	A new class of drug to treat type II diabetes
	Angina/ myocardial ischaemia	GR 53992	A calcium antagonist
	Anti-emesis/IBS	GR 87442	A $5-HT_3$ antagonist
	Injectable antibiotic	GR 63116	Powerful antibiotic for hospital use
	Migraine	GR 40370	Same class as sumatriptan
	Anti-inflammatory	GR 80907	Novel class (5–LO inhibitor)

Source: County Natwest, *Glaxo Research and Development Update*, 4 December 1991.

turnover over the last twenty years, showing a rise from an initial 3.7 per cent to 14 per cent in 1991.

Patents

As previously mentioned when discussing competition, relatively little information is given on patents and patent challenges in Glaxo's annual report. The Chief Executive's review of activities refers to a patent action in respect of the new product Zofran and a patent challenge in respect of the established Zantacs's second patent. According to the note to the accounts on contingent liabilities, appearing in the annual report, it appears that Glaxo has made what it feels are adequate provisions relating to 'product liability and intellectual property rights', however, no further details are provided (see Table 7.21).

Product liability

Table 7.21 also refers to potential liabilities arising from company products. This may include provision for claims in respect of

Table 7.20 Glaxo's research and development expenditure over the last twenty years

Year	Total (£m)	% of group turnover
1972	7	3.7
1973	7	3.2
1974	8	3.1
1975	12	5.5
1976	14	3.4
1977	17	3.5
1978	20	3.7
1979	25	4.6
1980	32	5.2
1981	40	5.6
1982	50	5.8
1983	60	5.8
1984	77	6.4
1985	93	6.6
1986	113	7.9
1987	149	8.6
1988	230	11.2
1989	323	12.6
1990	420	13.2
1991	475	14.0

Source: Glaxo Holdings plc, *Annual Report and Accounts*, 1991.

Table 7.21 Contingent liabilities in Glaxo

Note 23 Contingent liabilities	1991 (£m)	1990 (£m)
(a) Group		
Borrowings guaranteed	6	6
Other	30	20
(b) Holding company		
Borrowings guaranteed of subsidiary and associated undertakings	13	5

Unquantified claims have been made against group undertakings relating to product liability and intellectual property rights. In the opinions of the Directors the amounts provided in these accounts against such claims are adequate.

Although the taxation liabilities of certain UK and overseas subsidiary undertakings have not been finally agreed with the appropriate revenue authorities for a number of years, the Directors consider that the amounts provided in these accounts are adequate to meet any uncertainties.

No provision has been made for taxation which would arise on the distribution of profits retained by overseas subsidiary and associated undertakings, save as shown in these accounts.

Source: Glaxo Holdings plc, *Annual Report and Accounts*, 1991.

Myodil, where sixty back sufferers in Ireland were reported to be taking action against Glaxo, alleging side effects after the drug was injected into them prior to spinal X-rays (*Observer*, 2 December 1990; *Evening Standard*, 7 January 1991; and *European Chemical News*, 14 January 1991), and in respect of asthma and arthritis sufferers in Britain, who had experienced side-effects from long-term treatment with cortico-steroids (*European Chemical News*, 6 May 1991; and *The Northern Echo*, 15 August 1991). The myodil case commenced in July 1991 (*The Times*, 20 July 1991).

Quality

Connected to such concerns is the overall matter of product quality. Pharmaceuticals corporations are subject to various controls and inspections. Food and Drug Administration (FDA) inspectors from the USA regularly review production facilities located outside the USA which are supplying that market. Yet, despite this and the general climate of regulation focusing on quality and health and safety, virtually no mention is made of this in Glaxo's annual report. On the other hand the continued existence of Glaxo as a supplier of major markets and the absence of news of any restrictions will be taken by some as a sign that, in general, standards are achieved. No news is perhaps good news.

A second aspect of quality concerns the impact of a product. Nowadays there seems to be greater emphasis on the wider benefits which can be derived from a product, such as reduced time off work. In part this seems to be outlined by firms in order to justify higher prices. There are clear indications that Glaxo is pursuing wider economic and social evaluations of its products, yet little reference and certainly no quantifications are presented in the annual report or in any of the other sources we consulted.

Training

Surprisingly, training is one aspect of employment not addressed directly in Glaxo's reporting despite the corporation's reputation for qualified staff and technical and professional employment. Information on training is absent from the annual report and in general any wider discussion of the group, yet there are reasons to believe that in such a research- and marketing-oriented organisation investment in training may be significant, and that in one particular case reports of the reorganisation of the site (at Speke, in Britain) just before the beginning of our period suggested new approaches to work and the need for training (*Financial Times*, 1 May 1990).

Employment and industrial relations

This category included concern with the rate of exploitation, interest in job quantity, quality and security and conditions of work and life, equality of opportunity and impact on industrial relations. Our discussion is divided up as follows. We begin by considering remuneration and exploitation, before looking at information on the conditions of employment, health and safety, job quality and quantity. Finally we consider the matters of equal opportunities and employee involvement.

Before going on to consider these matters it is worth commenting on an issue which could be of general relevance to this entire section. Apart from a very brief reference to the 'many' employees who are members (contained in the 20F report), we have very little data on trade union membership, in total or national terms.

Employees' remuneration

Disclosure of employees' remuneration is restricted to the legally-required Directors' details and the overall employee details. A comparison of the two is shown in Table 7.22. This illustrates an average salary for non-executive Directors of £26,900, for Executive Directors £552,600 and all other employees £18,300. This produces a ratio of remuneration of 30:1 for executive directors to all other employees. However, given the location of research activities largely in developed countries and the indications of significantly higher returns outside of Europe and North America (see Table 7.7), together with the likelihood, as brokers' reports suggest, of location being determined by profit considerations (reducing costs), this is likely to show only part of the picture. National data on employment levels and remuneration would offer information of greater interest. In Table 7.22 we have calculated a ratio of highest paid to lowest on the basis of a figure of £8,000 per annum for the latter. This is likely to greatly exceed the lowest paid in many of the countries in which Glaxo operates, yet still produces a ratio of 133.5:1.

Only in the case of South African employees is any comparison

Table 7.22 Directors' remuneration and other employees' wages in Glaxo

	Total (£m)	Average (£000)
Non-executive Directors (8)[a]	0.215	26.9
Executive Directors, including Chairman (9)[b]	4.973	552.6
	5.188	305.2
All other employees (35,623)	650.812	18.3
	656.000[c]	18.4

Ratio of Executive Directors' salary to all other employees 30.2 : 1.0

It is not possible to calculate the ratios of the top paid director, the Chairman to the lowest paid in the group, but assuming a lowest salary of £8,000 the ratio would be 133.5 : 1.0

Source: Glaxo Holdings plc, *Annual Report and Accounts*, 1991.
Notes:
a Non-executive directors are assumed to be the lowest paid (up to £65,000 maximum)
   Total wage is calculated using the midpoint of the range disclosed
b Executive Directors are the rest, with total wages calculated on the basis of midpoints
c The wages figure used here excludes social security and pension contributions made by Glaxo, which could add a further 23.6% in the wages figure

Table 7.23 Index of average earnings of all employees in Coalite

	Coalite[a]	Chemicals and Allied Industries[b]
1967/68	100	100
1968/69	104	108
1969/70	116	117
1970/71	145	122
1971/72	156	138
1972/73	182	154
1973/74	188	168

Source: Social Audit (1974) A report on Coalite and Chemical Products Ltd, *Social Audit* 2 (2).
Notes:
a Information derived from *Coalite* annual reports.
b Information from *Monthly Digest of Statistics*, HMSO, *Coalite*'s financial year ends on 31 March, but for the purposes of comparison it is assumed to end on the preceding 31 December.

available with a desirable minimum. In the case of the 1990/91 EC Code Report all employees there were paid above the minimum living level + 50 per cent, indicating that there is no problem regarding defined poor wages in the South African subsidiary (EIRIS, 1992). We have no data for wages in any other country.

An example of an attempt to measure pay and fringe benefits is seen in the Social Audit Avon Report (Social Audit, 1976). This looks not only at the wage levels etc., but also describes payment systems, differentials and job evaluation, wage negotiations, earnings and hours. It is concerned, therefore, with not only data but also policies and structures. A table summarises weekly earnings and hours worked for different grades of staff at certain locations, including Directors. In the same organisation's report on Coalite (Social Audit, 1974) a table is presented as an index of average earnings of all employees in Coalite and the Chemical and Allied Industries from a base 1967/68 to 1973/74 (see Table 7.23). These illustrate the potential for firms to report or data to be collected on remuneration.

Rate of exploitation

Information on the rate of exploitation is most relevant at the local level because of the power of transnationals to locate production in low wage economies, or at least use that threat to play off locations against each other. Clearly, as indicated above, such detail is not available. However, some attempt can be made to calculate an overall rate of exploitation, based on the relationship between profit before deducting wages and the wages cost, as shown in Table 7.24. This shows that profit before wages is 2.69 times the total wages bill. The probability (drawing on Table 7.7) is that in certain parts

Table 7.24 Rate of exploitation in Glaxo

Wages and salaries	£656 millions
Trading profit	£1,104 millions

If one adjusts trading profit to add back wages and salaries as stated and Directors' remuneration (because of the question of whether such is a return to shareholders/owners and is in part performance related) of £6.65 millions, a rate of exploitation can be calculated by:

$$\frac{\text{Trading profit before wages and directors' remuneration}}{\text{Wages and salaries}}$$

$$\frac{£1,767 \text{ millions}}{£656 \text{ millions}}$$

$$= 2.69 \text{ times}$$

Source: Glaxo Holdings plc, *Annual Report and Accounts*, 1991.
Note: If one excludes Directors' remuneration from the wages figure above, the ratio becomes 2.72 times (£1,767m : £649m)

of the world the rate of exploitation is significantly higher, and in other parts lower.

Conditions of employment

Clearly other aspects of the employment relationship are important. Various conditions of work and life are central to people's everyday experiences. Recently the matter of pensions has received great attention. The annual report reveals that there is a shortfall, although elsewhere Glaxo reports that it has one of the best pension schemes (*Glaxonews*, June 1991). The pension scheme covers the majority of staff, though few specific details are given. Similarly, we are not informed of any worker representation or trade union representation on pension schemes. Nor is it clear whether pensions is accepted by the company as an area on which it is willing to negotiate with trade unions.

Other conditions of employment may also be worth looking at closely. For example, the following were examined in Social Audit's Avon report (Social Audit, 1976): holidays, sick pay, disability insurance, share option scheme, canteens, social and sports facilities, subsidised transport, removal allowances and pre-retirement courses. While these may be seen as often less essential conditions, the following section deals with the widely-acknowledged matter of health and safety.

Health and safety

Glaxo recognises the importance of health and safety in its annual report without providing any specific data. Elsewhere various policies are reported (in-house journals) and mention is made of improvement in statistics. However, there is nowhere any disclosure of any data, no reporting of any incidents or prosecutions. This is surprising since elsewhere (*Glaxonews*, February 1990) Glaxo acknowledges that its health and safety record is inferior to another transnational, Du Pont, leading it to introduce new measures.

Some corporations have voluntarily reported on health and safety matters. For example, Atlantic Richfield produced a graph of lost working days due to accidents per 100 employees per year over the period 1972–9, showing its performance compared to all manufacturing. Its eight-point safety and health policy was also reproduced. In another example Dow Chemicals reported on a number of matters, including the existence of its employee health surveillance scheme.

More specific details of health and safety performance are found in the Social Audit reports of Coalite, Tube and Avon. The Coalite report (Social Audit, 1974) contains details of the number of reportable incidents and accident frequency (see Table 7.25). Similarly the Tube report (Social Audit, 1973) contains details of the average annual number of reportable accidents, the average per 1,000 employees, and the average in comparable industries for companies or works in the group. Similar details are calculated for Avon plants (Social Audit, 1976), although this time the number of accidents investigated by Her Majesty's Factory Inspectorate (HMFI) is noted. Discussion of health and safety in this report extended beyond accidents to procedures and consultation. The report discussed relations with HMFI (noting inspections per plant), noise and chemical hazards. A table is included which lists suspected and recognised carcinogens used in the Avon Group at November 1974. A much larger list of hazardous materials used at Avon is produced with details of dangers (Social Audit, 1976). Such examples illustrate the potential for firms such as Glaxo to extend their accountability, and can be seen as an

Table 7.25 Incidence of reportable accidents in Coalite works per 1,000 employees, 1970–3[a]

Year	Industry average[b]	Bolsover 'Coalite'	Askern	Rossington	Grimethorpe
1970	99.8	130.6	159.3	–	325.0
1971	96.0	119.9	98.7	–	317.8
1972	93.2	102.1	96.1	264.3	278.1
1973	98.7	n.a.	93.8	264.7	n.a.

Source: Social Audit (1974) 'A Report on Coalite and Chemical Products Ltd'. *Social Audit* 2(2).

Notes:

a These data were made available to us by local union officials – together with estimates of the numbers of works employees at each *Coalite* plant needed to compare the Company's record with the industry average. (No annual figures were available for accident levels at Bolsover Refinery.)
The table compares levels of 'reportable accidents' – those which involve a worker in three or more days absence from work.

b The average is for the 'coke ovens and manufactured fuel' industry (Minimum List Heading 261) as published in the annual reports of HM Chief Inspector of Factories.
According to HMFI, the standard of accident reporting in this industry is 'well above average'.

indication to a monitoring Centre of what might be valuable information.

Job quality

Details of job quality are not reported in the Glaxo annual report, although perhaps it is assumed that functions such as marketing and research are generally perceived to be satisfying, are well remunerated and offer opportunities for progression. There is no indication of job categories, nor of staff turnover. And perhaps most importantly in the absence of some classification of jobs, with reference to skills needed etc., we know little about the location of such jobs (except for research), a matter of particular significance when examining a transnational corporation.

Job quantity

Some information on job quantity is given, with an analysis of UK and overseas figures. This information is provided for the last

Table 7.26 Analysis of employment changes in Glaxo, 1972–91

Year	UK employees	Overseas	Total	% change in UK	% change in Overseas	% change in total
1972	17,000	13,107	30,107			
1973	16,568	13,197	29,765	−2.5	+0.8	−1.1
1974	16,344	13,735	30,079	−1.4	+4.1	+1.1
1975	17,084	14,436	31,520	+4.5	+5.1	+4.8
1976	16,132	14,551	30,683	−5.6	+0.8	−2.7
1977	15,944	14,596	30,540	−1.2	+0.3	−0.5
1978	15,881	15,020	30,901	−0.4	+2.9	+1.2
1979	15,602	14,179	29,781	−1.8	−5.6	−3.6
1980	14,816	14,371	29,187	−5.0	+1.4	−2.0
1981	13,725	14,493	28,218	−7.4	+0.8	−3.3
1982	13,188	14,918	28,106	−3.9	+2.9	−0.4
1983	13,605	14,163	27,768	+3.2	−5.1	−1.2
1984	13,685	11,368	25,053	+0.6	−19.7	−9.8
1985	13,463	12,171	25,634	−1.6	+7.1	+2.3
1986	11,815	12,913	24,728	−12.2	+6.0	−3.5
1987	10,867	14,087	24,954	−8.0	+9.1	+0.9
1988	11,035	15,388	26,423	+1.5	+8.5	+5.9
1989	11,444	17,266	28,710	+3.7	+12.2	+8.7
1990	12,291	20,934	33,225	+7.4	+21.2	+15.7
1991	12,422	23,218	35,640	+1.1	+10.9	+7.3

Source: Glaxo Holdings plc, Annual Report and Accounts, 1991.

twenty years. Table 7.26 analyses UK and overseas employment, identifying annual percentage changes. Recent years indicate some contrast between the UK and overseas. The ratio of UK to overseas has changed dramatically since 1972, when it was 1.30 to 1991's 0.54. Although the total work-force is now approximately 5,500 greater than it was in 1972, the UK numbers are down by 4,500 while overseas are up 10,000. The scope for transnational corporations to relocate to low wage economies or to replace home production and exports by imports, suggests a need to monitor such change. Unfortunately there is little information available on the location of jobs.

Equal opportunities

Glaxo's annual report contains a statement of non-discrimination (referring to colour, race, ethnic or national origin, sex, marital status or religious belief) and that the group gives full consideration to job applications from disabled people. Section 9 of Schedule 7 of the 1985 Companies Act requires companies to describe their policy in regard to disabled people. However, no specific reporting of how this policy turns out in practice is detailed. There is no reporting of the actual equal opportunities impact of Glaxo.

An example of the kind of detailed analysis of equal employment opportunity which could be reported is provided by General Motors. This matrix covers job category and minorities and women (see Table 7.27), analysing their numbers in each job category. The table illustrates the substantial differences between office and clerical employment and officials and managers, as well as between craftsmen (sic) and labourers. An interesting inclusion in the same General Motors report is the narrative on programmes for Minorities and Women, which covers dealings with minority suppliers and auto dealerships. A focus on relative wages is also seen in the Avon report where wages and hours worked are calculated in terms of male and female (see Tables 7.28 and 7.29). This report also presents statistics on the employment of registered disabled people at different plants (see Table 7.30).

Employee involvement

We are informed in the annual report, as required by Paragraph 11, Schedule 7 of the 1985 Companies Act, that employees are

Table 7.27 General Motors US employment at 31 December 1981*

Job category	Year	Total employment	Total women Employment	%	Black	Asian	American Indian	Hispanic	Total employment	%
							Minority employees			
Officials and managers	1979	56,844	3,610	6.4	4,453	127	219	524	5,323	9.4
	1980	51,918	3,252	6.3	3,956	112	196	444	4,708	9.1
	1981	51,145	3,303	6.5	4,030	136	185	499	4,850	9.5
Professionals	1979	38,264	5,896	15.4	2,192	614	101	389	3,296	8.6
	1980	36,206	5,727	15.8	2,135	632	111	406	3,284	9.1
	1981	38,593	6,731	17.4	2,270	658	97	472	3,497	9.1
Technicians	1979	13,254	2,192	16.5	1,160	135	37	223	1,555	11.7
	1980	11,971	2,065	17.3	1,083	128	42	192	1,445	12.1
	1981	11,140	1,908	17.1	983	116	36	164	1,299	11.7
Sales workers	1979	4,789	436	9.1	402	25	20	76	523	10.9
	1980	4,155	384	9.2	369	25	22	58	474	11.4
	1981	3,712	301	8.1	342	24	17	57	440	11.9
Office and clerical	1979	37,998	22,165	58.3	5,867	220	140	1,034	7,261	19.1
	1980	33,949	19,946	58.8	5,033	211	134	940	6,318	18.6
	1981	32,963	19,596	59.5	4,963	212	112	924	6,211	18.8
Total white-collar employees	1979	151,149	34,299	22.7	14,074	1,120	517	2,246	17,957	11.9
	1980	138,199	31,374	22.7	12,576	1,108	505	2,040	16,229	11.7
	1981	137,553	31,839	23.1	12,588	1,146	447	2,116	16,297	11.8
Craftsmen (skilled)	1979	100,020	1,211	1.2	6,571	129	232	1,415	8,347	8.3
	1980	99,136	1,305	1.3	6,706	140	221	1,402	8,469	8.5
	1981	89,659	1,175	1.3	5,496	132	213	1,215	7,056	7.9

	Year									
Operatives (semi-skilled)	1979	332,663	71,736	21.6	69,868	833	780	11,310	82,791	24.9
	1980	301,302	66,664	22.1	63,277	718	675	10,046	74,716	24.8
	1981	272,399	57,759	21.2	56,223	657	550	10,291	67,721	24.9
Labourers (unskilled)	1979	21,543	2,687	12.5	4,239	87	46	904	5,276	24.5
	1980	22,275	3,095	13.9	4,127	73	39	898	5,137	23.1
	1981	21,252	3,456	16.3	3,744	78	42	835	4,699	22.1
Service workers	1979	17,894	2,507	14.0	4,265	32	39	660	4,996	27.9
	1980	16,723	2,339	14.0	3,742	36	50	583	4,411	26.4
	1981	15,546	2,079	12.4	3,495	25	38	632	4,190	26.9
Total blue-collar employees	1979	472,120	78,141	16.6	84,943	1,081	1,097	14,289	101,410	21.5
	1980	439,436	73,403	16.7	77,852	967	985	12,929	92,733	21.1
	1981	398,856	64,469	16.2	68,958	892	843	12,973	83,666	21.0
Grand totals	1979	623,269	112,440	18.0	99,017	2,202	1,614	16,535	119,368	19.2
	1980	577,635	104,777	18.1	90,428	2,075	1,490	14,969	108,962	18.9
	1981	536,409	96,308	18.0	81,546	2,038	1,290	15,089	99,963	18.6

Source: General Motors, *Public Interest Report*, 1982.
Notes:
* Includes employees on short-term leave and temporary layoff, as required for statistical reporting purposes.
EQUAL EMPLOYMENT. Even though GM's total US employment at year-end 1981 was 41,226 below the 1980 level, the representation of women and minorities was virtually unchanged from 1980.

Table 7.28 Numbers of full-time male and female Avon employees

| | Works | | Staff | |
	M	F	M	F
Melksham[a]	2,273	169	844	283
Bradford[b]	692	147	251	86
Bridgend[c]	447	18	125	52
Medicals[d]	55	420	40	33
Inflatables[e]	51	225	35	29
Motorway (works + staff)	847	174		

Source: Social Audit (1976) 'On the Avon Rubber Company Ltd', *Social Audit* 2 (3 & 4).

Notes:
[a] November 1974.
[b] September 1974/works and July 1974/staff.
[c] October 1974.
[d] September 1974.
[e] September 1973.

Table 7.29 Female average earnings (and hours worked) as a percentage of male earnings (and hours) at Avon companies, 1972–4

| | For works employees only[a] | | | | | |
	1972 (%)	(hours) (%)	1973 (%)	(hours) (%)	1974 (%)	(hours) (%)
Melksham	58.0	(91.2)	61.7	(87.6)	62.0	(83.6)
Bradford	52.8	(76.5)	65.5	(92.2)	63.3	(83.2)
Bridgend	56.7	(96.6)	56.1	(91.7)	42.0	(68.8)
Rubber Industry average	55.0	(91.4)	57.2	(88.5)	62.0	(89.6)

Source: Social Audit (1976) 'On the Avon Rubber Company Ltd', *Social Audit* 2(3 & 4).

Note:
[a] No figures supplied for Avon Inflatables or Avon Medicals.

encouraged to become involved in various ways. However, those ways mentioned appear in general to be means of management informing staff, rather than obvious ways of consulting or allowing staff to be represented. There is no reference to how practices differ across the group. Little is actually said about the structures in place for consultation. No information is given on disputes and bargaining procedures, actual disputes or redundancy agreements, except in the 20F statement where we are informed that Glaxo has not experienced any work stoppages in recent years. Some specific detail is given in the media and Glaxo's own publications, such as a charter at one plant (Speke), and the setting up of an employee

Table 7.30 Employment of registered disabled people by Avon companies

	Total number in work-force (approximate) number at 1.1.75)	Percentage of work-force who are RDPs
Melksham	3,500	1.5
Bradford	1,200	3.0
Bridgend	640	3.0
Medicals	565	1.77
Inflatables	385	0.78
Motorway	1,100	0.45

Source: Social Audit (1976) 'On the Avon Rubber Company Ltd', *Social Audit* 2(3 & 4).

consultation committee, for the discussion of environmental operational changes at the Ware plant (*Glaxonews*, February 1990). However, in general little is reported in both the annual report and in the media on employee involvement.

Balance of payments

Concern with the impact of transnational corporations has also centred on the balance of payments effects of decisions and the questions of capital flows and repatriation of profits. Overall, particularly in smaller countries, there is likely to be a concern with the impact of such flows on currency stability.

Flow of funds

In general transnational corporations in their annual reports will say very little about such trade and flows. As indicated on a number of occasions earlier in this chapter, the annual report of the Glaxo group and discussion in the media and in brokers' reports concentrates on the group as a whole. The segmented information is extremely limited, and certainly does not extend to describing flows of capital and profits or imports and exports of particular companies or in respect of particular countries. This is obviously a significant omission for a monitoring Centre, given the extent to which the corporation not only produces and sells overseas but also researches. It is also clear that Glaxo actively shifts funds around the globe, in order to obtain the best returns. The annual report details liquid funds of £2,095,000,000, and the statement 20F confirms this is held in different currencies.

Table 7.31 Glaxo's principal subsidiaries and associated undertakings' operations

Company	Co-ordinating	Holding	Production	Exporting	Research	Marketing	Trading	Finance	Insurance	Administration
Glaxo Group	✓									
Glaxochem		✓								
Glaxo Export				✓						
Glaxo Group Research					✓					
Glaxo International Research					✓					
Glaxo Manufacturing Services		✓	✓							
Glaxo Operations			✓							
Glaxo Pharmaceuticals UK			✓			✓				
Glaxo Pharmazeutika Ges						✓				
Glaxo Belgium						✓				
Glaxo Danmark						✓				
Glaxo Pharmaceuticals Oy						✓				
Laboratoires Glaxo			✓		✓	✓				
Cascan GmbH & Co KG (50%)										
Glaxo GmbH			✓			✓				
Glaxo A.E.B.E.			✓			✓				
Glaxo Ltd			✓			✓				
Glaxo S.p.A.			✓			✓				
Duncan Farmaceutica S.p.A.						✓				
Glaxo Bv						✓				
Glaxo Norway						✓				
Glaxo Farmaceutica Lda						✓				
Glaxo S.A.			✓		✓	✓				
Glaxo Sweden						✓				
Adechsa S.A.							✓			

Glaxo A.G.

Glaxo Institute for Molecular
Biology

Glaxo S.U.S.T.A.S. (87%)

Glaxo Finance Bermuda

Glaxo Insurance (Bermuda)

Glaxo Trading (Bermuda)

Glaxo (Bermuda)

Glaxo Canada

Glaxo American Inc

Glaxo Inc

Glaxo (Latin America)

Laboratorios Glaxo
(Argentina)

Glaxo do Brasil

Glaxo Parmaceutea Chilena

Laboratorios Glaxo de
Colombia

Glaxo del Ecuador

Glaxo de Mexico

Glaxo Centro America

Glaxo del Peru

Glaxo Caribbean

Glaxo Uruguaya

Laboratorios Glaxo de
Venezuela

Glaxo ABI (69%)

Glaxo East Africa

Glaxo South Africa

Table 7.31 Continued

Company	Co-ordinating	Holding	Production	Exporting	Research	Marketing	Trading	Finance	Insurance	Administration
Glaxo Bangladesh			✓			✓				
Glaxo China						✓				
Glaxo Hong Kong			✓			✓				
Nippon Glaxo (50%)			✓			✓				
Glaxo-Sankyo (25%)*						✓				
Glaxo Malaysia			✓			✓				
Glaxo Laboratories (Pakistan) (70%)			✓			✓				
Glaxo Phillipines						✓				
Glaxo Singapore						✓				
Glaxo Far East		✓								
Glaxochem (Pte)								✓		
Glaxo Development plc							✓			
Glaxo Pharmaceuticals Pte			✓			✓				
Glaxo Ceylon (78%)			✓			✓				
Glaxo Taiwan						✓				
Glaxo (Thailand)						✓				
Glaxo-Vidhyasom			✓			✓				
Glaxo Australia						✓				
Glaxo New Zealand			✓			✓				
Changqing Glaxo Pharmaceuticals (50%)			✓			✓				
Glaxo India (40%)			✓			✓				
Glaxo Korea (50%)						✓				
Glaxo Nigeria (40%)						✓				

Source: Glaxo Holdings plc. *Annual Report and Accounts*, 1991.
Note:
* Nippon Glaxo holds 50% of the Ordinary Capital of Glaxo-Sankyo, which results in the Glaxo Group having an indirect interest of 25%.

Financing

The financing of Glaxo is relatively simple and debt free (based on the levels of long-term debt). Profits generated from operations have been sufficient to finance recent expansion. The balance sheet at 30 June 1991 reveals current assets investments of £2,095 million tied up in short-term government and equivalent investment, other investments and deposits at banks. On the other hand during the year 1990/91 Glaxo raised £90 million in Japanese Convertible Bonds for reasons which are not fully explained in the report. However, Japan is the second largest pharmaceuticals market in the world according to Glaxo's own statistics and Glaxo is obviously keen to expand operations there.

Trade flows

With the limited information available on trade flows, but the knowledge that research is conducted in at least ten countries and that trade in bulk pharmaceuticals is conducted within the group, as well as sales from one country to another (see Table 7.31 which indicates that marketing is the sole operation in a large number of companies and countries) the volume of imports and exports, as well as allocated overheads and profit repatriation seem likely to be very significant.

The only specific mentions of intra-group trade on a geographical basis is seen in Table 7.6, where inter-segment turnover is clearly significant (20%, being £838 millions of a total £4,235 millions) even using such enormous continental segments). Clearly the situation will likely be extremely complex, yet one which could lend itself to a concise presentation in the form of a matrix, with entries representing the value of flows in and out of countries.

On imports and exports, only Glaxo's exports from the UK (£641 million) is disclosed in the Chief Executive's Review of Activities, being more than a quarter of all UK exports of pharmaceuticals in the year. A ten-year summary of exports is presented in Table 7.32.

A proposal for the disclosure of transactions in foreign currency was contained in the Corporate Report (Boothman Committee, 1975). Although the suggestion is apparently more concerned with national prosperity through direct exports and returns from overseas investment, clearly a monitoring Centre would wish a more complete picture of imports and export activity, flows of funds

Table 7.32 Glaxo's exports from Britain 1982–91

Year	£m
1991	641
1990	653
1989	618
1988	485
1987	395
1986	393
1985	332
1984	262
1983	240
1982	207

Source: Glaxo Holdings plc, various Annual Reports and Accounts.

Table 7.33 Index of UK exports of Tube Investments

	Tube Investments	*Manufacturing industry*
1972	118.5	146.5
1971	112.0	145.0
1970	99.8	136.0
1969	92.2	134.0
1967/8	69.5[a]	111.5
1966/7	91.0	104.5
1965/6	93.0	104.0
1964/5	100.0	100.0

Source: Social Audit (1973) 'The first social audit; Tube Investments Ltd,' *Social Audit* 1(3).

Note:

[a] The sharp drop in 1967/8 was not due to nationalisation of *TI*'s steel interests – they accounted only for about 10 per cent of the group's exports. *TI*'s figures have been adjusted using the price index for exported goods and services.

for investment and remittance of profits. In fact, the Corporate Report's specific proposal is for a statement of cash transactions in foreign currency containing at least the following information:

1 UK cash receipts for direct exporting of goods and services;
2 Cash payments for direct imports to the UK, distinguishing between capital and revenue;
3 Transactions in respect of overseas borrowings remitted to or repaid from the UK;
4 Similarly investments and loans from or repaid to the UK;
5 Overseas dividends and interest, etc. received in the UK and remitted overseas.

Yet for a transnational corporation clearly the need is for information, not only concerning the activities of British firms, but also of all other parts since a monitoring Centre will be concerned, amongst other things, with not only the activities in and involving British subsidiaries etc. Our matrix suggestion for trade flows would seem reasonable for investment and lending flows.

Examples of firms reporting on such activities are extremely limited. However, one case of the use of exports information is illustrated in the Tube Investments report (Social Audit, 1975). Table 7.33 taken from that report sees the level of exports from the UK being compared to those in manufacturing industry from a base year of 1964/5.

'Basics'

A consistent concern of most governments at almost all times has been to exclude foreign transnationals' involvement in specific industries. What constitutes a key or basic industry can clearly differ from country to country and over time, although it often includes defence, energy and/or public services/utilities.

In some respects Glaxo as a pharmaceuticals company does not appear to be involved in a basic industry, but can be seen as a major supplier to one, the health and welfare industry. Although only a relatively small participant, the drugs industry does have a potentially-significant role to play. We have referred to several governments' concern with pharmaceutical prices. However, in return we have seen, in part through Glaxo's pursuit of the idea of pharmacoeconomics, the potential for the drugs industry to reduce health and welfare costs and increase working time. To that extent Glaxo may be seen to be an important part of the industry which keeps workers fit and healthy for employment.

POLITICAL ISSUES

The second category of issues of concern we suggested was referred to as political. Such concerns could be as important as the core issues above at any point in time, but would not be established concerns. This is not to say they would not become core in the future. They might, in our situation, drawing on the review of the three countries represented by the matrix Table 5.1 in Chapter 5. We have classified the following as political issues: compliance/

co-operation with wider industrial and economic policy, regional impact/development policies, and environmental impact. Each is dealt with below.

Compliance/co-operation with wider industrial and economic policy

Although some detail is known under this heading, many of the matters identified are discussed elsewhere in this chapter. Our analysis of government concerns has revealed issues for which it is difficult to identify what might be considered useful information for a monitoring Centre. For example, concern with the national interest, interest in the extent to which a transnational contributes to the self-support and sound development of the economy, impact on the smooth running of the economy or its rehabilitation and maintenance of order in native business all need to be explored further before we can begin to suggest what might be more useful information. Other matters are a little more specific, such as the desire to see transnationals supplement domestic investment (although perhaps wishing to see this not become too large a proportion of total investment), compliance with monetary policy, economic independence, the inflationary impact and impact on national income.

However, the point needs to be made that the information we have collected does not analyse Glaxo's national impact in sufficient detail to address these matters. Virtually no national data is presented or reported on, except for some sales and investment data. Table 7.34 brings together the information scattered throughout the annual report on both of these matters. This shows that 24 per cent of turnover is not specified in terms of country, and that none of the capital expenditure is attributable to any country directly. The position is much worse in respect of cost data, where no national analysis is conducted. To do so would enable one to calculate profitability.

Similarly, virtually no information is available which might enable one to assess compliance with monetary policy. Later, under the heading of balance of payments, we will comment on the absence of detail on financial flows and to that we can add that very little is known about price changes and cost changes, including wage rates. The exceptions include the broker's analysis of reported sales growth in Table 7.11 which identifies the global price increases of

Table 7.34 Segmental sales and investment data of Glaxo

		£m	
Sales in:	USA	1,245	
	UK	385	
	Italy	292	
	Germany	195	
	France	190	
	Spain	70	
	Japan	200	
		2,577	
		820	being 24% unexplained other than in terms of contracts
	Total	3,397	
Investment			
	Manufacturing	177	
	Research and development	236	
	Other	208	
		621	
	Land and buildings	43	
	Plant and machinery	27	
	Fixtures and equipment	63	
	Assets in construction	488*	
		621	

Source: Glaxo Holdings plc, *Annual Report and Accounts*, 1991.
Note:
* Some of these assets may have been completed and reclassified.

recent years, the various press reports on negotiations over prices of Glaxo products in a number of countries, and Glaxo's own announcements to the press (e.g., *Scrip* 8 March 1991).

One example of interest, perhaps illustrating a willingness to co-operate with national industrial strategy, did come to light. Though not reported by Glaxo, we read of the likely closure of a Glaxo India plant, which had been kept open, despite losses, due to the country's requirements (*Chemical Weekly*, 13 August 1991). Glaxo India is an associate company with Glaxo holding a 40 per cent shareholding. Accounting treatment of the firm as an associate implies that Glaxo has significant influence in the firm's operation, though this may indicate that the remaining shareholders or government were able to exercise greater influence.

Regional impact/development policies

In the previous section we noted the absence of national data on investment. In a later section we comment on the absence of reporting of government grants or assistance, much of which is offered to attract firms to particular locations. As a consequence little can be said about Glaxo's willingness to locate in regions of countries where industry, employment etc., are much sought after.

In this section we deal first with the extent of Glaxo's purchase of local supplies, before considering treatment of the local community, location policy and finally disinvestment.

Suppliers

Little or no specific information on the extent to which Glaxo uses and consumes local supplies is revealed in the annual report or other public sources. Some indication of the consumption of local supplies would be given by a detailed national analysis of costs and similar analysis of imports and exports, but this is not available.

Increasingly the importance of supplier connections is being recognised for attracting foreign direct investment, unfortunately sometimes as a result of disinvestment rather than investment, when expected job losses are multiplied by a supplier knock-on effect. Although there appear to be significant problems measuring the impact of reduced consumption of local services (part of the multiplier effect) some closure audits did address the problem in trying to ascertain the wider consequences of corporate actions (Harte and Owen, 1987). However, social audit reports examining continuing operations have largely ignored this significance.

Treatment of the community

The treatment of the local community is addressed briefly by Glaxo in its annual report. The Chairman's Statement reports that companies should be active and responsible members of the communities within which they operate. He goes on to state that community contributions have 'steadily increased and are substantially above the target set by the Per Cent Club of UK companies [a philanthropic group who set targets for corporate giving], of which we are a founder member'.

The Chief Executive's Review of Activities ends with a section on the community which reaffirms Glaxo's commitment to 'good corporate citizenship'. This discloses total charitable donations in Britain (£3.6 million), with other community contributions of £2.4 million. Some of the largest donations are specified, each relating to the medical field. Few details are given of donations overseas, except in the USA, where US $7.6 million was donated. Specific mention of support for the arts is made. However, there is no indication of the Per Cent Club target. Further details of smaller charitable donations are often contained in Glaxo's in-house journals, as well as projects assisted and charitable donations of staff, and sizeable donations are widely reported in the press. Unfortunately, despite this, the annual report contains no attempt to contrast Glaxo's donations to those of other firms in general. Although there are clearly limitations in comparisons made with something which is in itself inadequate, the examination of charitable giving in the Avon and Tube reports (Social Audit, 1973, 1976) suggest that a little more can be provided to help appreciate the absolute figures (see Tables 7.35 and 7.36).

In general there is little analysis of Glaxo's giving. As indicated above, large sums have been committed to medical research and infrastructure (of the total £6.0 million referred to it appears that £4.05 million was given to four medical projects). In contrast, an

Table 7.35 Avon's donations to charity expressed as a percentage of pre-tax profits by various companies

	1972	1973
Avon group	0.39	0.37
Quoted manufacturing companies	0.14	0.17
Companies the same size as Avon[a]	0.10	0.07
Major companies in the rubber industry[b]	0.13	0.16

Source: Social Audit (1976) 'On the Avon Rubber Company Ltd'. *Social Audit* 2(3 & 4).

Notes:
[a] i.e., companies having the same net assets (± 3 per cent) as Avon.
[b] i.e., companies listed in *The Times 1000* (ranked by turnover) which belong to the British Rubber Manufacturers' Association. However, no data were available from Firestone or Uniroyal. Firestone had not filed accounts at Companies House since 1972 and, nevertheless, refused to give the information requested. Uniroyal's accounts were filed in Edinburgh, so the Company was approached directly – but they also refused to co-operate.

Table 7.36 Tube Investments' charitable donations

Year	TI charitable donations (excluding political contributions) (£)	Charitable donations as a percentage of profits before tax and interest[e]	
		TI	All UK companies[d]
1972	88,200[a]	0.30	n.a.
1971	71,800	0.29	0.51
1970	82,500	0.32	0.50
1969	93,000[b]	0.32	0.49
1967/8[c]	63,908	0.41	0.53

Source: Social Audit (1973) 'The first social audit: Tube Investments Ltd'. *Social Audit* 1(3).

Notes:
[a] Including BA, as in previous years.
[b] For a 17–month period.
[c] The first year these figures were disclosed.
[d] Taken from *National Income and Expenditure*, 1973.
[e] Including profits earned abroad.

Table 7.37 Dow Chemicals' charitable donations

	1983 Actual (US $)	1984 Estimated (US $)	1985 Projected (US $)
Health	2,680,000	3,068,000	3,442,000
Arts & cultural	149,000	248,000	361,000
Community projects	1,508,000	2,156,000	1,788,000
Aid to education	4,364,700	5,327,000	6,716,000
Other	1,057,700	1,100,000	1,200,000
Total	9,759,400	11,899,000	13,507,000
Corporate	935,300	1,500,000	2,950,000
Brazil	140,000	120,000	150,000
Canada	173,700	218,300	220,000
Europe	280,500	350,000	437,500
Latin America	72,100	104,800	107,800
Pacific	74,600	121,700	232,600
USA	8,083,200	9,484,200	9,409,100
Total	9,759,400	11,899,000	13,507,000

Source: Dow Chemical Company, *Public Interest Report*, 1984.
Note:
The Dow Chemical Company's financial contributions are devoted to five general categories.
The table illustrates the division of funds by category and geographic area.

analysis of contributions in category and geographic terms is presented by Dow Chemicals (Table 7.37), following some discussion under each heading. However, for communities, when analysed in national terms, such information can perhaps show what is being given elsewhere in the group and so can perhaps be used as a bargaining lever.

Location policy

Concern with the regional or community impact of any transnational corporation is heightened when there are difficulties attracting investment and jobs, and where a transnational is a significant agent in the local economy. Thus information on the location policy of a transnational and, in particular, whether it chooses to locate in relatively isolated and dependent communities, is likely to be of interest. The location of production and research facilities is not normally a matter for annual reports, despite the obvious significance to the community. A monitoring unit attempting to come to terms with the power of transnationals may need to know not only of levels of investment, jobs created and degree of movement, but also, in order to understand what management sees as a priority, locational policy. For example, does the transnational locate in small communities for added financial gain or security, and what does this mean for policy-making? In a later section on impact on the exchequer we refer to reasons for Glaxo locating in Singapore (and perhaps Puerto Rico), and in the section on fairness we discuss the possibility that Glaxo's locations may on some occasions be in relatively small communities where it may find itself in a strong bargaining position, particularly with the work-force. Some recognition of possible tension is recognised in an internal Glaxo publication, where it is suggested that some in local government in Montrose (Scotland) have their reservations about Glaxochem's location there, possibly due to the dependence and fears of the impact of run down or closure (*Glaxoworld*, October 1992).

Disinvestment

Finally Glaxo's annual report says very little about disposals of businesses. It refers to the sale of the bulk penicillin plant at Cambois in the UK, placing it in the context of overall strategy. However, there is no reference to the disposal of McFarlan-Smith, a British subsidiary, presumably on the grounds of materiality. Part of the cost of extraordinary items, charged against profits, appears to relate to this disposal, although details are limited. There is no mention of any redundancies during the year in the annual report. However, as a result of the disposal of the Cambois plant there were redundancies introduced by the new owners (*Scrip*, 19 June 1991).

Environmental impact

Although the Chief Executive and the Chairman both state Glaxo's concern with its environmental impact, very little is actually disclosed beyond policy and intentions. Although details of the Glaxo statement on environmental policy are summarised in the annual report, we discovered a six-point policy in Bernstein (1992). Unfortunately this is rather brief and is less specific than might be desirable, where one wished to see data reported on progress. This is surprising given the consequences Glaxo's operations can have on such matters as air (by plant emissions) and water (waste disposal). In-house journals appear to be relatively scarce of detail on environmental impact, despite the likelihood that employees who live in the community in which the firm operates will have an interest in this aspect of performance.

EIRIS (Ethical Investment Research Services), a research group providing information for ethical and environmental investment, has identified three aspects of Glaxo's environmental performance which merit attention. Firstly, EIRIS has estimated the value of the vehicle fleet of the Glaxo group to exceed £100 million, ranking it for special attention under its heading 'greenhouse gases'. The second relates to two products (aerosols) of the group which have a high Ozone Depletion Potential. Neither is referred to in such detail in Glaxo's annual report and as a consequence we do not know the quantity or value of sales. Lastly, Glaxo Laboratories Ltd has exceeded a water discharge consent from Ulverston on one occasion during the year to 31 March 1992.

Although these matters may not appear to be of too great significance, their reporting by EIRIS is in contrast to the apparent silence of Glaxo's own accounts, and the absence of such comment revealed by our review of trade journals etc.

RANDOM ISSUES

Our final section of issues of concern is described as random. This label is used to indicate that a monitoring Centre, with limited resources, would be selective in its monitoring. Hence a number of issues of interest may have to be monitored on a random basis. Clearly these should be less important issues. Using our matrix from Chapter 5 we have selected those issues which are neither classified as core nor political to be the random category. This means that this section reviews impact on productivity and efficiency, impact on the exchequer, impact on national competitive position, use of material, local components and resources processing, fairness, cultural issues, openness, accountability and information and a final miscellaneous category.

Productivity and efficiency

Our table of issues of concern reveals no specific details of what was of interest in terms of productivity and efficiency.

Although output in the pharmaceuticals industry is said to be growing faster than in either the chemicals sector or manufacturing as a whole, the nearest one gets to information on productivity or efficiency are those discussions referred to previously concerning the influence of exchange rates on turnover and profits. As the broker's table (see Table 7.12) indicates, exchange rates are one of three reasons for changes in turnover, price and volume being the other two. Some might argue that profit margins (profits related to turnover) and return on capital employed (profit related to capital or net assets) satisfy the desire for information on productivity or efficiency. Yet as the brokers' table indicates such, and particularly in the context of patent protection and monopoly or oligopoly profits, may represent power rather than productivity. Profit can be seen as a return to capital, which arises from the social relations of production (Tinker, 1980).

On the general question of the commercial risks of pharmaceuticals production, some have suggested that there are only a small number of examples of major research efforts coming to little or nothing or of firms going out of business (Alexander, 1969), and that the drug industry is not particularly risky (Abel-Smith, 1976). In fact, since the late nineteenth century it appears to have been the most profitable major manufacturing industry (Liebenau, 1987). One frequently hears the argument that profits are needed to finance investment in R&D. However, Glaxo's enormous profit figures are *after* R&D spending. Others might argue that researching, developing and getting a product to market before others and reaping the monopoly profits of doing so are *the* driving factors in stimulating R&D. Whilst the industry is characterised by being very competitive, it needs to be remembered that this is no open market. For example, products are protected by patents and the price is negotiated with the state.

Productivity is perhaps best measured by relating outputs (in physical terms) to inputs. The use of the plural here suggests a problem particularly when it is an aggregation of different types of input and output. The obvious case in respect of inputs is labour and machinery. In Glaxo's case productivity and efficiency is likely to be difficult to examine because of the high level of investment in research and development and marketing.

Our discussion of productivity focuses largely on value added, with some comment on sales and the subject of pharmacoeconomics. Although restricted to the available accounting information, value added is a reasonable measure of the size of the pie available for distribution to employees, investors, etc. Clearly its potential as a measure of productivity is limited by its financial focus and the imperfections of market prices.

Value added

In Glaxo's case, as with other British annual reports, it is possible to calculate some simple measures of productivity based on value added (the difference between the value of products sold and the cost of the materials and services, excluding labour). This can be done by taking the data in the Profit and Loss Account, and re-presenting it to calculate value added rather than profit (see Table 7.38).

Some simple measures of value added productivity which could be used are the following, where figures have been taken from the annual report to illustrate;

1 Value added/turnover : £2,063 m/£3,397 m = 60.7%
2 Value added/wage costs : £2,063 m/£804 m = 257%
3 Value added/total net assets : £2,063 m/£3,372 m = 61.2%

Table 7.38 Value added of Glaxo

Value added statement	£m	£m
Turnover		3,397
less bought in goods and services		1,331
Gross value added		2,066
less depreciation		151
Net value added		1,915
add investment income (net)		179
		2,094
less extraordinary items (closure and takeover costs)		31
Adjusted net value added		2,063
distributed as follows:		
Wages	804 (39%)	
Tax†	359 (18%)	
Shareholders*†	893 (43%)	
Directors' remuneration (say)	7 (0%)	
		2,063

Source: Based on information contained in Glaxo Holdings plc, *Annual Report and Accounts*, 1991.

Notes:

* Being minority interests 12, dividends 420 and retained profits 461.

† Part of the tax bill will take the form of an advance payment of corporation tax, being the company's payment of tax on dividends to shareholders. Since there is no write-off of Advance Corporation Tax we can assume that with a 25% income tax charge that ACT will be 33% of the dividend (£420m), being £140m. One could therefore argue for a division of value added as follows:

	£m	
Wages	804 (39%)	
Tax	219 (11%)	
Shareholders	1,033 (50%)	
Directors' remuneration	7 (0%)	
		2,063

4 Value added/number of employees : £2,063 m/£35,623 m = £57,912 per employee (see Table 7.38 for details of the calculation of value added).

The last of these calculations can be compared with the previously calculated average wage of £18,300 per employee.

Such an approach was taken in Social Audit's Avon Report (Social Audit, 1976). In examining the use of resources Social Audit calculated Avon's return on capital employed and compared this to quoted manufacturing companies, then calculated the same for three major subsidiaries of Avon. Similar calculations were also carried out concerning value added, in this case value added per employee

Table 7.39 Value added per employee of Avon

	Avon[a]		Rubber industry[b]		Manufacturing industry[b]	
	VA per employee (£)	VA per £ of wages/salaries (£)	VA per employee (£)	VA per £ of wages/salaries (£)	VA per employee (£)	VA per £ of wages/salaries (£)
1970	1,708	1.31	2,565	1.96	2,305	1.89
1971	2,130	1.37	2,721	1,93	2,536	1.88
1972	2,293	1.35	2,995	1.93	2,935	1.94
1973	2,465	1.32	3,344	1.85	3,312	1.97
1974	2,603	1.30	c	c	c	c

Source: Social Audit (1976) 'On the Avon Rubber Company Ltd'. *Social Audit* 2(3 & 4).
Notes:
[a] Avon's figures were derived from the Group's published accounts. As a result, the figures are not absolutely accurate because they could not be adjusted for differences in stocks of raw materials and fuels at the beginning and end of each year. The company promised, but failed to supply, this information as well as information relating to capital expenditure on vehicles, and net fixed assets overseas. However, the effect on the value added figures is almost certainly very small and would not affect the overall trend of Avon's performance.
[b] Report on the Census of Production, available from HMSO.
[c] Not available at time of going to press.

Table 7.40 Index of output (sales) per head of Coalite

Year	Coalite[a]	Coal and petroleum products[b]
1969/70	100	100
1970/71	94	100
1971/72	81	113
1972/73	85	119
1973/74	84	132

Source: Social Audit (1974) 'A report on Coalite and chemical products'. Social
   Audit 2(2).

Notes:
[a] These figures relate to 'Coalite' works – the refinery at Bolsover has been excluded.
   Price increases of 'Coalite' have been taken into account. However, the figures are
   for sales rather than production and this distorts the 1972/74 figures, when unsold
   stocks of 'Coalite' were much greater than in previous years.
[b] Figures taken from Monthly Digest of Statistics, HMSO, and relate to calendar years.

and value added per £ of wages/salaries. These were calculated for
Avon, the rubber industry and manufacturing industry as a whole
(see Table 7.39).

Sales

Earlier Social Audit reports on Coalite (Social Audit, 1974) and
Tube Investments (Social Audit, 1973) examined productivity by
reference to an index of output, taking the latter to be equal to sales,
and comparing this to industry figures. As we can see from the
notes to the relevant tables (Table 7.40 Coalite and 7.41 Tube) some
adjustment has been made to the sales figure. In the case of Coalite
it appears that price increases have been removed, while for Tube a
sectorial inflation rate has been taken into account in adjusting sales.
The latter is clearly easier to obtain in a multi-product firm. For Glaxo
exchange rates add a further complication, although the previous
broker's table, our Table 7.12, did identify the volume changes.

Pharmacoeconomics

Finally Glaxo itself offers an approach to the measurement of
productivity which could be considered. Possibly as a result of
increasing government pressure to reduce prices and the pharmaceuticals industry's objective to maximise profits, it is interesting to
note Glaxo's case for higher prices. For example, in the case of
Imigran, its new anti-migraine drug (e.g., Scrip, 18 September 1991),

Table 7.41 Index of output per head of Tube Investments

	Tube Investments[a]	Manufacturing industry[b]
1972	106	119
1971	99	111
1970	100	107
1969	100	106
1967/8[c]	100	100

Source: Social Audit (1973) 'The first social audit: Tube Investments Ltd'. *Social Audit* 1(3).

Notes:

[a] *TI*'s sales figures have been adjusted for inflation using the price indices for steel tubes, mechanical engineering, electrical engineering and aluminium goods.

[b] *TI*'s range of activities do not allow it to be fitted into any one industrial category for which statistics are available. The nearest classification – mechanical, instrument and electrical engineering – shows an identical increase in output per head to manufacturing industry as a whole.

[c] *TI*'s figures are not artificially depressed by the use of 1967/8 as a base year. It was the first year that the Company disclosed the number of its UK employees (in accordance with the 1967 Companies Act), and was in fact a very poor year for the Company. If anything, the use of this base is to *TI*'s advantage.

Glaxo has justified its higher price by allowing sufferers to treat themselves and therefore saving health service time and resources, and benefiting firms (investors) and the economy by reducing time off work. Such an approach to examining the costs and benefits of pharmaceuticals (pharmacoeconomics) is clearly not new, but it is of interest to see such advocacy of the internalising of externalities by the state when Glaxo and similar private sector firms fail to report on their wider social and economic impact, never mind take it into account in decision-making. Pharmacoeconomics raises the possibility of their being various outputs worth measuring if one wished to calculate the community or welfare benefits of Glaxo's products, and so could be said to offer an alternative approach to measuring a welfare productivity, although *The Economist* warned its readers to watch out when this sort of 'guesswork' is conducted by the pharmaceuticals industry (26 September 1992).

Perhaps this is an indication of the type of accounting we can expect from Glaxo in future, namely, one which seeks to measure the wider economic and social net benefits or costs of its activities.

Impact on the exchequer

Not surprisingly government concerns have extended to the direct impact of transnational corporations on the state's cash flows. This has taken the form of interest in the taxation consequences, primarily income and corporation tax, transfer pricing (presumably because of the tax consequences and the impact on flows in and out of the country) and the receipt of government funds.

Corporation tax

Details of the corporation tax charge (analysed between UK and overseas), amounts paid, deferred taxation and advance corporation tax are reported in the annual report (see Table 7.42). Following a professional accounting standard (SSAP 15), only that part of deferred tax which will be payable in the foreseeable future is provided for as a liability in the balance sheet (£141 million), with a note stating that legally the full potential liability is actually £72 million greater at £213 million. There is, however, only limited analysis of the group's corporation tax. Little or no detail is provided of where taxation is paid by Glaxo in the annual report, although brief details are provided in the 20F statement for the SEC.

Corporation tax: 20-year review

The statistical review of results over the last twenty years actually omits the tax charge from its summarised presentation of profits information. However, it can be calculated as shown in Table 7.43. This assumes the corporation tax to be the difference between profit before tax (pbt) and profit before extraordinary items, and expresses this as a percentage of profit before tax. Although taxable profits will rarely equate with profit before tax (the former is calculated from the latter, making adjustments to reflect tax legislation), over a period of twenty years it is a fair enough basis on which to consider company taxation. Clearly a significant fall in the relative corporation tax revenues can be seen, while the absolute amount raised by governments has significantly increased. No analysis of British versus overseas taxation can be offered here, though obviously it is of interest, as would be the case with any transnational.

Our discussion also raises the matter of the existence of adjustments between accounting profits and taxable profits. Such is calculated in the tax computation, which is submitted to the tax authorities. This is likely to be something of interest to the Centre, in part because it reveals the disallowance of non-business items and may reveal any tax-avoiding schemes, but also because it will, once

169

Table 7.42 Corporation tax details of Glaxo

Note 7: Taxation	1991 £m	1990 £m
		(restated)
On profits for the year:		
UK corporation tax at 33.75% (1990 – 35%)	136	151
Deduct: Double taxation relief	12	19
	124	132
Overseas taxation	179	199
Deferred taxation	56	26
	359	357
Attributable to:		
Holding company and subsidiary undertakings	358	355
Associated undertakings	1	2

Note: Taxation has been significantly affected by reliefs in certain overseas undertakings. It has also been reduced by £32 m (1990 – £36 m) because of accelerated capital allowances for which no deferred taxation has been provided in respect of profit on inter-company stocks; if it had been provided the taxation charge would have been increased by £4 m (1990 – £2 m).

Note 19: Provisions for liabilities and charges

(c) The deferred taxation provision at 30 June 1991, included above, is in respect of

	1991 £m	1990 £m
		(restated)
Unremitted foreign investment income	122	69
Accelerated capital allowances	10	6
Stock valuation adjustment	9	7
Other timing differences	–	1

The full potential liability for deferred taxation is in respect of:

Accelerated capital allowances	222	196
Unremitted foreign investment income	122	69
Stock valuation adjustment	9	7
Inter-company profit in stock	(45)	(51)
Advance corporation tax recoverable	(97)	(75)
Other timing differences	2	6
	213	152

Source: Glaxo Holdings plc, *Annual Report and Accounts*, 1991.

Table 7.43 Corporation tax charges of Glaxo

Year	Profit before tax (£m)	Profit before extraordinary items (£m)	Tax[a]	Tax/Pbt %
1972	27	15	12	44
1973	34	18	16	47
1974	43	22	21	49
1975	41	20	21	51
1976	74	35	39	53
1977	87	42	45	52
1978	86	42	44	51
1979	72	47	25	35
1980	66	42	24	36
1981	87	61	26	30
1982	134	80	54	40
1983	186	109	77	41
1984	256	169	87	34
1985	403	277	126	31
1986	612	400	212	35
1987	746	496	250	34
1988	832	571	261	31
1989	1,006	688	318	32
1990	1,182	807	375	32
1991	1,283	912	371	29

Source: Glaxo Holdings plc, *Annual Report and Accounts*, 1991.
Note:
[a] Tax is assumed to be profit before tax (Pbt) minus profit before extraordinary items.

Notes: To Table 7.42
In addition:
a An extraordinary item charge of £20 million is included in calculating profits for the year. This is described as the taxation payable by Nippon Glaxo Ltd on the purchase by Glaxo Group Ltd of a 5% interest in Glaxochem (Pte) Ltd owned by Nippon Glaxo Ltd. Nippon Glaxo is a principal subsidiary of Glaxo Group, in which the latter holds 50% of the shares. The amount of £20 millions is Glaxo's half of the total tax payable.
b Advance Corporation Tax (ACT) recoverable at 30 June 1991 amounted to £97 millions, and is included in debtors in the group balance sheet.
c Taxation payable is included in creditors falling due within the year at the year end, totalling £294 millions.
d Taxation payable is included in creditors falling due after more than one year, totalling £20 millions.
e Deferred tax provided for as a liability is included under provisions for liability and charges, totalling £141 millions at the year end.
f Further details of the deferred tax provision are included in Note 19 on the accounts.

agreed with the tax authorities, reveal any adjustments made for transfer pricing. This may in fact be the very reason why the tax position of some Glaxo subsidiaries had not been resolved by the time the 1990/91 accounts were finalised (see note 23 on contingent liabilities in the annual report, reproduced here as Table 7.21).

Other taxes

There is almost no mention of other taxes, such as VAT and local taxes. There is also no indication of how much income tax has been collected from employees on behalf of governments.

Transfer pricing

Clearly transfer pricing is likely to be an important issue in preparing accounts for a transnational corporation such as Glaxo. For example, Glaxochem, a subsidiary, which produces bulk active ingredients and so is engaged in primary production, supplies other Glaxo companies in Britain and overseas for further processing. Such transfer prices can be seen as administered, rather than market prices, where there is some scope for specific profit to be declared in a particular country according to tax rates and incentives (Murray, 1981). The tax authorities will be seeking to ensure that such pricing is fair and is not set in order to minimise taxation in their country. Given the extent to which transnational pharmaceutical corporations are seen to operate different pricing policies across the globe and the existence of intra-group trade flows (sometimes in bulk chemicals, sometimes in finished products), it is perhaps not surprising to see that Glaxo says very little about its policies. Even where we obtain segmented information (see Table 7.6) which includes references to inter-segment trading, we are still not informed of the basis for such pricing. Clearly intra-segment trading will also likely have occurred, and be of importance in any national analysis of Glaxo's performance.

The importance of transfer pricing to tax authorities increases where a transnational corporation locates in a lower tax country. Glaxo makes no reference to having done so in 1990/91, although it reports on its investment and operation in many countries in the annual report. Elsewhere, in a broker's report (Morgan Stanley, 16 August 1991) we are informed 'Like most of the major pharmaceuticals companies, Glaxo manufactures drugs in tax-free or tax-advantaged locales'. It suggests that Glaxo has located in Singapore for UK tax purposes, rather than Puerto Rico which is more tax advantageous to US corporations (although the *Financial Times*, 14 August 1991, reports that, along with a host of other British and European companies, Glaxo has been attracted to Puerto Rico).

The Singapore tax advantages are staggering. Where a corporation opens a new plant it pays no tax on products made there for ten years, and then 15 per cent for the next five years, followed by the full tax rate of 33 per cent. Morgan Stanley reveal that the tax rate on Zantac production in Singapore is set to become 15 per cent in 1993 and 33 per cent in 1997. However, Glaxo is building a new plant for new products, a point confirmed by the Chief Executive's Review of Activities (which refers to approval having been given for a major multi-purpose facility) and so will benefit once again from lower tax rates. Morgan Stanley's forecasts are quite specific:

> This facility comes on stream in 1994, so in 1992 and 1993 the tax rate (for the group) is set to increase from the current 28.5% to somewhere in the region of 30.5–31%. Tax credits for the company's R&D facility in Stevenage (UK) should help offset the Singapore effect.

Some specific details of these benefits are illustrated in the 20F report's analysis of taxation, including the important deferrals of tax.

Government grants

Virtually no references are made to the receipt of government grants and assistance, perhaps because government incentives have increasingly taken the form of lower tax rates and favourable taxation allowances in recent years. While grants would, if material, have to be accounted for in an open manner (under SSAP 4), tax allowances and favourable tax breaks need not be disclosed, except in their consequence of lower cost (tax) figures.

Relationship with the State

In addition to these examples of direct cash (tax) interests in transnational corporations (and the interest in transfer pricing for its indirect effect), the relationship between Glaxo and the State is becoming increasingly clear yet complex. We have so far encountered the State as customer, tax collector, regulator, protector and advocate (particularly as regards patents). As a consequence the British government has, in the case of Glaxo, an interest in lower prices as a consumer through the NHS, but higher prices as a tax collector through the Inland Revenue. The picture is complicated further by the scope for higher prices to benefit the British balance of payments. By agreeing to higher prices as a customer (through the health service), the British government can support Glaxo's efforts to have similar higher prices accepted in other markets. This would benefit the British economy, particulary where profits are remitted and taxes can be levied. Yet clearly the latter is not as straightforward, as the lower costs of a Singapore location suggest. Overall, given the many facets to the relationship, it can be argued that 'in effect the pharmaceuticals industry operates within the framework of a *de facto* industrial policy' (*The Guardian*, 8 August 1992).

There does in this situation, because of the complex and significant relationship, seem to be some value in the preparation and presentation of a Statement of Money Exchanges with Government as envisaged by the Corporate Report (Boothman Committee, 1975). This proposed disclosure of details of money exchanges with local and central government (distinguishing between home and overseas governments) includes:

(a) income taxes collected on behalf of revenue authorities;
(b) value added taxes collected;
(c) corporation taxes paid;
(d) rates and other local taxes;
(e) other payments to government departments;
(f) money receipts, including grants, from government.

A partial statement was prepared by General Motors in 1981 (see Table 7.44), which presents details of taxes payable by the corporation, taxes payable by customers and employee's taxes. Obviously such is a partial statement, omitting to state what, if any, amounts were received as grants from the State or turnover resulting from the State's purchase of GM products.

Earlier we revealed the complex relationship Glaxo has with the State, suggesting perhaps an even greater need to account. In a similar vein General Motors, in the same report present financial details of the cost of government regulations on matters such as safety, emissions, noise and plant pollution. A second aspect of the

Table 7.44 Taxes generated by General Motors' activities

Taxes payable by GM to US and foreign tax authorities	1981	1980
	(US dollars in millions)	
Income taxes (credit)	(123.1)	(385.3)
Payroll taxes	1,548.7	1,377.5
Property taxes	403.9	388.2
Federal excise taxes	268.2	244.1
Miscellaneous taxes	210.1	185.0
Franchise, sales, and use taxes	72.6	54.0
Total	2,382.4	1,863.5
Note: Taxes per share of common stock.	7.97	6.37

US and Foreign taxes paid by customers purchasing GM products*	1981	1980
	(US dollars in millions)	
Franchise, sales, use and other local taxes	672.1	734.9
Federal excise taxes	719.0	776.0
Total	1,391.1	1,510.9

Note: * These taxes represent only the portion of taxes paid by customers which are collected by GM and remitted to the appropriate taxing authorities.

Employee US federal taxes withheld by GM**	1981	1980
	(US dollars in millions)	
Federal income tax	3,490.7	2,981.1
FICA tax	956.9	782.4
Total	4,447.6	3,763.5

Source: General Motors, *Public Interest Report*, 1982.
Note:
** This information does not include state, local and foreign employee taxes which are withheld by GM and its subsidiaries and remitted to the appropriate taxing authorities.

report is the statement of the cost in person hours (see Table 7.45). Once again Glaxo's regulation by the State can be compared to that of GM.

National 'competitive position'

Concern with the impact of transnational corporations on the national 'competitive position' as a matter of concern has not been

Table 7.45 The cost of government regulations to General Motors

Impact of government regulations on General Motors

| | | | | | Calendar year | | | | | Eight Year |
	1974	1975	1976	1977	1978	1979	1980	1981**	Total
				(US dollars in millions*)					
Regulation of vehicles									
Auto safety	414	347	354	423	466	512	529	550	3,595
Auto emission control	454	185	188	247	446	601	719	635	3,475
Vehicle noise control	16	15	14	17	23	21	25	25	156
TOTAL	884	547	556	687	935	1,134	1,273	1,210	7,226
Regulation of plant facilities									
Plant pollution control									
Air	77	57	58	83	146	211	299	299	1,230
Water	56	54	56	72	95	114	131	126	704
Solid waste control	48	38	57	79	75	88	75	90	550
TOTAL	181	149	171	234	316	413	505	515	2,484
Occupational safety and health	79	62	75	88	103	104	114	120	745
Government reports and administrative costs related to regulation	190	185	215	249	266	292	323	330	2,050
GRAND TOTAL	1,334	943	1,017	1,258	1,620	1,943	2,215	2,175	12,505

Notes:
* Includes estimated research and engineering, reliability, inspection, testing, facilities, tools, and rearrangements costs. Does not include the direct cost associated with the product (except direct inspection).
** Estimated expenditures.

Equivalent employees'† efforts required to meet government regulations

	Calendar year							
	1974	1975	1976	1977	1978	1979	1980	1981
Regulation of vehicles								
Auto safety	12,300	10,400	10,500	11,800	11,100	11,800	10,600	10,000
Auto emission control	4,800	4,000	3,900	4,000	4,300	4,900	4,900	4,700
Vehicle noise control	400	300	300	300	400	300	300	300
TOTAL	17,500	14,700	14,700	16,100	15,800	17,000	15,800	15,000
Regulation of plant facilities								
Plant pollution control								
Air	800	800	800	800	700	1,100	1,100	1,000
Water	500	500	500	600	800	800	800	700
Solid waste control	500	500	600	600	600	700	700	700
TOTAL	1,800	1,800	1,900	2,000	2,100	2,600	2,600	2,400
Occupational safety and health	1,100	1,100	1,100	1,200	1,400	1,400	1,500	1,500
Government reports and administrative costs related to regulation	4,900	4,700	5,200	5,200	5,500	5,500	5,400	5,100
GRAND TOTAL	23,500	22,300	22,900	24,500	24,800	26,500	25,300	24,000

Source: General Motors, *Public Interest Report*, 1982.
Notes:
† These estimates of employment, including technical, clerical, and other support personnel, were based on total hours worked as a result of regulations. Those hours were then converted to the equivalent number of employees working a calendar year.

outlined in further detail, but simply stated as a matter of concern. Presumably many of the other issues identified here can be related to this more general concern, for example, attracting (or not losing) research and development activities, the extent of imports and exports, pricing (including transfer pricing) policies, etc.

One matter, however, could be argued to relate to this issue in a different way. Whereas the previous examples may be seen to have a direct effect in improving a national economy's competitive position, the very trade of Glaxo, in pharmaceuticals, could be argued to be vital to the efficient operation of the modern capitalist state. Thus rather than being seen as a welfare cost, the price paid for pharmaceuticals can instead be seen as an investment in terms of cost savings elsewhere in the welfare system and in terms of reduced lost productive time of employees. In particular the latter's benefit to firms (and so owners), in a capitalist economy could be argued to be, and is increasingly by Glaxo in its interest in and advocacy of pharmacoeconomics, essential to a nation's 'prosperity'.

Use of national/local components and resources

Under this heading we grouped four issues. Firstly, the concern that transnationals' investment use local resources and components, secondly, that a transnational does not locate in order to simply export raw materials, thirdly that, particularly in a country which is not well favoured with raw materials, the transnational secures raw materials from abroad, and lastly the question of energy use.

Once again most of these issues have been discussed, however indirectly, in previous sections. In particular our identification of the absence of country specific information, particularly in trade flows, suggests that little information on the physical volume will be available on the use of components and resources. In addition it is also worth noting the emphasis on financial values in reporting the performance of transnational corporations. Traditionally, accounting has little place for non-financial measures. In this respect it is unlikely to be very helpful in explaining the movement of raw materials, particularly intra-group because of the subjectivity of transfer prices. Finally, on the matter of energy consumption, we were unable to trace any meaningful data, either in total, national or local terms.

'Fairness'

Various concerns have been expressed concerning the fairness or equity of transnational corporations' behaviour. Some are phrased in the most general manner or refer to avoiding unfairness or not being unethical. Other concerns are more specific such as being free from fraud, duress or undue influence, bribery or speculation.

For Glaxo and many other transnational corporations problems might arise for governments and communities because of their size and power. Being in a monopoly or oligopolistic situation may lead to potentially exploitative relations. So despite Glaxo's portrayal of itself as a very important player in the industry, the fastest growing of the top five and in the eyes of some brokers about to eclipse Merck as number 1, it can still point to its only controlling just over 3 per cent of the world drugs market. Such indicators are, as we have suggested, misleading. Glaxo's best segmented detail, the therapeutic analysis of group pharmaceuticals and food turnover (see Table 7.13) indicates its involvement in more than six therapeutic classes. It is this involvement, seen in relation to particular national markets, which is more likely to determine dominance.

Our earlier discussion of marketing also revealed widespread concerns, particularly as regards advertising and communication with doctors through sales representatives ('the detail men'). In general we have no information on the group's relationship with doctors or government, no indication of any internal code of conduct or external statement. Such a code would presumably cover the matter of bribery and other illegal acts. However, as we noted in our discussions of marketing, Glaxo has as an objective no references under the ABPI marketing code.

This absence of information is particularly disappointing since the drugs industry has a poor record in this respect. Although extreme examples, recently US pharmaceutical firms are said to have had more than three times as many serious or moderately serious law violations as other companies (Braithwaite, 1984). The international pharmaceuticals industry is also said to have a worse record of international bribery and corruption than any other industry, a greater history of fraud in safety testing and a disturbing record of criminal negligence in the unsafe manufacture of drugs (ibid.).

On the wider matter of the ethics of its business behaviour several aspects have been identified by EIRIS (Ethical Investment Research Service), an information service collecting data on pre-selected ethical aspects of corporate behaviour. Glaxo's performance falls foul of the EIRIS review in terms of its operations in countries with oppressive regimes (see below where this is discussed further), its involvement in South Africa, use of animals in testing, its impact on greenhouse gases and its impact on water quality (the last two previously dealt with under the environment) (EIRIS, 1992).

Our review of Glaxo has also raised a number of other matters which call to mind questions of fairness. Glaxo's position is not clear cut. In all instances the point is that there may well be a case for reporting more before concluding as to Glaxo's impact. For example, it does seem that Glaxo, particularly Glaxochem in Britain, has located some of its facilities in small communities, where it is a very important employer and can perhaps exercise a substantial degree of power over the community and work-force.

Our analysis of value added also reveals, even on a global basis, a division of wealth created which seems somewhat inconsistent with the Chairman's view that it is the contribution of the staff throughout the world 'which has ensured the Group's continued success'. We have also identified an absence of individual company or costing data, and the failure to discuss the basis of related party transactions (transfer pricing) or its effects.

The power of a transnational such as Glaxo may be seen in looking at particular overseas operations. For example, Chetley (1986), drawing on Muller (1982), outlines the substantial return to the British holding company and its investors from a relatively small initial investment in Glaxo India. Yet details of overseas subsidiaries and associate companies are limited in the annual report and other public sources.

'Cultural issues'

The specific matter identified here was a concern that the incoming transnational corporation would not disrupt the local way of doing things. Little can in fact be said about such a matter given our information, particularly as it is so specific to the country and time.

One concern identified under the marketing heading concerned the potential for transnational pharmaceuticals corporations to exploit different regulatory standards. Drugs which fail to meet standards in one country may be offered for sale elsewhere. Studies have shown that some drugs on sale in different countries have been described differently (e.g., Medawar, 1979).

Openness, accountability, information

The overall impression of Glaxo's reporting, as evidenced by the annual report, is of compliance with legislation and professional accounting requirements and with a little more. Some discussion and analysis seems better than might be expected as a minimum (particularly of products and research and development).

Yet it appears that despite the filing of a more detailed 20F form with the Securities and Exchange Commission, such information does not all appear in the annual report, which is intended for British consumption. Neither the 20F nor the Form 8 to be filed with the Japanese Ministry of Finance as a result of the bond issue are offered to readers directly or indirectly through the annual report. Our review of the former document suggests that a number of important matters appear to be dealt with in more detail, including principal discoveries, major patent expiration dates, statement on compliance with regulation, statement of legal proceedings, analysis of overseas taxes and advertising costs.

One further document is offered by application to the Secretary. The EC Code of Conduct for companies with operations in South Africa is available.

Miscellaneous

Our final section captures remaining issues of importance, and so includes a number of diverse issues ranging from political donations or involvement to concern with the country from which investment has come or is going to and location in countries with oppressive regimes. We focus on two of these matters here.

Political donations and involvement

Brief details of political donations in Britain are given in the Report of the Directors contained in the annual report, in accordance with Schedule 7 of the Companies Act 1985. These comprise £60,000 to the Conservative Central Office and £12,000 to the Centre for Policy Studies. No explanation is offered for these payments (none is required by law). And no comment is made on whether any assistance has been given beyond cash donations (again disclosure is not required).

However, perhaps most importantly, there is no mention of, or requirement to report, political donations overseas. Surely this is a glaring omission for transnational corporations. Nor is there any mention of political lobbying services used. In Glaxo's case these are likely to be not insignificant due to the complex relationship it has with the government (described above), a case perhaps confirmed by the politicians on the main Board (Howe, Armstrong and Arculus).

CONCLUDING COMMENT

This chapter has attempted to explore the usefulness of publicly-available information for the construction of an economic and social account of the performance and impact of one transnational, Glaxo. In the following chapter we will discuss the general matters raised by this exercise. Once again we will tentatively put ourselves in the position of a monitoring Centre, although the majority of the chapter will be taken up with discussion of matters regarding the collection of information rather than questions of industrial strategy. Thus the focus is very much on the Centre's ability to construct economic and social accounts of transnationals' impact and performance.

8

DISCUSSION OF THE GLAXO CASE STUDY

So far we have been concerned with building a case for the monitoring of transnational corporations. This has involved examining practice in various industrialised countries over the last thirty or so years in order to illustrate how British governments have differed in their attitudes to transnational corporations. We agreed that if fear has been the main reason for failing to act in some way to control transnationals, Britain should take heart from the interests and activities of other industrialised nations.

In Chapters 5 and 6 we began to address in some detail the question of information, suggesting that our proposed Centre could monitor transnationals by preparing economic and social accounts of their performance and impact. This construction of the Centre's own account was likened to the work of institutional investors, who take the annual corporate report prepared by management together with a variety of other quantitative and qualitative information, and construct their own account of the performance of individual firms. This economic and social account would differ significantly from the financial statements we are used to seeing as accounting reports, since it would be more consistent with the objectives of the Centre. In order to examine the sorts of things which could be of interest to the Centre we considered a transnational, Glaxo, by reference to the list of interests expressed in France, Japan and the USA over the last thirty years. These interests were explored in Chapter 5.

Our case study, in Chapter 7, was not intended to be the preparation of an economic and social account the Centre could prepare, nor an illustration of a monitoring Centre in practice, but our attempt to explore further its work with a real life case. For reasons explained in Chapter 7, we restricted our review to publicly-available information. The case study is therefore a limited attempt to identify further issues relevant to the Centre's work.

The purpose of this chapter is to discuss some matters arising from the case study. Included in this discussion we will consider lessons to be learned for the proposed construction of economic and social accounts by the Centre. Before turning to this, however, the following section explicitly sets out our view of transnationals and transnationalism. Up until now our own perspective has taken something of a back seat. Since our position informs our selection of this as an area of study, the questions we ask and the interpretation we offer of the literature and government policies (we eschew the positivist view that we are dealing with solely facts here) we offer a brief statement of our perspective. The reason we do this now is because discussion of the case study is influenced so strongly by discussants' perceptions, and because it is no longer necessary to maintain our self-imposed shackles.[1] Put another way, until now we have deliberately tried to develop an argument in a way that depends upon our own perspective as little as possible; our proposal and most of its detailed exploration is consistent with wide-ranging views across various perspectives on transnational corporations and transnationalism. With this aim there has been no need to outline our own perspective. Nevertheless, our proposal for a monitoring strategy is in no way undermined by relaxing this constraint when discussing the case study. On the contrary, by explicitly relaxing the constraint and discussing Glaxo from our own viewpoint, we effectively illustrate how a Centre's analysis function (see again Chapter 4) would be especially influenced very strongly by the perspective it develops.

However, once more it is important to stress that in this chapter we are not attempting to mimic a Centre. For example, our proposal is that a Centre constructs and analyses accounts. We have not attempted to construct the sort of account a Centre could construct. Likewise, we are not attempting the sort of analysis a Centre would undertake, not least because three academics with a limited economic, legal, business and other experience are unable to seriously act like the Centre we envisage.

A PERSPECTIVE ON TRANSNATIONALS AND TRANSNATIONALISM

The essential feature of transnationals is their production in more than one country. Such firms operate strategies seeking capital accumulation and growth on a global scale (Sklair, 1991). Although theories of the transnational have been put forward (see again Chapter 1) our preference is for a view which is rooted in the analysis of monopoly capitalism (Baran and Sweezy, 1966; Cowling, 1982). This criticises the Coasian assumption of an even distribution of power, going beyond the Coasian limiting emphasis on markets and focusing on distributional issues rather than Pareto efficiency (Cowling and Sugden, 1987a). Under the monopoly capitalism approach, a transnational corporation is seen as 'the means of coordinating production from one centre of strategic decision making when this co-ordination takes a firm across national boundaries' (ibid.). This definition emphasises the importance of control rather than market exchange and sees firms becoming transnationals in order to defend against or attack oligopolistic rivals (ibid.).

Transnationals are argued to behave in a manner of divide and rule (Sugden, 1993 drawing on Marglin's analysis (Marglin, 1974)). In this respect they are seen to be in a powerful position in relation to nation states, communities and employees. Transnationalism, and in particular the threat of mobility (e.g., withdrawing investment or refusing to invest) gives firms additional leverage and leads to such problems as monopolisation, deindustrialisation and the undermining of democracy (Cowling and Sugden, 1987a, 1993b). Transnationals are seen to have the power to challenge the state's capacity to control national economic activity (Held, 1988; Murray, 1981; Wilms-Wright, 1977). In this context we find it especially interesting that governments, and in particular recent British ones, appear to have so little information on the operations and impact of transnationals. This is in marked contrast to transnationals themselves. They collect substantial information on the performance of divisions and subsidiaries (Labour Party, 1977) as well as on rivals.

Thus we take a view of transnationals which suggests that largely as a result of their pursuit of private profit, their size and their transnational flexibility (where they, unlike communities, are at least potentially highly mobile), they pose problems for nation states by seeking to reduce costs and increase revenue in the name of capital accumulation. Such strategies can and do impose costs on the community. This asymmetry of power between transnationals and nations suggests that the latter should adopt a coherent economic strategy to counter such control (Cowling, 1990). Our view is that communities need to know more about transnationals so as to have a better chance of protecting themselves and not being played off against each other. Though states have considerable formal regulatory powers, transnationals possess real economic power, such as withdrawal of investment, redundancy or the promise of investment as a counter to government desires to impose some control (Murray, 1981, specifically discussing control of transfer prices).

TOWARDS AN ANALYSIS OF PERFORMANCE AND IMPACT

In the light of our perspective on transnationals, the following section is presented as a discussion of the case study, rather than the kind of analysis a Centre would undertake. To this extent it draws attention to matters which could be investigated further, rather than offering detailed evaluation. Our approach is to concentrate largely on the six core issues from the seventeen issues of concern identified in Chapter 5 (namely ownership and control, competition, research and development/technology, employment and industrial relations, balance of payments and 'basics') and comment on the extent to which publicly-available information threw some light on these matters. We have also raised some questions as a result of the absence of information.

In general, since the issues of concern were more about the overall impact of transnationals on the economy, it did not come as a surprise to find that some of the publicly-available information was of limited value. This is because such information tends to be that which facilitates the operations of the capital markets. In particular we confirmed the influence of financial accounting reports on publicly-available data. Financial accounting reports tell one more about how an organisation has performed in terms of profitability and liquidity. They say much less about the wider impact of the organisation, except to the extent that performance (profitability) affects investors' financial welfare. Thus reports concentrate on indicating matters such as how profits have been calculated and distributed (or retained). Some reference is made to the financial impact on the state (taxes paid), employees (wages) and suppliers (purchases of goods and services). However, this information is disclosed because of its relevance to investors in the calculation of profits. In contrast there is very little public information on matters such as the employment relationship and environmental impact.

This is not intended to suggest that financial reports were irrelevant, only that the perspective taken in their preparation reflected other than that of the community. For example, we discovered some useful information in brokers' reports, particularly their attempts to construct forecasts of likely future performance. These forecasts tended to say little or nothing about the location of production or employment consequences. Such matters are not unimportant in the construction of profit forecasts, but are secondary, needed in preparing estimates of costs and revenues, but not something to be reported unless material to the financial prospects of the group as a whole, as viewed from an investor's perspective.

At the present time there seems to be a great deal of uncertainty facing the pharmaceuticals industry as a whole. Whereas the 1980s was a boom period for the industry and Glaxo in particular, when it grew to become the second largest pharmaceuticals company in the world, there are signs that the 1990s are unlikely to be as rewarding. Drug companies will likely find it increasingly difficult to discover, finance and develop the kind of blockbuster drugs of the past. There is concern within the industry that there may be growing threats to patents, and that there will be increasing pressure to get drugs to the market more quickly. There are also signs that some governments, particularly those without a strong domestic drugs industry, are keen to erode the benefits of patents and accelerate the development of generic equivalents. Governments are also seeking greater control over prices, particularly of the new wave of drugs and despite the pharmacoeconomic arguments used by firms like Glaxo. Recent efforts to restrict the range of prescribed drugs are likely to continue, and there are signs of tougher government attitudes to the promotion of drugs.

These comments on the industry are drawn substantially from a reading of the business press and brokers' reports. Their emphasis is specifically on the consequences of such change for the capital markets. Yet the points they make are of significance to governments and any potential monitoring Centre. Such increased pressures on firms are likely to have the consequence of tighter cost control, increased concentration in the industry by means of takeover – in the pursuit of economies of scale – and perhaps an increased mobility as firms seek low cost environments. Such behaviour will place more pressure on the community and in particular employees of firms such as Glaxo. It is in this context that we consider the results of the case study from Chapter 7.

The following discussion of matters raised in the Glaxo case study is presented under the appropriate headings of the core issues of concern. Two types of comment are made. First there are those comments which arise from the discovery of information, which we suggest is of some interest. To these are added comments which indicate the absence of information.

Ownership and control

Our discussion of the matters of ownership and control raised an important question regarding the location of Glaxo's corporate headquarters. Our search for information revealed an increase in the scale of American share ownership (26 per cent, although this was not new), increased American Board participation (particularly with the appointment of a former US Ambassador to Britain), and significant investment of resources on research and development in the USA (15 per cent of staff are now located there, a slight increase over the previous year). In addition the USA is the most important market for Glaxo, accounting for 37 per cent of sales, by far the largest country. Taken with the uncertainty regarding the use of its cash pool and general strategy (will it move into over the counter drugs by means of a takeover of an American corporation?), there is sufficient here to concern a British Centre on Transnational Corporations.

On the matter of issues on which we were unable to trace much, if any, information, at least two are worth commenting on: the first refers to the independence of local management and the second to employee involvement in the running of the business. In the case of Glaxo there was little to be found on the structure of the group and the extent to which there was local autonomy. This is likely to be an important matter to a national monitoring Centre, since local plants which are co-ordinated from the centre are less likely to survive a restructuring than those which have retained some independence. Subsidiaries are more easily controlled than associate companies. The point for a monitoring centre to suggest may be that the latter should be encouraged as a means of transnational involvement.

On the matter of employee involvement in the running of the firm, this appears to exist solely through the small-scale ownership of shares in the holding company. Thus in the absence of further information there is little to indicate that Glaxo allows its employees to become involved in the running of its business, particularly at the local level.

Competition

Our review of this issue raised some questions as a result of our obtaining limited details of the geographical segmentation of financial results. Although the data on profitability is limited, taken together with the information on investment, it may offer a Centre some indication of the incentives to relocate operations. In the case of Glaxo, despite the substantial investment in Britain (judging by narrative reports and indications of research staffing), there is also significant activity overseas. For example, the location of production in Singapore, taking advantage of tax concessions, suggests a possible willingness to locate according to fiscal incentives. Although there are no indications that the company is seeking to locate in other countries to take advantage of cheap labour or lower production, health and safety or environmental standards, the possibility is raised by the location in Singapore.

A second aspect of competitive implications concerns the extent to which Glaxo has entered into agreements with other drug companies. Although there was nothing of significance in the period we examined, shortly after there were examples of co-operation with other large drug companies and we know nothing of continuing agreements. Such collaborations appear to be relatively common in the industry yet, given the potential to be exploited contrary to the interests of the community, it is a matter in which one would expect a Centre to take an interest.

As for issues on which there appeared to be little information or comment, we identified two. Firstly, there is the absence of forecast information. A monitoring Centre, like other parties interested in transnationals, would find it difficult to operate if restricted to historic data, much of which is over one year old when disclosed to the public. There appears to be a case for the Centre obtaining plans from transnationals, particularly where there is a likely significant impact on the community. Secondly, there was little comment on the marketing performance of Glaxo. Despite the general concerns with marketing in the pharmaceuticals industry and some specific criticisms of Glaxo in the press, there was very little detail on this aspect of the firm's performance. There seems little doubt that a Centre wishing to back winners would need to concern itself with the marketing performance of firms, since this can, particularly in the drugs industry, be crucial to overall performance, as well as being so significant to society's welfare. In this respect there is particular concern expressed about the marketing performance of transnational drug companies in developing countries. Our suggestion would be that, as with other issues, a British Centre on Transnational Corporations be concerned, not only with the impact in Britain, but also with the impact overseas, whether or not there is formal co-operation with other countries.

Research and development/technology

The disclosure of details of location of research staff enabled us to identify changes over the years. There is little doubt that a Centre would be interested in the extent to which, despite the increase in numbers employed in Britain, the percentage was declining. Although the changes are relatively small, taken with our earlier comments on the possible increasing importance of the USA, they would be of interest. Again this is not intended to be seen in narrow, nationalistic terms. A monitoring Centre would not necessarily oppose the transfer of jobs to other countries, particularly if those were poorer countries or countries where Glaxo had important markets. However, a Centre would realistically be interested in proposed changes as a contribution to assessing change in the British economy, and perhaps because it would suggest that government negotiate over transfers which are arranged purely to benefit the controllers of capital.

Similarly the information we obtained on the matter of product liability might be of interest to a Centre wishing to form an overall opinion as to the type of firm Glaxo is. Despite limited reporting of product liability issues, the Centre would be concerned to see how such matters are handled, and whether the cases suggest that there is a need to seek information on matters of quality control, research processes, or health and safety.

On the question of the absence of information, two matters seemed particularly important. Firstly, we have no information on training, something of a surprise given the knowledge-based nature of the business. This may well be due to the informal nature of much training in the company. On the other hand it may be a function of the different perspectives being brought to bear in our analysis. Although the skills of a work-force are essential to the financial performance of a firm, and therefore of interest to controllers of capital, the issue is, like the matter of location of production referred to previously, of secondary importance. Whilst information on training could be of interest to investment analysts, it is likely that such would be only a small part of the larger picture of interest. In contrast the Centre, with an interest in the impact of transnationals on the community, would be concerned with quality of jobs, the investment in skills and the personal development of workers.

Secondly, we know little about the quality of the products of Glaxo. Above we comment on the possible importance of product liability. To this we can add the absence of public reporting of the Food and Drugs Administration (FDA) and other government inspections of Glaxo's production. Whilst ultimately one would expect serious problems with inspections to be made public, or at least the consequence of a product being withdrawn from certain markets, a Centre monitoring transnationals' performance should not be expected to wait until such a late stage. If a monitoring Centre is intended to have an active role in industrial policy it must be sufficiently well informed to be able to influence directly and indirectly the performance of transnationals, not simply have to pick up the pieces of poor performance, in whatever respect.

Employment and industrial relations

Our calculations of the ratio of directors' salaries to employees' wages (30.2:1) and the calculation of a rate of exploitation (profits being 2.69 times returns to labour) were of limited value, particularly given the assumptions which had to be made and that we had only overall data for the Glaxo group. The absence of national data precludes much comment here. However, there is in such calculations an illustration of the scope to use traditional accounting information to show the distribution of rewards. Similarly, the calculation of value added in the section on productivity revealed that only 39 per cent of the wealth created went to employees, with 43 per cent going to investors. Such figures can be compared to other drug companies and firms in general by a Centre, as could the returns to workers if further details were provided, classified according to grades and countries of location. Such would undoubtedly be of interest to a Centre wishing to ensure fair returns to workers, both here and abroad.

In the case of matters which were barely covered in publicly-available information it is worth singling out two. The first we have referred to above when addressing the question of ownership and control, that is, the absence of detail on the matter of employee involvement and industrial democracy as a whole. As we pointed out in this section there is not even information on trade union membership in total never mind on a national basis. Indications are that employees are informed, rather than involved.

In addition there is virtually no information on conditions of employment. For example, although there are indications that Glaxo takes health and safety extremely seriously, and there are no incidents reported during the year, there is almost no information publicly available on the matter. This concern with the absence of health and safety data can be linked to the limited reporting on FDA and other inspections. If our earlier comments are accurate, and the industry is heading for a tougher time ahead, then there may be reason to take a greater interest in such matters. Transnationals are often seen to use wage costs as a reason for shifting the location of production. Increasingly, however, in an environment of strict regulation, there may also be an incentive to locate in countries where there are less strict health and safety and other regulations. Moreover, such location decisions would be influenced by attempts to divide and rule employees and communities.

Balance of payments

Little information was reported by Glaxo on trade, capital and investment flows around the world, despite the obvious significance of these for a transnational group. The only detailed indicators of trade flows was provided by the segment data of Table 7.6 and the reporting of exports from Britain (in Table 7.32).

This seems wholly inadequate for the purposes of monitoring. Yet fuller reporting of flows would simply reflect overall funds flows, unless accompanied by substantial detail particularly on transfer pricing. Our suggestion of a compact matrix for trade, capital and investment flows is made in the knowledge that such could only be the beginning of an attempt to acquaint oneself with the activities of Glaxo.

Perhaps this issue, more than any other, has illustrated the difference between the 'group' perspective of investors and Glaxo itself and a monitoring Centre's need to obtain disaggregated data. Without such detail a Centre would be in a poor position to anticipate a transnational's strategy and policies.

'Basics'

Little can be said under this heading, given the different nature of the concern. Whereas most other issues of concern identified in our matrix in Chapter 5 were of general concern regarding some aspect of corporate performance, the matter of basics was about the very nature of the business. In this case France, Japan and the USA had restrictions on foreign involvement in certain specific, allegedly essential industries. As far as we can see Glaxo, and drug companies in general, do not fall within the usual definition (although health and welfare is sometimes included as a basic industry in which foreign involvement is restricted). As a result there is little comment to make here on this issue.

Although our discussion is limited here to matters which were classified as core, this should not be interpreted as suggesting that there was little to be said about the remaining issues. For example, despite the existence of an environmental policy there is virtually no reporting of the firm's performance in this respect. We also noted that there was very little information on productivity, having to construct our own value added information.

LESSONS FOR THE CONSTRUCTION OF AN ECONOMIC AND SOCIAL ACCOUNT

In Chapter 6 we outlined a number of potential difficulties which might be experienced by a Centre wishing to construct an economic and social account. These problems were drawn from the literature on social accounting. Here we comment on them in the light of our case study, although in general, in the absence of a Centre's economic and social account, little can be added.

One matter of some difficulty for social accounting was seen to be the calculation of externalities, the wider economic and social consequences of actions which are not reflected in market prices. Our discussion above raised two matters which might be considered as such, but which were referred to briefly and certainly not quantified. Both environmental impact and health and safety are matters which could result in impact beyond the traditional market view of the firm. Whilst one can capture both effects by referring to legal cases, fines etc., this seems inadequate as a means of reporting impact. Such emphasis relies on satisfactory legislation, rather than a recognition that the interests of particular groups in society may not be particularly well served by the law.

Health and safety and environmental impact are examples worth using further. In both cases there is so little information that it is not possible to discuss the pros and cons of financial versus non-financial reporting. At the moment there is so little information disclosed on these matters that there can be no comparison. Given the dominance of the financial accounting report there can be no worthwhile discussion of the question of appropriate measures from the case study. Yet in general, given the concerns of a Centre with the power of transnationals, it would seem rather inappropriate for the basis of some economic and social accounting to reflect the legal status of issues and to apply market prices to quantifications. Our clear preference is for an accounting which is in a large part non-financial.

This limited disclosure highlights the emphasis on investors' needs rather than those of governments or a Centre wishing to monitor transnationals. Although it must be remembered that we have confined ourselves to publicly-available information, and in particular did not ask Glaxo for more material, our research clearly raises the question of regulatory change, either involving wider public disclosure or the giving of powers to a Centre in order to obtain information direct from transnationals. Such change could well result in opposition from managers and controllers of capital, on the basis of the increased financial cost it would impose on them, or due to the potential reduction in power which might result. On the other hand some increase in publicly-available information might well be welcomed by investment analysts.

Whatever the outcome there is no doubt that disclosure is likely to continue to be at least strongly influenced by management. Given this, the wider accounting of transnationals might then be used to legitimate their activities, rather than facilitate monitoring (Hamilton, 1984; Puxty, 1986). Yet managerial co-operation is clearly needed, particularly since information systems may not be geared to collecting, never mind reporting, the necessary economic and social information.

It would not be surprising to see transnationals objecting to the increased disclosure of information on the basis of its commercial confidentiality. Much of the history of attempts to increase financial disclosure for investors is dogged by corporations stonewalling on the basis of the commercial confidentiality argument, particularly emphasising the disadvantage home companies feel in relation to overseas competitors. Recognising this, although we envisage a British Centre on Transnational Corporations which would seek to make information on transnationals publicly-available, there may well be circumstances in which confidentiality must be respected. There are important precedents in this respect, including the Inland Revenue and the Customs and Excise. They regularly obtain information from corporations which would be of great interest to the stock market but which remains confidential.

CONCLUSION

This discussion of the case study has focused on the problems likely to be faced by a monitoring Centre. It can only be seen as a start in identifying these, since as we have stressed we are not a transnationals Centre.

What we have set as a task, namely the construction of economic and social accounts, may not appear to have been progressed significantly by our case study. However, we have revealed the difficulty of constructing accounts, brought the successful realisation of the designated task a step nearer, and, although the most important lesson concerns the general inadequacy of publicly-available information for monitoring, we have raised a number of questions regarding Glaxo's activities.

There is scope to monitor transnationals in a limited way even with publicly-available information.

There is, however, also a need to address the problems arising from the partisan disclosure rules we have at the present time. Ours is a belief that the social and political dimension of transnationals' performance is as important as their narrowly-defined economic or accounting performance. This would appear to be reflected in the requests for firms to provide more and different information to that which is currently required. If needs be it should be reflected in new requirements for firms to disclose information.

However, it is clear that there remains an underlying difficulty caused by the contrasting organisation of capital and the community. The increasing internationalisation of commerce is in marked contrast to the organisation of communities, government and politics (Murray, 1971). It is with this in mind that we will now turn in Chapter 9 to emphasising the need for governments to co-operate in the monitoring of transnationals.

NOTE

1. These shackles will be reimposed in Chapter 9.

9

CO-OPERATION BETWEEN COUNTRIES

Although various countries have been considered in the course of this volume, until now we have been proposing a strategy for one country to pursue in isolation. This chapter is another (and the final) turning point in our argument. It will extend our proposition to encompass the possibility of countries acting together. We are still advocating that Britain creates its own Centre on Transnational Corporations. However, we are now also suggesting that Britain should promote supranational co-operation over monitoring.

Co-operation could be pursued with various countries. For example, an obvious possibility, bearing in mind the discussion of Chapter 3, is to work with the United States, where the history of concern with information suggests there could be some support for such an initiative. Another option is to encourage a United Nations initiative. However, for Britain an even more obvious possibility is to promote co-operation amongst European Community members, given that the Community is the most sophisticated supranational institution with which Britain is involved and upon which it can therefore build. It is co-operation at the European Community level that will be the concern of this chapter. However, we recognise the importance of co-operation more widely, not least to ensure that weaker, developing countries do not suffer as a result of policies in so-called advanced industrialised nations. Accordingly, the chapter should also be seen as illustrating the sort of argument that should be applied to co-operation more widely.

Our basic intention is to argue for monitoring at the Community level and, in so doing, to explain why this may appeal to member states. In suggesting something that Britain should promote within the Community, our concern will be to establish both how Britain would gain from such an initiative and how other member states would benefit. Thus we will show why Britain should promote the initiative and why it may succeed in persuading other members to participate.

We suggest that Britain advocates creation of a European Centre on Transnational Corporations. The intention is that this would feed into and from the British Centre – and indeed similar bodies in other nations – contributing to the latter's activities but also compiling economic and social accounts at the Pan-European level and analysing these in a Pan-European context. The idea of national and supranational Centres co-existing, rather than one co-operative body, is partly that this would leave individual countries with greater freedom. For example, a European Centre would have to operate along lines acceptable to all Community members and therefore might be less active than Britain ideally desires; Britain would remain free to be more active via its own Centre. Furthermore the co-operative body would focus on transnationals at the Pan-European level, leaving the British Centre to pursue its national and intra-national concerns. Hence if it came to discussing future strategy possibilities, for instance, the European Centre would concentrate on Pan-European options, which are likely to be different from relevant options at the national level. In other words, the British and European Centres would perform related but different tasks.

Some readers may wonder why we have taken until the volume's penultimate chapter to raise the co-operation issue. Indeed, faced with a proposal for monitoring by a particular country, a common reaction is to argue that any monitoring would have to be carried out at a supranational level. In contrast we suggest that, whilst a co-operative initiative is desirable, it is a complement to rather than a substitute for a British Centre. Moreover, our suggestion is that Britain advocates a European Centre whilst immediately creating a British Centre. In this sense and although it is not important, analysis of a strategy for one country to pursue in isolation can sensibly precede analysis of co-operative ventures. Perhaps it may also be argued that it is easier for a government to begin monitoring at a national level and, using this valuable experience, build up to multilateral initiatives; it is easier for a government to walk before it can run. This may effectively be the best justification for the ordering of the volume.

By way of background, the chapter[1] begins with an examination of previous Community concerns with transnationals. This is important to explaining why Community members might co-operate over monitoring. Drawing on existing literature, the first section will characterise events in the context of the Commission's 1973 Spinelli Report,[2] the Vredeling proposals and so on. Key features and hence lessons for future Community initiatives will be highlighted. In the light of this discussion, the second and third sections will advocate and explore the European Centre on Trans-national Corporations option. The second section will outline the option and consider some of its attributes. The section will also return to previous Community concerns, commenting on specific monitoring related initiatives and proposals in the light of our suggestion. However, it will ignore crucial issues associated with member states co-operating rather than acting unilaterally; these will be taken up in the third section.

PREVIOUS EUROPEAN COMMUNITY CONCERNS

Our intention in this section is to characterise first the general position and then the attitudes of member states. Those wanting details of particular policies and so on are referred in the first instance to Robinson (1983) and Tempini (1989, 1992).

The general position

European Community concerns about transnationals have a long history. For example, European Management Forum (1973) refers to a 1963 French proposal for a common policy on foreign investments and foreign transnationals. It also reports the European Commission's 1965 proposals for gathering information and for consultation over capital movements into and out of the Community.[3] Yet nearly thirty years since the airing of these proposals, a coherent Community framework has not emerged. Community initiatives have been essentially piecemeal and no overall strategy for approaching transnationals has been formulated. This conclusion is also reached by Tempini (1989), following her survey of events, and by Robinson (1983), who goes so far as to venture that 'a global European policy exclusively addressed to multinationals *per se* does not exist, never has and, short of unforeseeable political earthquakes, never will'.

The lack of an overall strategy does not imply that transnationals are given a completely free hand. Indeed Robinson (1983) argues that there was much activity to curb the alleged disadvantages of transnationals in the 1970s and he predicted a lot more for the 1980s. However, he seems to overstate what actually happened in the 1970s and he certainly overestimates what was to come in the 1980s. Perhaps he was influenced by the prominence being given to the Vredeling proposals when he was writing. In many ways there seems to have been more talk than action, as illustrated by the Vredeling saga, and since that petered away in the mid-1980s there has been relatively little activity on the transnationals' issue, piecemeal or otherwise. This is clear from the listing of relevant Directives in Tempini (1989) and from a glance at the *European Access* bibliography.

This garrulous inactivity is perhaps surprising given the apparently quite widespread and long-held belief that, whilst the presence of transnationals has its advantages and is desirable, there are disadvantages which require attention.[4] This pros and cons approach can be seen in European Commission (1973), the famous Spinelli Report suggesting a policy line which Tempini (1989) argues is very close to the current Community perspective. The Report suggests that 'the growing hold of multinational undertakings on the economic, social and even political life of the countries in which they operate, gives rise to deep anxieties which . . . demand the attention of the public authorities'. When discussing general guidelines for regulating transnationals, it goes on to observe that 'the measures to be undertaken should not impede the development of a phenomenon with recognised economic and social advantages, but that they should merely aim at guarding the Community against its harmful effects'. More recently, for example,[5] the pros and cons approach is seen in European Parliament (1989). This reports the submission of a motion to the Parliament referring to the need for the 'progressive formulation of international rules and codes of conduct, in order to optimise the positive effects [of transnationals] while keeping the negative effects to a minimum'.[6]

The attitudes of member states

The garrulous inactivity is perhaps less surprising, however, when it is remembered that Community Directives need to satisfy member states. Indeed, this may also mean that the piecemeal approach and the lack of overall strategy are unsurprising characteristics. Agreement on a common approach requires a common denominator, something countries might find hard or even impossible to find if they are sufficiently varied in their views. Moreover, whilst the precise attitude of every European Community member towards transnationals is very difficult to characterise, the existing literature clearly shows that there is considerable variation.

In so far as it is possible to generalise, France has been the most prominent supporter and proponent of transnationals regulation. For example, the French unsuccessfully sought Community controls on inward investors in both the 1960s and 1970s (European Management Forum, 1973; Hamilton, 1976; Graham, 1982). At the other extreme (in the past[7]) Britain has been very much against regulation (although compare Hamilton, 1976[8]). For instance, McDermott (1986) tells of Britain being the major opponent of the Vredeling proposals for improved employee information and consultation in transnationals (see, in addition, Crane's (1984) report of a Council of Ministers' discussion on this issue). McDermott also mentions the allegation that Britain's government even master-minded an international lobbying campaign by transnationals against the proposals.

The other Community members have taken positions somewhere between France and Britain. The existing literature on the European Community is somewhat sparse on members' attitudes but some tentative comments can be made about some countries. Germany has clearly taken an in between position. It has supported some initiatives, for example, Vredeling, but opposed others, for instance, the 1965 measures concerning information and capital movements that we commented upon earlier (European Management Forum, 1973; Graham, 1982; Robinson, 1983; Thomsen and Nicolaides, 1990). From Robinson (1983), it looks as though Ireland and Luxembourg have been relatively unenthusiastic about regulation whereas Belgium and Denmark have been more in favour. However, Hamilton (1976) effectively sees Belgium as comparatively unenthusiastic and it is interesting to note McDermott's (1986) observation that by June 1984 Denmark was alone with Britain in finding the Vredeling proposals unacceptable. There is also uncertainty about the positions of Italy and the Netherlands. It appears from Robinson (1983) that Italy has been relatively cool on regulation but there is at least a suspicion from Hamilton (1976) and Thomsen and Nicolaides (1990) that greater controls on foreign investors were desired. In contrast, the suggestion from Robinson (1983) is that the Netherlands has been comparatively keen on regulation whereas European Management Forum (1973), Hamilton (1976) and Thomsen and Nicolaides (1990) suggest otherwise. The problem could well be that different authors are writing at different times and that countries' attitudes can change – for instance, Robinson (1983) argues that Greece has been relaxing its traditionally restrictive attitude towards foreign investment.

Whatever the precise position, however, for our purposes this discussion reveals two points. Firstly, it is very clear that different European Community members have different attitudes towards regulating transnational corporations; some are more-or-less sympathetic, others are more-or-less unsympathetic. Secondly, there is at least the strong possibility that countries' attitudes have changed over time. Assuming these patterns are replicated in the future – and there is nothing to suggest otherwise – there are two corresponding lessons for any new initiative. Firstly, it must accommodate countries which are relatively hostile to the regula-tion of transnationals. Secondly, it would at least be very useful to create a flexible strategy capable of evolving in various directions and thus of serving different member state requirements as these change over time.

The literature on member state attitudes is also interesting in so far as it identifies three fears which have reined back any inclination to regulate. Similar worries at least may plague governments in the future and therefore will need to be addressed when making new proposals. The most widely reported concern is that regulation would discourage potential investors (see also earlier chapters commenting on such a fear in a national rather than community context). For instance, Graham (1982) claims that Germany opposed French initiatives in the 1960s for fear of discouraging US invest-ment. Similarly, Tom King, then British Employment Minister, said of the Vredeling proposals: 'The Government believes that if these proposals were to become law they could discourage investment in the Community'.[9] See also Crane (1984) on Britain's attitude to Vredeling, Graham (1982) on French reluctance to act alone in case investors locate elsewhere in the Community yet still access French markets, and Robinson (1983) on Belgium and Italy. Fear of discouraging investors is likely to affect at least most countries in the future. It needs to be taken very seriously. Less widespread, but nevertheless significant, has been the fear that constraining (so-called) foreign firms would hamper the performance of (so-called) domestic transnationals. This will be a greater worry for those countries which are 'home' to a more powerful set of transnational corporations. In line with this, it is raised by Robinson (1983) in terms of France, Germany and Britain. Furthermore, a subset of European Community members may have another concern. European Management Forum (1973) claims that Community members opposed the aforementioned 1965 initiatives covering information and capital movements because of worries that France would try to impose a policy restricting foreign investors. This thin end of the wedge argument can be seen more generally in Braun (1973). Should new proposals come before the Community in the future, a similar fear may haunt those countries which are comparatively unsympathetic to a new strategy for approaching transnationals.

EUROPEAN MONITORING

Our characterisation suggests Britain is a member of a Community that has approached transnationals in a piecemeal, fragmentary manner. The absence of a strategic, systematic (and therefore inherently superior)[10] alternative despite the widespread pros and cons attitude implies that any future change addressing this defect will have to come relatively slowly and carefully.[11] Experience does not favour anything bold. In such an environment, we suggest that policy-makers who accept the argument for a British Centre on Transnational Corporations should also promote the creation of a similar European Centre on Transnational Corporations. This would be the least that could be done to move the Community in a more suitable direction. Nevertheless, it would be a significant step benefiting member states and, as far as Britain is concerned, would be an ideal complement to a national body.

The remainder of this section will outline and begin to explore this suggestion. In doing so it will echo Chapter 4's comments on the proposed British Centre. We will ignore issues that arise from countries co-operating rather than acting unilaterally. These will be considered in the third section. This is analytically convenient because it enables this section to concentrate on our proposal's first basic dimension: the idea of European monitoring. The third section will then examine the second basic dimension: co-operation (over European monitoring).

Like our envisaged British Centre on Transnational Corporations, the European Centre would collect information, prepare economic and social accounts, and use these to influence economic policy and attitudes of and towards transnational corporations. This would be a simple approach, potentially of significant direct benefit and the start of an evolutionary process of policy development which would allow the Community to feel its way at its own pace. The Centre would have the ability to collect information on important issues relating to transnationals; it would continuously monitor especially important issues in a set of larger corporations and randomly monitor other areas and other firms; it would analyse its economic and social accounts very broadly.[12] Unlike our envisaged British Centre on Transnational Corporations, the European Centre would concentrate on Pan-European accounts and analysis.[13]

Concern with information is not new in a European Community context and indeed we have already referred to some related, earlier initiatives. However, our proposal is different. For instance, the 1973 Spinelli Report focuses on the need for 'better provision of information'. It advocates 'the most widespread possible distribution of an annual report . . . to allow all interested parties to arrive at their own judgement' of transnationals. This is a much narrower purpose than that of the Centre; Spinelli does not suggest information gathering and reporting as a means of influencing transnationals' attitudes nor as the start of an evolutionary process of policy development. Moreover, Spinelli's proposals fall well short of the continuous and wide-ranging compilation and analysis of economic and social accounts that we envisage. See also *Euroforum* (1976), Drew (1979) and Graham (1982) on the Commission's eighteen-month survey of transnationals which followed the Spinelli Report. The survey was very general, for example, looking at the aggregate turnover of large groups of firms. Drew refers to it as monitoring but it bears little resemblance to the monitoring we envisage. Similarly Tempini (1989) briefly advocates a policy of improving the information flow from transnationals[14] and of establishing a transnationals 'information bank'. This also differs in purpose, depth and breadth from our proposal; for instance, an information bank sounds more akin to a library than the proactive European Centre on Transnational Corporations that we are visualising.

By creating a Centre, members of the European Community would be taking a significant step. Ignoring for the moment any points that may arise from the first section's characterisation of member state attitudes, the significance that should be attached to a body compiling and analysing economic and social accounts is in some way analogous to the significance that equity investors attach to the preparation and analysis of conventional financial statements. We are proposing that the Community bases its pursuit of society's interests on a systematic approach with similarities to that used by equity investors as a foundation for their pursuit of private interests. More particularly, the monitoring strategy would provide a pool of knowledge which might enable the formulation of apt and more detailed strategies in the future. In addition, a Centre's analysis would provide a catalyst and stimulant for broad discussion of future strategy options. Moreover, the information a Centre would provide might have significant direct effects because it might influence transnationals' behaviour, assuming the argument that transnationals trade on ignorance.

These gains from monitoring might be to some extent offset by potential losses associated with two of the worries that we suggested have and will characterise European countries, fear of discouraging potential investors and fear of hampering domestic transnationals. However, neither fear should cause significant unease; a member state would at worst have little to lose on this basis. By its terms of reference, a monitoring body could be required to immediately explore its own impact on potential investors and on the perform-ance of domestic transnationals; economic and social accounts could be compiled and analysed with these fears paramount. On the one hand, if it reveals that the fears are indeed justified and in fact outweigh all of its offsetting benefits, the monitoring body could be instantly disbanded. At least Community policy would then have a solid foundation and, for instance, there would be no need to waste resources on garrulous inactivity in the future. Furthermore, the monitoring could be stopped without any significant loss in investment or in the performance of domestic firms. On the other hand, should the fears prove groundless, the Community might have set itself on a more suitable policy direction.

More generally, this illustrates an important feature of our proposal: it is especially flexible, leaving all future options open and positively facilitating their consideration. Hence, for example, it accommodates a country whose attitude towards transnationals is likely to change over time. As the first section suggests, this could be important in the European Community context.

Moreover, what is emerging from this discussion (although we still have to examine co-operation rather than unilateral action) is that the necessary and sufficient conditions for accepting that European level monitoring is worthwhile are extremely weak. Thus countries differing in their attitudes towards transnationals are very likely to find monitoring acceptable. This is undoubtedly important in the European context. It is necessary and sufficient merely to accept that: (a) transnationals are important actors in the Community; (b) there may be scope for the Community to influence their impact significantly. It is not necessary to believe that transnationals are villains of the peace; monitoring is even worthwhile if it is merely believed that the presence of transnationals only confers important advantages and that these may be made significantly more beneficial. As for (a), a glance at some reasonable texts on transnationals should satisfy most people that it is generally the case. Condition (b) is also easily satisfied. It is hinted at by the discussion of Chapters 2 and 3; although they referred to national initiatives, (b) only requires that there 'may' be scope and the disagreement over national possibilities surely spills over into dispute at the supranational level. Moreover, the long, garrulous history of concern over transnationals in the Community context itself implies that (b) would receive widespread acceptance in Europe.

CO-OPERATION OVER MONITORING

Assuming that a particular Community member accepts the view that Pan-European monitoring would be useful, in principle one option is to co-operate with other members in creating the sort of Centre we have outlined but another is to act unilaterally. For instance, if Britain establishes its own monitoring body, it could charge this with compiling Pan-European accounts and with analysing these accounts from the viewpoint of potential Community strategies that would best suit Britain's interests.[15] Put another way, if countries are to co-operate we need to explain why they should do so; following Gowland (1982), if there is to be co-operation we need to explain how it would benefit utility maximising nations. Indeed, this is especially important because co-operation contrasts with the way countries have often behaved in the past. They have tended to see themselves as rivals in their dealings with transnationals and appeared to do anything but co-operate. See, for instance, Sleuwaegen's (1987) comment on intra-European Community rivalry over inducements for incoming investors, and Buckley and Artisien (1987) on inward investment to Greece, Portugal and Spain.

To explore co-operation over monitoring we will make the

analysis manageable by focusing on a relatively narrow approach in various respects. Firstly, we will focus solely on the transnationals issue. In practice a government may view its set of potential policies as a whole and negotiate with others for the best package. This is illustrated by Gowland's (1982) discussion of French and German co-operation over agriculture and steel when the European Community was originally established. He argues that Germany agreed to participate in the agriculture plan even though, taken alone, participation was 'almost certainly against German interests'; the aim was to obtain French involvement in the steel plan. It is also reflected in European Management Forum (1973), which claims that the 1963 French proposal for a Community policy on transnationals was rejected because de Gaulle had vetoed Britain's membership application. To contemplate these sorts of trade-offs would take this analysis well beyond its remit. Secondly, in typical economists' fashion we will concentrate on the selfish scenario. When countries are deciding whether or not to co-operate the decision each makes could in principle be founded upon benefit to the others as well as benefit directly to itself. Indeed, this might be realistic for members of the European Community if they genuinely saw themselves as part of a real community. In contrast, our lifelike assumption is that each country is only concerned with itself in a narrow sense. Thirdly, analysis will be implicitly based on a simple Paretian social welfare model; attention will be on whether a particular country gains or loses and will even ignore, for instance, the possibility of gainers compensating losers.[16]

Moreover, our approach will be narrower still because it will pursue a framework associated with transactions costs analysis. There are other options. For example, one is to explore in detail the alleged disadvantages identified with transnationals and thus to consider the advantages that co-operation might bring. Another is to draw an analogy with the theory of rivalry and collusion amongst firms; this would suggest that countries may co-operate over monitoring precisely because they see themselves as rivals.[17] However, there is a limit to what can be pursued in one volume and, as the forthcoming discussion will reveal, a framework centred on transactions provides a useful basis for interesting comment. In addition, one of the aims of this volume is to present and justify a strategy with as wide an appeal as possible. Hence, for instance, we have avoided pinning our proposal to specifically alleged disadvantages of transnationals. It seems appropriate to continue in this spirit, if only to see how far the argument can be pushed. Similarly, developing a rivalry and collusion analogy would probably provoke more controversy than developing a transactions approach. It is therefore fitting for this volume to pursue the latter, providing the analysis offers valuable and convincing insight.

In fact the analysis can offer valuable insights from two angles and taken together these provide a positive case for European Community members creating a European Centre on Transnational Corporations. It also implies that the latter would be an ideal complement to the sort of national body we have outlined and explored in earlier chapters.

The first angle examines the costs of carrying out a particular transaction. This is in the spirit of the vast transactions costs literature (see, for instance, Coase, 1937, and Williamson, 1975, on the theory of the firm). We suggest that co-operation would almost certainly allow countries to carry out the same monitoring at less cost. To illustrate, consider two countries, x and y, contemplating European level monitoring of transnationals. They have two choices. One is to act alone, in which case denote their total costs by $C_x(\cdot)$ and $C_y(\cdot)$ respectively. The other is to co-operate; to compile exactly the same economic and social accounts and to analyse these to exactly the same extent, but to do so in co-operation. In this case, denote their total combined costs by $C_{xy}(\cdot)$. Assuming co-operators divide total costs proportionately to their compilation and analysis of accounts, it seems extremely likely that $C_x(\cdot) > \alpha_x C_{xy}(\cdot)$ and $C_y(\cdot) > \alpha_y C_{xy}(\cdot)$, where $\alpha_x(\alpha_y)$ is the share of co-operators' costs borne by country $x(y)$.

There are two basic reasons to expect this outcome. The first relates to information gathering, particularly remembering that the concern is with specific firms' activities in various countries. Different countries will have easier and perhaps exclusive access to different sources of information. When countries co-operate, this may enable a particular point to be unearthed more quickly and/or with less trouble. The second refers to information processing. A truly co-operative venture should bring different dimensions to the analysis of information. Co-operation should entail a pooling of minds and ideas from different nations hence different perspectives being brought to the transnationals issue. Consequently, the analysis of economic and social accounts may be achieved more speedily.[18]

Moreover, still concentrating on the costs of carrying out a particular transaction, suppose there is a British Centre on Trans-national Corporations along the lines we have envisaged. A European Centre would almost certainly allow the national body to carry out the same monitoring as when there is no Community initiative but at less cost. Again there are two basic reasons: the co-operative venture would have easier and perhaps exclusive access to different sources of information which it could make available to the national body – which, it should be stressed, is concerned with transnationals' activities in Britain and thus to some extent, necessarily, trans-nationals' activities more widely – and it could communicate with the British Centre in ways that contribute different perspectives to the latter's analysis. What we have in mind is that a British Centre on Transnational Corporations would interact with a European Centre as it compiles economic and social accounts and as it analyses those accounts. This should cut the costs of a particular transaction for the British Centre. Furthermore, the interaction should be two-way, hence the European Centre should be able to decrease its trans-actions costs by feeding from the national body. (Indeed, it is easy to visualise a network of national monitoring bodies throughout Europe, each linked to a European Centre acting as a hub.)

Perhaps more to the point, however, these considerations also suggest that co-operation might change the content of monitoring, in the sense of allowing outcomes which could not otherwise occur. This brings us to the second aspect of our transactions approach: examination of the contents of a particular transaction. Compare Cowling and Sugden (1987a, 1987b, 1993a) on the theory of the firm. They criticise the failure of transactions costs analysis to probe beyond mere costs and to look at what is actually going on in a transaction. We must avoid a related error.

Consider first the interaction between British and European monitoring bodies. Compared to when there is no European Centre, the existence of both bodies might enable each to compile otherwise unobtainable accounts and to analyse these accounts to an otherwise unobtainable extent. These changes are not associated with costs (other than in a trivial sense).[19] It is possible that the quality and quantity of raw information available to each monitoring body would be improved in otherwise unachievable ways as a result of their actively pooling their different information sources. This might yield unique improvements in the quality and content of both their accounts and their analysis. These might similarly be better due to a pooling of their minds and ideas.

Similarly, if we concentrate solely on European level monitoring, compared to when they act unilaterally countries which co-operate might be able to compile otherwise unobtainable accounts and to analyse these accounts to an otherwise unobtainable extent. Again, for example, it is possible that the quality and quantity of raw information would be improved in otherwise unachievable ways by countries pooling their different sources. Accounts and their analysis might also be uniquely improved by co-operators pooling their minds and ideas. Moreover, co-operation would change the transaction content in other, more fundamental ways. We have argued that a European Centre could be created in a way that left a country with little to lose if its fears of discouraging potential investors and of hampering the performance of domestic trans-nationals were realised. Thus the fears do not warrant excessive attention. Nevertheless, it is worth noting that, in some senses, the fears are totally removed when European countries co-operate. Fear of discouraging investors partly means worry that they will locate in rival countries. For a member of the European Community a large part of this worry refers to location elsewhere in the Com-munity, especially with events surrounding the Single European Market; recall Graham's (1982) comment about French reluctance to act unilaterally in case investors were pushed to another part of the Community. Yet firms cannot discriminate against specific nations if all nations follow the same approach. Similarly, fear of hampering performance is in part worry that other nations will somehow retaliate against a particular approach. This cannot happen amongst a group of co-operating nations. In both situations, without co-operation at least some policy-makers will have nagging doubts and will foresee the possibility of adverse consequences, however slight; only by genuine co-operation can these worries be totally eliminated.[20]

In contrast, co-operation may introduce a fear which would otherwise be absent: the aforementioned thin end of the wedge argument might come into play. This should be noted because it could be important but it is not worth a lot more attention in this volume. Without co-operation there can be no fear that another country will try to turn a strategy into something unwanted. With co-operation this is possible. Our monitoring strategy is not designed to be the thin end of an unwanted wedge and it has been carefully set up to avoid that connotation. For example, it has not been based on a negative view of transnationals and it has been explicitly designed as a minimalist approach. It has even been argued that the proposed Centre could be disbanded if countries' other fears were realised. If this is accepted, it would be stretching a point to believe that monitoring would be the start of something unwelcome. Nevertheless, it could undoubtedly be seen and used in that way. This cannot be eradicated by anything we might say because, if there is a problem, it is ultimately political. Suffice it merely to observe that politicians may need to satisfy worried colleagues.

This illustrates how the essence of a transaction can be determined by its means. Likewise there is another issue that co-operation would introduce. Assume countries x and y see themselves as rivals in their dealings with transnationals. If x monitors alone it might believe it can benefit at y's expense. In so far as gathering and processing information is the only strategy for dealing with transnationals this is not an especially important issue but suppose, for instance, governments also negotiate systematically with transnationals for improved benefits. In this case, x might value asymmetric information and therefore unilateral monitoring, for example, if it sees itself and y as rivals for a particular investment. Furthermore, co-operation in such circumstances would again raise the fear of hampering domestic firms' performance. If country x acts alone it might obtain information which y would use to bargain with firms from x. If the countries co-operate this information might be shared.

Accordingly this is a second argument against co-operation. However, it should be emphasised that the same holds for all countries. Co-operation might make country x share information that it would have liked to keep secret but equally might provide x with information that y would have liked to keep secret. In short, disadvantages that x might foresee might be offset by parallel advantages.

Bringing all of this together, the arguments are not all one way but intimate that in general European Community members would be well advised to co-operate if they believe Pan-European monitoring would be useful. The transactions analysis suggests that co-operation might enable countries to monitor more cheaply than they otherwise would, to compile otherwise unobtainable accounts and to analyse these accounts to an otherwise unobtainable extent. It would also remove a significant part of European Community members' fears. Against these factors, co-operation could introduce the thin end of the wedge worry, although probably less so than any other strategy. Cutting both ways, co-operation might also raise advantages and disadvantages for countries believing they might benefit at each other's expense. These points add up to a positive case for co-operation. Furthermore, the case is even stronger for Britain (and likewise any other nation) if it creates a national monitoring body; the transactions analysis implies that a European Centre on Transnational Corporations would be an excellent complement to our envisaged British Centre.

CONCLUSION

This chapter has suggested that Britain should promote supranational co-operation over monitoring. Its detailed analysis has focused on European Community members. We have attempted to establish how both Britain and other member states would benefit from such an initiative.

By way of background, we examined previous Community concerns with transnationals. It was suggested that there is a long history of concern and a quite widespread belief that transnationals have their pros and cons. Yet there has been more talk than action and the Community has merely had a set of piecemeal initiatives. A consideration of member state attitudes pointed to variation and to three fears: of discouraging potential investors, of hampering the performance of domestic firms and of introducing measures which would snowball out of control.

Building on this experience, it was argued that policy-makers who accept the case for a British Centre on Transnational Corporations should also promote the creation of a similar European Centre on Transnational Corporations. This would be the least that can be done to move the Community in a more suitable direction yet would be a significant step benefiting member states and, as far as Britain is concerned, would be an ideal complement to a national monitoring body. Like our envisaged British Centre, the European Centre on Transnational Corporations would collect information, prepare accounts and use these to influence economic policy and attitudes of and towards transnationals. Unlike the British Centre, it would concentrate on Pan-European accounts and analysis.

As regards benefits from adopting our proposed European Centre for member states in general, the chapter pointed to various sources of gain associated with a simple, systematic pursuit of society's interests. We suggested that the proposal accommodates variations in Community member attitudes. This is partly because the strategy is very flexible, leaving all future options open and positively facilitating their consideration. It is also because the necessary and sufficient conditions for accepting that such monitoring is worthwhile are merely acceptance that transnationals are important actors in the Community and that there may be scope for the Community to influence their impact significantly. We also argued that some of the countries' fears could be overcome. In part this was based on the strategy's flexibility but also on a transactions analysis. This analysis went beyond transactions costs studies. It focused on gains from co-operation over monitoring as well as potential disadvantages. Nevertheless, we suggested that Community members in general would find it beneficial to adopt our proposal.

These general arguments are relevant to Britain but we also pointed to particular reasons why a British Centre on Transnational Corporations (and indeed other, similar national bodies) would benefit from the existence of a European Centre. This was also part of our transactions analysis.

Our overall conclusion is that, when it comes to designing a strategy for approaching transnationals, membership of the European Community offers something that can be built upon and used for mutual advantage. In this sense membership broadens the available strategy options and should be seen very positively; it offers exciting and useful possibilities.

NOTES

1 Much of this chapter draws heavily on Harte and Sugden (1992).

2 European Commission (1973).

3 See also Braun (1973): 'As early as January 1965 the EEC Commission ordered the gathering of a working group to establish . . . a comprehensive analysis of the facts related to American investment in the countries of the EEC'.

4 This again echoes the assertion in Chapter 1 that there is widespread agreement that there may be some disadvantages to transnationals' presence. See also Chapter 4.

5 See also *European Community News* (1979), reporting a speech from the Commissioner for industrial policy.

6 This motion amended an earlier submission which merely stressed the positive effects, see European Parliament (1988).

7 This discussion of Britain refers to the past; our volume as a whole is an explicit attempt to encourage a new attitude in the future! However,

even if Britain changes its approach along the lines we advocate, this would not alter the thrust of our comments in this section.

8 Hamilton (1976) suggests that '"tension" levels between host countries and multinationals' in the Community have been greatest in countries like France and, when under a Labour Government, Britain. In contrast see Chapter 2, although this does not comment on the European Community.

9 Quoted in a press release, Department of Employment and Department of Trade and Industry (1983).

10 By its nature, a strategy implies a systematic, coherent, thorough approach. In contrast, piecemeal initiatives run an extra risk of doing things which are inappropriate and not doing things which are appropriate, precisely because they are piecemeal; a set of piecemeal measures will constitute the full set of apposite policies by luck rather than judgement. This is not to say that a strategy for controlling transnationals necessarily implies more 'intervention' by governments, more legislation or more items of policy. It is to say that those items of policy which are pursued within a strategy are part of a coherent plan of action. To obtain a feel for the difference, albeit in an essentially national context, see essays in Cowling and Sugden (1990).

11 Even in 1977, a time when the prospects for designing a Community strategy were comparatively bright, when the European Parliament called for controls on transnationals it emphasised the need for a gradual approach, a point reported in Drew (1979).

12 See earlier chapters for futher comment on such characteristics. Likewise, see earlier discussion for further comment on many of the points being raised in this section.

13 This is not to deny that, in preparing accounts focusing on Britain, the British Centre would need to look beyond Britain, to Europe and elsewhere. Likewise a European Centre would look beyond Europe.

14 See also Drew (1979) on the Lange-Gibbons code.

15 If there is an interest in Community strategies, it would be advisable to compile European level accounts if only because strategies best suiting Britain's interests should be designed in ways appealing to broader Community interests. Otherwise the strategies would be unlikely to gain Community acceptance.

16 See Dosser, Gowland and Hartley (1982) for a more general discussion of the basis for co-operation.

17 This possibility is raised in Harte and Sugden (1990), which also raises other aspects of co-operation and indeed monitoring generally. See also Sugden (1990b), looking at transnationals strategy in general.

18 We are not suggesting that co-operation is easy. For instance, it could be very difficult to marry together different perspectives on transnationals. We are suggesting that the end result would be improved by facing and overcoming such difficulties.

19 If a transaction yields an outcome unobtainable by any other means, it could be argued that the transaction has finite costs and its alternative infinite costs. In this trivial sense, transaction costs are relevant.

20 Response to a particular approach need not be directed at hampering

the performance of domestic firms. It may try to impede the approach itself. Thus McDermott (1986) reports that, in response to the Vredeling proposals, the US Congress discussed a bill to protect US transnationals from being forced to disclose information to foreign nations. This sort of reaction can also be eliminated by co-operation.

10

A SIGNIFICANT STEP FOR BRITAIN

Transnational corporations are very important players in the British economy. In manufacturing, for instance, foreign enterprises and a mere twenty-eight leading UK transnationals were responsible for 36 per cent of total sales in the early 1980s. At the same time, foreign enterprises and forty-five leading domestic transnationals had 43 per cent of manufacturing employment. More generally, there is broad agreement that the impact of transnationals may be sometimes negative, without denying the possibility that offsetting advantages may yield net benefits. Hence the possibility of a government strategy for approaching transnationals needs careful examination. Only a closed mind would reach another conclusion.

That was our judgement in Chapter 1, which laid relatively brief foundations for the detailed analysis which was to come. We went on to justify and explore a constructive strategy that would see the creation of two unique monitoring bodies, the British Centre on Transnational Corporations and the related European Centre on Transnational Corporations. This chapter draws together our analysis. The chapter essentially summarises the view that introducing our proposed strategy towards transnationals would be a significant step for policy-makers in Britain.

LESSONS FROM EXPERIENCE

Our proposals attempted to learn from experience, both in Britain and in countries which British policy-makers are likely to see as direct competitors in international markets. We suggested that Britain's recent approach is questionable, both in the light of arguments about transnationals' effects, and in the light of experience in France, Japan and the US.

216

As regards Britain's policy towards British transnationals, there has been relatively little discussion in the literature. Our assessment is that these corporations have essentially been given free rein to do as they wish (although their activities have been influenced in the ways applicable to firms in general). Governments have seen this as beneficial for Britain, a view which is not undisputed. For example, the activities of British transnationals are arguably associated with deindustrialisation, and with divide and rule tactics against employees. Moreover, the free rein has not been based on good information; governments have been ignorant about transnationals' effects.

Similar information problems have undermined British policy towards overseas transnationals. They have generally received a warm, unrestricted welcome that has seen governments increasingly active in encouraging investors. True, Britain has had some restrictions over incoming investment. Many of these constraints have focused on non-manufacturing activity, but not all. Nevertheless the instances of restrictions are relatively isolated. Very importantly, it seems that the basic justification for policy is the belief that foreign-controlled firms have a beneficial presence. This view has persisted despite, perhaps because of, governments' very poor information. Furthermore, the alleged sources of benefit are once more open to challenge, arguably revealing very insecure foundations for Britain's attitude; there are serious questions over foreign firms' impact on technology, employment and the balance of payments. Moreover, even if we ignore a possible downside to such firms' presence, there are queries about government's failure to maximise perceived advantages of transnationals' activities.

These doubts about the appropriateness of British policy are reinforced when we look at experience in Japan, France and the United States. Japanese policy over recent years has responded to international pressures to open up to investment flows but any alterations have been carefully planned. They have also been influenced by an awareness of potential problems associated with transnationals' activities. Before 1967 Japan tightly controlled firms using the 1949 Foreign Exchange and Foreign Trade Control Law and the 1950 Foreign Investment Law. A series of alleged 'liberalisations' began in 1967. Nevertheless, we characterise Japan as having a relatively tight rein on transnationals in the 1970s. Further changes were introduced in the 1980s but foreign investors are still faced with potentially significant hurdles, the concept of 'administrative guidance' being especially important.

France has also experienced a trend towards more leeway for transnationals. Before 1967, the formal position was that investors required prior authorisation under complex exchange control measures. In 1967 a declaration procedure came into use – a change we characterise as a liberalisation more apparent than real – and further alterations have since occurred, for instance the introduction of a notification procedure. However, our overall impression is that it would be wrong to label the French stance as either obstructionist or liberal; even though its attitude has become more relaxed, the French government still does not follow a hands-off approach, as recent cases illustrate.

A different picture can be drawn for the United States. It has an open-door policy towards inward direct investment, for instance, but has also experienced a fascinating debate involving politicians in and around government. This debate seems to have gone in cycles: Congressional and public concern over transnationals mounts, the administration reluctantly agrees to a limited measure to thwart more ambitious proposals, and then implements it in such a narrow manner that concern soon mounts again that it was inadequate. This has happened with both the Committee on Foreign Investment, a monitoring initiative introduced in the mid-1970s, and more recently with the Exon-Florio provisions.

Compared to Britain, the Japanese and French approaches have been very different, not necessarily better but certainly causing us to question the appropriateness of British policy. Moreover, a query over Britain's attitude also originates from events in the US. In Britain, governments and politicians have given policy towards transnationals very little attention. In contrast there has been a lively US debate, suggesting Britain should review its approach. It is also interesting to consider the views underlying different countries' experiences. The idea of benefiting from transnationals' activities underpins policies in Britain, Japan, France and the United States, and the alternative approaches raised in the United States' debate. An implication of this is that to adopt an alternative approach to Britain's is not necessarily to dispute that transnationals' presence can be beneficial. Perhaps even more importantly, an interesting contrast with Britain is that policies in Japan and France, and the US debate, reflect a greater willingness in these countries to consider and act against transnationals' alleged disadvantages. This contrast should again raise questions in Britain, for example, amongst those who fear that the cost of a country making any attempt to significantly influence the activities of overseas transnationals is that the firms will take their investment elsewhere. Experience in Japan, France and the United States casts doubt on the rationality of this view.

A conclusion that we draw from all of this is that Britain's recent attitude towards transnationals needs to be re-examined.

However, a further point which should be recognised is that the reasons for Britain's attitude, though open to question, none the less impose a real constraint on the relatively-immediate policy options. We have already maintained British governments' basic belief that foreign-controlled firms have a beneficial presence. For the vast majority of people what this actually means is that their advantages outweigh their disadvantages. Believing this, yet nevertheless extending inward investors the sort of welcome we have described for British governments, is to do very little about either minimising the disadvantages or maximising the advantages. There are various reasons for this approach. One is the belief that leaving resource allocation to a set of markets free from government influence is the way to maximise welfare. Another is the fear that if inward investment is not given a free rein, it will disappear. If we are to design a new strategy which appeals to today's policy-makers, it is important to address these views; whilst arguments about transnationals' effects and experience in Japan, France and the US will hopefully cause policy-makers to doubt such beliefs, these beliefs are unlikely to be overturned by such analysis. In short, we need to design a strategy which directly accommodates the beliefs.

A signal to an appropriate way forward is given by yet another contrast between Britain and similar economies. Britain's free rein for transnationals has not been based upon good information about their activities. Compared to Japan, France and the US, Britain has failed to take the information issue seriously. The need for good information has figured very prominently in the US debate and is the area where the US government has been most willing to act. This suggests a pertinent question for those in and around British government: if even the United States – one of the most relaxed countries when it comes to worrying about transnationals – takes the information issue more seriously than Britain, is Britain making a mistake? Furthermore, the relevance of this question is reinforced by experience in Japan and France; an inherent feature of their tighter rein on transnationals is the belief that information on certain matters is essential.

MONITORING IN BRITAIN AND EUROPE

Recognising that Britain's attitude towards transnationals needs to be re-examined but that there is a real belief amongst many British policy-makers in the benefits of free markets and/or the strong likelihood of discouraging investors, we suggest that Britain should learn from concern over information in other countries. More specifically, it would be worthwhile for Britain to adopt a monitoring strategy that can be seen and presented as following in the footsteps of Japan, France and the US: the government should establish a British Centre on Transnational Corporations and advocate creation of a European Centre on Transnational Corporations. This would be a significant break from Britain's past and be doing something extremely important, yet would hardly be doing anything particularly radical. Although a unique approach, it would be a logical development from events elsewhere. This might appeal to policy-makers wary of changing Britain's recent stance.

A British Centre on Transnational Corporations would collect information on transnationals' performance and impact, prepare accounts and use these to influence economic policy and attitudes of and towards transnational corporations. Focusing on transnationals operating in Britain, we have in mind a Centre that continuously monitors especially important issues in a set of larger corporations and randomly monitors other issues and other firms. It is envisaged that the Centre would compile economic and social accounts of particular corporations, and then analyse these accounts; the impact of transnationals on Britain would be explicitly highlighted and policy possibilities for Britain discussed. We suggest that the value of these activities is in some way analogous to the value that equity investors attach to the preparation of conventional financial statements for particular firms and then to investment analysts discussing these accounts. In other words, we propose that society bases the pursuit of its interests on a systematic approach with similarities to that used by equity investors as a foundation for their pursuit of private welfare.

The necessary and sufficient conditions for accepting that such monitoring is worthwhile are extremely weak. Thus policy-makers with very different attitudes towards transnational corporations could find monitoring acceptable. It is necessary and sufficient merely to accept that, in Britain: (a) transnationals are important actors; (b) there may be scope to significantly influence their impact in the interests of society. Monitoring is worthwhile if it is felt that transnationals only have important positive benefits and that these may be made significantly more beneficial. It is not necessary to believe that transnationals are the big baddies of the modern world. Nor is it necessary to believe that they can undoubtedly be influenced to yield better effects.

More particularly, both policy-makers with a strong belief in free markets and those hampered by fear that investors will be pushed elsewhere would at worst have little to lose by creating a British Centre, at best a lot to gain. For instance, by its terms of reference the Centre could be required to explore immediately its own impact on potential investors in Britain; if this reveals that the fear is justified and in fact outweighs all off-setting benefits, the monitoring body could be instantly disbanded, but should the fear prove groundless a government might have set itself on a more suitable policy direction. Either way, government policy would have a solid foundation, unlike in the past. Furthermore, assuming the Centre is not disbanded, its creation would have constructive implications in three respects. Firstly, its accounts and analysis would supply a pool of knowledge which might enable the formulation of coherent, detailed and successful strategies for Britain in the future. Secondly, its analysis would provide a permanent catalyst and focal point for broad discussion of strategy options. Thirdly, the information a Centre would supply might have significant direct effects because it might beneficially influence transnationals' behaviour.

In part for similar reasons, forming a European Centre on Transnational Corporations would also be beneficial. It, too, is an extremely flexible strategy, not only leaving all future options open but actually facilitating and encouraging their consideration.

We envisage that the European Centre would be created by members of the European Community. It would perform similar tasks to the British Centre but with a European focus; economic and social accounts of transnational corporations' performance and impact would be prepared and analysed with a Pan-European concern. If it came to discussing future strategy possibilities, for instance, the European Centre would concentrate on Pan-European options, which are likely to be different from relevant options at the national level. Moreover, the European Centre would feed into and from the British Centre – and indeed similar bodies in other nations – contributing to the latter's activities but also compiling economic and social accounts at the Pan-European level and analysing these in a Pan-European context by, in part, drawing on the British Centre's information and expertise. In other words, the two Centres would perform related but different, interacting tasks.

The idea of European monitoring may appeal to Community members in general because it would replace a piecemeal and fragmentary Community approach to transnationals with a strategic, systematic alternative that would cautiously move the Community in a more suitable direction. It would imply a relatively slow and careful change, the sort of change that experience suggests is needed. To create a European Centre on Transnational Corporations would be to accommodate variations in Community member attitudes. It could overcome some of these countries' fears when it comes to policies towards transnationals – fear of discouraging potential investors and fear of hampering domestic transnationals – and would almost certainly allow a particular country to monitor at the Pan-European level more cheaply and more effectively than if it acted unilaterally. As for the appeal to Britain in particular, it is also worth noting that a European Centre would be an ideal complement to a British Centre; the latter would almost certainly prepare and analyse its accounts more cheaply and more effectively as a result of interaction with a European counterpart.

ECONOMIC AND SOCIAL ACCOUNTS

Precise details about the operation of these Centres need careful consideration. To some extent such details have been explored in this volume, concentrating explicitly on the British Centre but in ways that are often generalisable. We have considered a range of points, for example, the number of firms to monitor and the overall cost, in fact suggesting that a British Centre could operate on a relatively small budget. However, we have focused in particular on the preparation of economic and social accounts.

A British Centre on Transnational Corporations would be concerned with society's interests. Precisely which aspects of transnationals' performance and impact this puts in issue is not clear cut but the sort of items that would be on its agenda can be illustrated by looking at the concerns of similarly-placed countries to Britain. For instance, the main issues that have concerned France, Japan and the United States when they have looked at transnationals over recent years include the following: ownership and control; competitive implications; research and development/technology; impact on productivity/efficiency; impact on the exchequer; employment and industrial relations; balance of payments/international trade; impact on national 'competitive position'; compliance/co-operation with wider industrial and economic policy; regional impact/development policies; use of national/local components and resource processing; 'basics'; 'fairness'; 'cultural issues'; openness/accountability/information; environmental impact. Even if similar concerns were on Britain's agenda, we are not suggesting that the Centre would examine all of these issues in every case; at a point in time, for each monitored transnational the Centre would always examine a given set of core issues – those which continually arise whenever governments and researchers contemplate the performance and impact of transnational corporations, and/or issues that would prove to be especially relevant in the British context as the Centre's work progressed – and always examine a given set of political issues – those which are currently important for political reasons but are not established concerns – leaving other important items to be explored on a random basis. Nevertheless, it is clear that a Centre would be concerned with a wide range of economic and social matters.

This range raises questions regarding the accountability of transnational corporations, and in particular doubts as to the adequacy of corporate annual reports and accounts for monitoring purposes. Not least, most of the issues that have interested France, Japan and the US over recent years are excluded from corporate annual reporting. More generally, traditional accounting reports reveal less about the impact of a transnational corporation than about the firm's financial performance as it affects controllers of capital and their investment. To use traditional reports as the basis for monitoring transnationals, rather than to acknowledge monitoring as an alternative objective of reporting, would allow the nature of extant accounting practices to dominate the interests underlying the desire to monitor.

Thus both the British Centre on Transnational Corporations and the European Centre need to construct their own accounts of transnationals' performance and impact, drawing information from traditional accounts but also spreading their enquiries more widely. In advocating this we recognise potential problems. It is not being suggested that the work of the Centres would be easy, particularly in their attempts to decide what would be useful information and how to collect it. In particular we caution against seeking perfect measures, stress the limitations of quantitative measures and especially too narrow a financial focus, and warn of the dangers of capture by accountants or by transnational corporations themselves. However, there is no cause for pessimism. There is value in the use of subjective and imprecise indicators which improve upon the current, limited corporate reporting and go some way to accounting for the economic and social matters likely to be of interest to the monitoring Centres. There is even value in focusing solely on information that is publicly available and that has been obtained without asking corporations for more, as revealed by our detailed examination of Glaxo.

This case study illustrates the difficulty of constructing economic and social accounts, and its most important lesson concerns the general inadequacy of publicly-available information for successful monitoring. Yet it enables us to raise various questions regarding Glaxo's activities, because of the information that both is and is not available. For example: may Glaxo shift its corporate headquarters to the US?; are there worries over its outward investment to, say, Singapore?; is the relative decline of Britain as a location for Glaxo's research activity a worry?; are there concerns about Glaxo deliberately locating production in smaller communities?; are communities adversely affected by Glaxo co-operating with other drug companies?; given little indication that Glaxo allows its employees to become involved in the general running of its business, does this suggest a less than ideal organisation?

Such questions are likely to be of considerable interest to a British Centre on Transnational Corporations, although it is not at all clear what they may or may not lead to in terms of future industrial strategy. Perhaps a Centre's analysis would entail recommendations that, for instance, a British government negotiates with Glaxo over potential transfers of research activity. Perhaps it would suggest initiatives close to recent French or Japanese experience.

FUTURE DEVELOPMENTS

Uncertainties surrounding industrial strategies that our envisaged monitoring approach might spawn are obviously not an issue for this volume; in the context of monitoring, these potential strategies are primarily for consideration in the years to come, if and when the Centres are operating successfully. As for the suggested monitoring approach *per se*, however, it raises various issues which could be usefully explored in considerable depth before Centres are created.

One set of issues refers to the information on transnational corporations currently collected by government departments in Britain. As explained in Chapter 7, when looking at Glaxo we did attempt, at one stage, to extend our analysis beyond publicly-available information by investigating the collection of information by government departments. After all, we envisage a British Centre being related to the Department of Trade and Industry in some way, thus the potential for co-operation with government departments seemed worth exploring. Our experience was that most government departments have no single source of details of requests to corporations for information, and that our enquiries could not be dealt with in a reasonable time, if at all by some departments. Hence it is not clear what information firms are already providing yet it is clear that they are providing some. It is also clear that there is no coherence within government on this matter. These points are well worth exploring before a British Centre is created. Indeed, it would also be interesting to investigate the information currently gathered by different governments across Europe, to provide both further comparisons for our envisaged British Centre and a firmer basis for the creation of a European Centre on Transnational Corporations.

Another area for future research focuses on the accountability of transnational corporations which have received government aid to invest in particular areas. The provision of financial assistance by the state opens up a very good argument for better accountability to communities and appears to us to be a potentially very useful lever for ensuring transnationals' co-operation in providing this accountability. This co-operation could be important, given the limited value of publicly-available information. Hence it would be very interesting to examine the scale of assistance to transnationals, its importance to these corporations and, more significantly for us, what information government does and might get back in return. It would be useful to review how transnational corporations account for and disclose government assistance. In Chapter 4 we referred to the National Audit Office (1988) report on government departments' information on use of regional aid. The idea is to build upon such work. Again, European comparisons would be interesting.

Without denying the usefulness of such research projects to the monitoring argument, they are nevertheless for the future. Meanwhile, this volume has put forward a detailed case for a much needed government industrial strategy and has begun to explore that strategy. Even though further research would be worthwhile, we suggest our analysis is persuasive. We have attempted to provide a solid intellectual foundation for monitoring of transnational corporations as a means of appraising and influencing the activities of such firms in Britain (and elsewhere). We have advocated the strategy by a series of steps designed to maximise appeal and acceptance amongst policy-makers. Our own perspective on transnationals has been deliberately put to one side as much as possible. The proposal and most of its detailed exploration is consistent with wide-ranging views across various perspectives on transnational corporations and their consequences.

We suggest that if Britain and Europe adopts our strategy, it will be taking a significant step towards ensuring more successful industrial development in the future.

BIBLIOGRAPHY

Abel-Smith, B. (1976) *Value for Money in Health Services*, London: Heinemann.

Adams, R. (1992) 'Why is the environmental debate of interest to accountants and accountancy bodies?' in D. Owen (ed.), *Green Reporting: Accountancy and the Challenge of the Nineties*, London: Chapman & Hall.

Alexander, K. J. W. (1969) Foreword, in G. Teeling-Smith (ed.), *Economics and Innovation in the Pharmaceuticals Industry*, London: Office of Health Economics.

American Accounting Association (1975) 'Report of the Committee on Concepts and Standards for External Financial Reports', *Accounting Review Supplement*, XIX.

American Chamber of Commerce in Japan (1991) *Trade and Investment in Japan: the Current Environment*, Tokyo: The American Chamber of Commerce in Japan.

Ames, W. L. (1986) 'Buying a piece of Japan, inc.: foreign acquisitions in Japan', *Harvard International Law Journal* 27, 541–69.

Anderson, R. H. (1979) *The Usefulness of Annual Reports to Australian Investors*, paper presented at the Accounting Association of Australia and New Zealand Conference, University of Melbourne.

Anell, B. (1985) 'Exercises in arbitrariness and ambiguity – a study of twelve cost-benefit analyses of industrial disinvestment decisions', *Accounting, Organizations and Society* 10 (4), 479–92.

Arnold, J. and Moizer, P. (1984) 'A survey of the methods used by UK investment analysts to appraise investments in ordinary shares', *Accounting and Business Research* 14 (55), 195–207.

ASB (Accounting Standards Board) (1991) *The Objective of Financial Statements and the Qualitative Characteristics of Financial Information* (Exposure Draft), London: Accounting Standards Board.

Atlantic Richfield (1980) *Participation III, Atlantic Richfield and Society*, Los Angeles: Atlantic Richfield Inc.

Averyt, W. F. (1986) 'Canadian and Japanese Foreign Investment Screening', *Columbia Journal of World Business* 21 (4), 47–54.

Ayres, M. and Chubb, J. (1989) 'Exon-Florio: US power to block foreign acquisitions', *International Financial Law Review* 8 (4), 19–22.

227

Bachtler, J. (1990) 'Grants for inward investors: giving away money?', *National Westminster Bank Quarterly Review* May, 15–24.

Bailey, D., Harte, G. and Sugden, R. (1991a) 'Dirigisme at the core of the French approach to inward investment', *Multinational Business* Summer, 34–43.

Bailey, D., Harte, G. and Sugden, R. (1991b) 'A description of recent French policy towards transnational corporations', *Occasional Papers in Industrial Strategy* 1, Birmingham: University of Birmingham.

Bailey, D., Harte, G. and Sugden, R. (1992a) 'A description of Japanese policy towards transnational corporations', *Occasional Papers in Industrial Strategy* 4, Birmingham: University of Birmingham.

Bailey, D., Harte, G. and Sugden, R. (1992b) 'US policy initiatives towards transnational corporations', *Occasional Papers in Industrial Strategy* 5, Birmingham: University of Birmingham.

Bailey, D., Harte, G. and Sugden, R. (1992c) 'Japan – a legacy of obstacles confronts foreign investors', *Multinational Business* Spring, 27–36.

Bailey, D., Harte, G. and Sugden, R. (1992d) 'US policy debate towards transnational corporations', *Journal of World Trade* 26 (4), 65–93.

Bailey, D., Harte, G. and Sugden, R. (1994) *Transnationals and Governments: Recent Policies in Japan, France, Germany, The United States and Britain*, London: Routledge.

Baker, H. K. and Haslem, J. A. (1973) 'Information needs of individual Investors', *Journal of Accountancy* November, 64–9.

Bale, H. E. jr. (1983) 'US Federal Government's policy towards foreign direct investment', in E. H. Fry and L. H. Radebaugh (eds), *Regulation of Foreign Direct Investment in Canada and the United States*, Provo Utah: Brigham Young University/David M. Kennedy International Center.

Baran, P. A. and Sweezy, P. M. (1966) *Monopoly Capital*, Harmondsworth: Penguin.

Barwise, P., Higson, C. Likierman, A. and Marsh, P. (1989) *Accounting for Brands*, London: London Business School.

Bauer, R. A. (1973) 'The state of the art of social auditing', in M. Dierkes and R. A. Bauer (eds), *Corporate Social Accounting*, New York: Praeger.

Beaver, W. H. (1981) *Financial Reporting: An Accounting Revolution*, Englewood Cliffs, N.J.: Prentice-Hall.

Behrman, J. N. (1970) *National Interests and Multinational Enterprise*, Hemel Hempstead: Prentice-Hall.

Behrman, J. N. and Fischer, W. A. (1980) *Overseas R&D Activities of Transnational Companies*, Cambridge MA: Oelgeschlager, Gunn & Hain.

Benston, G. J. (1982) 'Accounting and Corporate Accountability', *Accounting, Organizations and Society* 7 (2), 87–105.

Bergsten, C. F., Horst, T. and Moran, T. H. (1978) *American Multinationals and American Interests*, Washington DC: The Brookings Institution.

Berle, A. A. and Means, G. C. (1932) *The Modern Corporation and Private Property*, New York: Macmillan.

Bernstein, D. (1992) *In the Company of Green*, London: Incorporated Society of British Advertisers Publications.

Bertin, G. Y. (1977) 'Foreign investment in France', in I. A. Litvak and C. J. Muale (eds), *Foreign Investment: the Experience of Host Countries*, New York: Praeger.

Birembaum, D. and Zackula, S. K. (1988) 'Foreign investment in Japan: current limits and restrictions', *East Asian Executive Reports* October, 9, 15–20.

Boddington, S., George, M. and Michaelson, J. (1986) *Developing the Socially Useful Economy*, Basingstoke: Macmillan.

Boothman Committee (1975) *The Corporate Report*, London: Accounting Standards Steering Committee.

Booz, Allen and Hamilton Inc. (1987) *Direct Foreign Investment in Japan: The Challenge for Foreign Firms*, a study for the American Chamber of Commerce in Japan and the Council of the European Business Community, Tokyo: The American Chamber of Commerce in Japan.

Braithwaite, J. (1984) *Corporate Crime in the Pharmaceutical Industry*, London: Routledge & Kegan Paul.

Braun, F. (1973) 'International control from the standpoint of the European Economic Community', in D. Wallace, jr. and H. Ruof-Koch (eds), *International Control of Investment*, New York: Praeger.

Brech, M. and Sharp, M. (1984) *Inward Investment: Policy Options for the United Kingdom*, London: Routledge.

Breugel, I. (1989) 'Needs more than a surface gloss', *Interlink* February/March, 19–20.

Bridges, Lord (1964) *The Treasury*, London: Allen & Unwin.

British North-American Committee (1970) 'Guidelines for multinational corporations: the government view', *British North-American Committee Paper*, BN/M-12, London: British North-American Committee.

Buckley, P. J. and Artisien, P. (1987) 'Policy issues of intra-EC direct investment: British, French and German multinationals in Greece, Portugal and Spain, with special reference to employment effects', *Journal of Common Market Studies* xxvi (2), 207–30.

Buckley, P. J. and Casson, M. (1976) *The Future of the Multinational Enterprise*, London: Macmillan.

Bullock, A., Stallybrass, D. and Trombley, S. (1988) *The Fontana Dictionary of Modern Thought*, 2nd edn, London: Fontana.

Cantwell, J. (1991) 'A survey of theories of international production', in C. Pitelis and R. Sugden (eds), *The Nature of the Transnational Firm*, London: Routledge.

Carey, A. (1992) 'A questioning approach to the environment', in D. Owen (ed.), *Green Reporting: Accountancy and the Challenge of the Nineties*, London: Chapman & Hall.

Carsberg, B. V. and Hope, T. (1984) *Current Issues in Accounting* (2nd edn), Deddington: Philip Allan.

Caves, R. E. (1982) *Multinational Enterprise and Economic Analysis*, Cambridge: Cambridge University Press.

Chang, L. S. and Most, K. S. (1977) 'Investor uses of financial statements: an empirical study', *Singapore Accountant* 12, 83–91.

Chenhall, R. H. and Juchau, R. (1977) 'Investor information needs – an Australian study', *Accounting and Business Research* 7 (28), 280–91.

Cherns, A. B. (1978) 'Alienation and accountancy', *Accounting, Organizations and Society* 3 (2), 105–14.

Chetley, A, (1986) 'Not good enough for us but fit for them – an examination of the chemical and pharmaceutical export trades', *Journal of Consumer Policy* 9, 155–80.

Chick, M. (1990) 'Information, politics and the defence of market power', in M. Chick (ed.), *Governments, Industries and Markets. Aspects of Government-Industry Relations in GB, Japan, West Germany and the USA since 1945*, Gloucester: Edward Elgar.

Clift, R. C. (1973) *An Investigation in the Nature and Quality of Information Utilized by Advisers in the Stockbroking Industry in Victoria*, unpublished PhD dissertation, University of Melbourne.

Coase, R. H. (1937) 'The nature of the firm', *Economica* 4, 386–405.

Cooper, D. J. and Sherer, M. (1984) 'The value of corporate accounting reports: arguments for a political economy of accounting', *Accounting, Organizations and Society* 9 (3/4), 207–32.

Cowe, R. (1987) 'Glaxo can still make money out of drugs', *The Guardian*, 13 October.

Cowe, R. (1993) 'Zantac keeps away Glaxo shareholders' ulcers', *The Guardian*, 19 February.

Cowling, K. (1982) *Monopoly Capitalism*, London: Macmillan.

Cowling, K. (1986) 'Internationalisation of production and de-industrialisation', in A. Amin and J. Goddard (eds), *Technological Change, Industrial Restructuring and Regional Development*, London: Allen & Unwin.

Cowling, K. (1987) 'An industrial strategy for Britain: the nature and role of planning', *International Journal of Applied Economics* 1, 1–22.

Cowling, K. (1990) 'A strategic approach to economic and industrial policy', in K. Cowling and R. Sugden (eds), *A New Economic Policy for Britain. Essays on the Development of Industry*, Manchester: Manchester University Press.

Cowling, K. and Sugden, R. (1987a) *Transnational Monopoly Capitalism*, Brighton: Wheatsheaf.

Cowling, K. and Sugden, R. (1987b) 'Market exchange and the concept of a transnational corporation: analysing the nature of the firm', *British Review of Economic Issues* 9 (20), 57–68.

Cowling, K. and Sugden, R. (eds) (1990) *A New Economic Policy for Britain. Essays on the Development of Industry*, Manchester: Manchester University Press.

Cowling, K. and Sugden, R. (1993a) 'Control, markets and firms', in C. Pitelis (ed.), *Transactions Costs, Markets and Hierarchies: Critical Assessments*, Oxford: Basil Blackwell.

Cowling, K. and Sugden, R. (1993b) 'A strategy for industrial development as a basis for regulation', in R. Sugden (ed.), *Industrial Economic Regulation. A Framework and Exploration*, London: Routledge.

Crane, P. (1984) 'Britain is out of step on workers' rights', *Europe*.

Cripps, F., Griffith, J., Morrell, F., Reid, J., Townsend, P. and Weir, S. (1981) *Manifesto: A Radical Strategy for Britain's Future*, London: Pan.

Davidow, J. and Schott-Stevens, P. (1990) 'Anti-trust merger control and national security review of foreign acquisitions in the United States', *Journal of World Trade* 24 (1), 39–56.

Day, J. F. S. (1986) 'The use of annual reports by UK investment analysts', *Accounting and Business Research* 16 (64), 295–307.

Dearing Committee (1988) *The Making of Accounting Standards: Report of the Review Committee under the Chairmanship of Sir Ron Dearing*, London: Institute of Chartered Accountants in England and Wales.

Defense Science Board (1990) in L. Spencer (1991) *Foreign Investment in the United States: Unencumbered Access*, Washington DC: Economic Strategy Institute.

de Marsac, X. T. (1976) 'Restrictions on foreign investments: France', *International Business Lawyer* 4 (1), 51–8.

Department of Employment and Department of Trade and Industry (1983) 'Government seeks views on EC proposals on employee participation and company law', *Press Notice* 9 November.

Dicken, P. (1986) *Global Shift. Industrial Change in a Turbulent World*, London: Harper & Row.

Dicken, P. (1992) *Global Shift. The Internalization of Economic Activity*, London: Paul Chapman.

Dierkes, M. and Bauer, R. A. (eds) (1973) *Corporate Social Accounting*, New York: Praeger.

Dierkes, M. and Preston, L. E. (1977) 'Corporate social accounting for the physical environment – a critical review and implementation proposal', *Accounting, Organizations and Society* 2 (1), 3–22.

Dilley, S. C. and Weygandt, J. J. (1973) 'Measuring social responsibility – an empirical test, *Journal of Accountancy* September, 62–70.

Dosser, D., Gowland, D. and Hartley, K. (eds) (1982) *The Collaboration of Nationals. A Study of European Economic Policy*, Oxford: Martin Robertson.

Dow Chemicals (1984) *Public Interest Report*, Midland, Michigan: The Dow Chemical Company.

Drew, J. (1979) *Doing Business in the European Community*, London: Butterworth.

DTI (Department of Trade and Industry) (1989) *Barriers to Take-overs in the European Community, Volume 2, France*, London: HMSO.

Dunning, J. H. (1977) 'Trade location of economic activity and the multinational enterprise: a search for an eclectic approach', in B. Ohlin, P. Hesselborn and P. M. Wijkman (eds), *The International Allocation of Economic Activity*, London: Macmillan.

Dunning, J. H. (1979) 'Explaining changing patterns of international production: in defence of the eclectic theory', *Oxford Bulletin of Economics and Statistics* 41, 269–95.

Dunning, J. H. (1980) 'Towards an eclectic theory of international production: some empirical tests', *Journal of International Business Studies* 11 (1), 9–31.

Dunning, J. H. (1981) 'Explaining the international direct investment position of countries: towards a dynamic or developmental approach', *Weltwirtzchaftliches Archiv* CXVII, 30–64.

Dunston Community Workshop (1983) *Dunston: The Social Audit*, Dunston: Dunston Community Workshop.

EIRIS (Ethical Investment Research Service) (1992) *Factsheets: Glaxo Holdings plc*, London: EIRIS.

Estes, R. W. (1976) *Corporate Social Accounting*, New York: Wiley – Interscience.

Euroforum, (1976) 28/76, 13 July.

European Commission (1973) 'Multinational undertakings and Community regulations', *Bulletin of the European Communities Supplement*, 15/73.

European Community News, (1979) 'European Community policy toward multinationals', 4/1979.

European Management Forum (1973) 'The European company in the world. Report for the Third European Management Symposium', February.

European Parliament (1988) 'Report on the role of multinational undertakings in the Community and in its external trade', Committee on External Economic Relations, PE DOC A 2–235/88.

European Parliament (1989) 'Second report on the role of multinational undertakings in the community and in its external trade', PE DOC A 2–378/89.

FASB (Financial Accounting Standards Board) (1978) *Statement of Financial Accounting Concepts. 1. Objectives of Financial Reporting by Business Enterprises*, Stanford, Connecticut: Financial Accounting Standards Board.

Fayerweather, J. (1982) 'Elite attitudes towards multinational firms', in J. Fayerweather (ed.) *Host National Attitudes Toward Multinational Corporations*, New York: Praeger.

FIRA (Foreign Investment Review Agency) (1982) *Barriers to Foreign Investment in the United States*, mimeo.

Fry, E. H. (1983) 'Foreign investment in the United States and Canada: the setting', in E. H. Fry and L. H. Radebaugh (eds), *Regulation of Foreign Direct Investment in Canada and the United States*, Provo, Utah: Brigham Young University/David M. Kennedy International Center.

Gaffikin, F. and Nickson, A. (1984) *Jobs Crisis and the Multinationals: De-industrialisation in the West Midlands*, Birmingham: Third World Books.

Geddes, M. (1992) 'The social audit movement', in D. Owen (ed.), *Green Reporting: Accountancy and the Challenge of the Nineties*, London: Chapman & Hall.

Gereffi, G. (1983) *The Pharmaceutical Industry and Dependency in the Third World*, Princeton: Princeton University Press.

Gerowin, M. (1975) 'US regulation of foreign direct investment: current developments and the Congressional response', *Virginia Journal of International Law* 15 (3), 611–47.

Gillespie, R. W. (1972) 'The policies of England, France and Germany as recipients of foreign direct investment', in F. Machlup, W. S. Salant and L. Tarshis (eds), *International Mobility and Movement of Capital*, New York: Columbia University Press.

GLC (Greater London Council) (1985) *London Industrial Strategy*, London: Greater London Council.

Globerman, S. (1986) *Fundamentals of International Business and Management*, New Jersey: Prentice-Hall.

Gniewosz, G. (1990) 'The share investment decision process and information use: an exploratory case study', *Accounting and Business Research* 20 (79).

Gorz, A, (1989) *Critique of Economic Reason* (translated by G. Handyside and C. Turner), London: Verso.

Government of Canada (1976) 'Policies of governments towards foreign direct investment', in K. P. Sauvant and F. G. Lavipur (eds), *Controlling Multinational Enterprises*, Boulder, Colorado: Westview Press.

Gowland, D. (1982) 'The theory of international associations', in D. Dosser, D. Gowland and K. Hartley (eds), *The Collaboration of Nations. A Study of European Economic Policy*, Oxford: Martin Robertson.

Graham, N. A. (1982) 'Developed countries and multinational corporations: threat perception and policy response in France and the United Kingdom', in J. Fayerweather (ed.), *Host National Attitudes Towards Multinational Corporations*, New York: Praeger.

Gray, R. H. (1990a) *The Greening of Accountancy: The Profession after Pearce*, London, Chartered Association of Certified Accountants.

Gray, R. (1990b) 'The accountant's task as a friend to the earth', *Accountancy* June, 65–8

Gray, R. (1992) 'Accounting and environmentalism: an exploration of the challenge of gently accounting for accountability, transparency and sustainability', *Accounting, Organizations and Society* 17 (5), 399–425.

Gray, R., Owen, D. and Maunders, K. (1987) *Corporate Social Reporting: Accounting and Accountability*, Hemel Hempstead: Prentice-Hall.

Gray, S. J. (1981) 'Segmental or disaggregated financial statements', in Lee, T. A. (ed.), *Developments in Financial Reporting*, Deddington: Philip Allan.

Gray, S. J. with McSweeney, L. B. and Shaw, J. C. (1984) *Information Disclosure and the Multinational Corporation*, Chichester: John Wiley.

Griffiths, I. (1986) *Creative Accounting: how to make your profits what you want them to be*, London: Unwin Hyman.

Hamilton, F. E. I. (1976) 'Multinational enterprise and the European Economic Community', *Tijdschrift Voor Economische En Sociale Geografie* 67 (5).

Hamilton, G. (1984) *The Control of Multinationals: What Future for International Codes of Conduct in the 1980s?* Geneva: IRM Multinational Reports.

Harte, G. F. and Owen, D. L. (1987) 'Fighting de-industrialisation: the role of local government social audits', *Accounting, Organizations and Society* 12 (2), 123–41.

Harte, G. and Sugden, R. (1990) 'A proposal for monitoring transnational corporations', in K. Cowling and R. Sugden (eds), *A New Economic Policy for Britain. Essays on the Development of Industry*, Manchester: Manchester University Press.

Harte, G. and Sugden, R. (1992) 'Cooperation in the European Community to regulate transnational corporations', in N. Koubek, H. Gester and G. R. Wiedemeyer (eds), *Richtlinien für das Personal-Management in Internationalen Unternehmungen*, Baden-Baden: Nomos Verlagsgesellschaft.

Health Action International (1992) *Promoting Health or Pushing Drugs?*, Health Action International.

Held, D. (1988) 'Farewell national state', *Marxism Today* December, 12–13, 15–17.

Hellman, R. (1977) *Transnational Control of Multinational Corporations*, New York: Praeger.

Hennart, J. F. (1991) 'The transaction cost theory of the multinational enterprise', in C. Pitelis and R. Sugden (eds), *The Nature of the Transnational Firm*, London: Routledge.

Herzel, L. and Shepro, R. W. (1990) *Bidders and Targets. Mergers and Acquisitions in the US*, Cambridge MA: Basil Blackwell.

Hines, R. D. (1982) 'The usefulness of annual reports: the anomaly between the efficient markets hypothesis and shareholder surveys', *Accounting and Business Research* 12 (48), 296–309.

Hines, R. D. (1989) 'The socio-political paradigm in financial accounting research', *Accounting, Auditing and Accountability Journal* 2 (1), 52–76.

Hines, R. D. (1991a) 'The FASB's conceptual framework, financial accounting and the maintenance of the social world', *Accounting, Organizations and Society* 16 (4), 313–31.

Hines, R. D. (1991b) 'On valuing nature', *Accounting, Auditing and Accountability Journal* 4 (3), 27–9.

Hodges, M. (1974) *Multinational Corporations and National Government*, Farnborough: Saxon House.

Hood, N. and Young, S. (1979) *The Economics of Multinational Enterprise*, London: Longman.

Hood, N. and Young, S. (1981) 'British policy and inward direct investment', *Journal of World Trade Law* 15, 231–50.

Hopwood, A. (1986) 'Economics and the regime of the calculative', in S. Boddington, M. George and J. Michaelson, *Developing the Socially Useful Economy*, Basingstoke: Macmillan.

Hymer, S. H. (1976) *The International Operations of National Firms* (written in 1960), Cambridge, MA: MIT Press.

Hymer, S. H. (1972) 'The multinational corporation and the law of uneven development', in J. N. Bhagwati (ed.), *Economics and World Order*, London: Macmillan.

Ing, B. (1992) 'Developing green reporting systems: some practical implications', in D. Owen (ed.), *Green Reporting: Accountancy and the Challenge of the Nineties*, London: Chapman & Hall.

Ishizumi, K. (1990) *Acquiring Japanese Companies: Mergers and Acquisitions in the Japanese Market*, Cambridge MA: Basil Blackwell.

Johnson, C. (1981) 'The internationalization of the Japanese economy', in H. Mannari and H. Befu (eds), *The Challenge of Japan's Internationalization*, Tokyo/New York: Kwansei Gakuin University/Kodansha International.

Johnson, C. (1982) *MITI and the Japanese Miracle*, Stanford: Stanford University Press.

Jones, D. T. (1985) *The Import Threat to the UK Car Industry*, University of Sussex: Science Policy Research Unit.

Kaplan, R. (1984) 'Yesterday's accounting undermines production', *Harvard Business Review* July–August, 95–101.

Kassarjian, H. (1977) 'Content analysis in consumer research', *Journal of Consumer Research* 4 (June), 8–18.

Kindleberger, C. P. (1969) *American Business Abroad*, New Haven: Yale University Press.

Knee, J. A. (1989) 'Limiting abuse of Exon-Florio by takeover targets', *George Washington Journal of International Law and Economics* 23 (2), 475–99.

Kransdorff, A. (1991) 'Brand bonanza', *Accountancy Age*, November, 43, 45–7.

Labour Party (1977) *International Big Business. Labour's Policy on the Multinationals*, London: The Labour Party.

Lea, S. and Webley, S. (1973) *Multinational Corporations in Developed Countries: A Review of Recent Research and Policy Thinking*, Washington DC: British-North American Committee.

Lee, T. A. (1979) 'Company financial statements: an essay in business history 1830–1950', in T. A. Lee and R. H. Parker (eds), *The Evolution of Corporate Financial Reporting*, Sunbury on Thames: Thomas Nelson.

Lee, T. A. and Parker, R. H. (eds) (1979) *The Evolution of Corporate Financial Reporting*, Sunbury on Thames: Thomas Nelson.

Lee, T. A. and Tweedie, D. P. (1977) *The Private Shareholder and the Corporate Report*, London: Institute of Chartered Accountants in England and Wales.

Lee, T. A. and Tweedie, D. P. (1981) *The Institutional Investor and Financial Information*, London: Institute of Chartered Accountants in England and Wales.

Lehman, C. and Tinker, T. (1987) 'The real cultural significance of accounts', *Accounting, Organizations and Society* 12 (5), 503–22.

Levey, M. M. (1989) *Foreign Investment in the United States*, New York: John Wiley.

Liebenau, J. (1987) *Medical Science and Medical Industry*, Basingstoke: Macmillan.

Linowes, D. F. (1972) 'An approach to socio-economic accounting', *Conference Board Record* November, 58–61.

Lynn, M. (1991) *The Billion Dollar Battle: Merck v Glaxo*, London: Heinemann.

Marglin, S. A. (1974) 'What do bosses do? Part 1', *Review of Radical Political Economics* 6, 60–112.

Mason, S. (1971) 'Information for investment decisions – how efficiently is it used?, *Investment Analyst* September, 3–16.

McDermott, M. C. (1986) *Foreign Divestment and Employee Disclosure and Consultation in the UK, 1978–1985*, PhD thesis, School of Financial Studies, University of Glasgow.

McMonnies, P. (ed.) (1988) *Making Corporate Reports Valuable*, London: Kogan Page/Institute of Chartered Accountants of Scotland.

McSweeney, B. (1986) *Value for Money Auditing: Some Observations on its Origin and Theory*, Glasgow: University of Glasgow.

Medawar, C. (1976) 'The social audit: a political view', *Accounting, Organizations and Society* 1 (4), 389–94.

Medawar, C. (1979) *Insult or Injury*, London: Social Audit.

Medawar, C. (1984) *The Wrong Kind of Medicine*, London: Consumers' Association/Hodder & Stoughton.

Miliband, R. (1984) *Capitalist Democracy in Britain*, Oxford: Oxford University Press.

Miller, J. (1981) *Situation Vacant – The Social Consequences of Unemployment in a Welsh Town*, London: Community Projects Foundation.

Morgan, G. (1988) 'Accounting as reality construction: towards a new epistemology for accounting practice', *Accounting, Organizations and Society* 13 (5), 477–85.

Muller, M. (1982) *The Health of Nations*, London: Faber & Faber.

Murray, R. (1971) *Multination Companies and Nation States*, Nottingham: Spokesman.

Murray, R. (1981) *Multinationals Beyond the Market – Intra Firm Trade and the Control of Transfer Pricing*, Brighton: Harvester.

National Audit Office (1988) *Report by the Comptroller and Auditor General, Department of Trade and Industry, Scottish Office and Welsh Office: Arrangements for Regional Industrial Incentives*, London: HMSO.

OECD (Organization for Economic Co-operation and Development) (1979) *International Direct Investment. Policies, Procedures and Practices in OECD Member Countries*, Paris: OECD.

OECD (Organization for Economic Co-operation and Development) (1987) *Controls and Impediments Affecting Inward Direct Investment*, Paris: OECD.

Ogden, S. G. and Bougen, P. D. (1985) 'A radical perspective on disclosure of information to trade unions', *Accounting, Organizations and Society*, 10 (2), 211–24.

Owen, D. (ed.), (1992) *Green Reporting: Accountancy and the Challenge of the Nineties*, London: Chapman & Hall.

Parker, J. E. S. (1984) *The International Diffusion of Pharmaceuticals*, Basingstoke: Macmillan.

Parker, L. D. (1986) 'Polemical themes in social accounting: a scenario for standard selling', *Advances in Public Interest Accounting* 1, 95–111.

Pearce, D., Markandya, A. and Barbier, E. B. (1989) *Blueprint for a Green Economy*, London: Earthscan.

Pearl, A. R. (1972a) 'Liberalization of capital in Japan – Part I', *Harvard International Law Journal* 13, 59–87.

Pearl, A. R. (1972b) 'Liberalization of capital in Japan – Part II', *Harvard International Law Journal* 13, 245–70.

Peasnell, K. V. (1974) *Accounting Objectives: A Critique of the Trueblood Report*, Lancaster: International Centre for Research in Accounting, University of Lancaster.

Pitelis, C. N. and Sugden, R. (1986) 'The separation of ownership and control in the theory of the firm: a reappraisal', *International Journal of Industrial Organization* 4, 69–86.

Poggi, G, (1965) 'A main theme of contemporary sociological analysis: its achievement and limitations', *British Journal of Sociology* 16, 263–94.

Power, M. (1990) *Brand and Goodwill Strategies*, Cambridge: Woodhead Faulkner.

Power, M. (1991) 'Auditing and environmental expertise: between protest and professionalisation', *Accounting, Auditing and Accountability Journal* 4 (3), 30–42.

Puxty, A. G. (1986) 'Social accounting as imminent legitimation: a critique of technist ideology', *Advances in Public Interest Accounting* 1, 95–112.

Raby, J. (1990) 'The investment provisions of the Canada-United States Free Trade Agreement: a Canadian perspective', *American Journal of International Law* 84, 394–443.

Ramanathan, K. V. (1976) 'Toward a theory of corporate social accounting', *The Accounting Review* 51 (3), 516–28.

Robinson, J. (1983) *Multinationals and Political Control*, Aldershot: Gower.

Robock, S. H. and Simmonds, K. (1983) *International Business and Multinational Enterprises*, Homewood, Ill.: Irwin.

Robock, S. H., Simmonds, K. and Zwick, J. (1977) *International Business and Multinational Enterprises*, Homewood, Ill.: Irwin.

Safarian, A. E. (1983) *Governments and Multinationals: Policies in the Developed Countries*, London: British North-American Committee.

Schreuder, H. and Ramanathan, K. V. (1984) 'Accounting and corporate accountability – an extended comment', *Accounting, Organizations and Society* 9 (3/4), 409–15.

Shinmura, T. (1989) 'A few foreign firms now buying into Japan', *The Japan Economic Journal*, 20 May, 3.

Silverman, D. (1975) 'Accounts of organizations, in J. B. McKinlay (ed.) *Processing People: Cases in Organizational Behaviour*, Holt, Rinehart & Winston.

Silverman, M. (1976) *The Drugging of the Americas*, Berkeley: University of California Press.

Silverman, M., Lee, P. R. and Lydecker, M. (1982) *Prescriptions for Death: The Drugging of the Third World*, Berkeley: University of California Press.

Sklair, L. (1991) *Sociology of the Global System*, Hemel Hempstead: Wheatsheaf.

Sleuwaegen, L. (1987) 'Multinationals, the European Community and Belgium: recent developments', *Journal of Common Market Studies* XXVI (2), 255–72.

SMMT (Society of Motor Manufacturers and Traders) (1984) *The Motor Industry of Great Britain, 1984*, London: SMMT.

Social Audit (1973) *The First Social Audit: Tube Investments Ltd*, London: Social Audit.

Social Audit (1974) *Social Audit: A Report on Coalite and Chemical Products Ltd*, London: Social Audit.

Social Audit (1976) *Social Audit on the Avon Rubber Co. Ltd*, London: Social Audit.

Solomons, D. (1989) *Guidelines for Financial Reporting Standards*, London: Institute of Chartered Accountants in England and Wales.

Solomons, D. (1991) 'Accounting and social change: a neutralist view', *Accounting, Organizations and Society* 16 (3), 287–95.

Stanley, M. (1991) *Glaxo: A Tale of Two Headaches and Two Blockbusters*, London: Morgan Stanley, 16 August.

Steuer, M. D., Abell, P., Gennard, J., Perlman, M., Rees, R., Scott, B. and Wallis, K. (1975) *The Impact of Foreign Direct Investment on the United Kingdom*, London: HMSO.

Steward, F. (1989) 'New times, green times', *Marxism Today* March, 14–15, 17.

Stopford, J. M. (1982) *The World Directory of Multinational Enterprises 1982–1983*, London: Macmillan.

Stopford, J. M., Dunning, J. H. and Haberich, K. O. (1980) *The World Directory of Multinational Enterprises*, London: Macmillan.

Stopford, J. M. and Turner, L. (1985) *Britain and the Multinationals*, Chichester: Wiley-IRN.

Sugden, R. (1990a) 'The warm welcome for foreign-owned transnationals from recent British governments', in M. Chick (ed.), *Governments, Industries and Markets. Aspects of Government-Industry Relations in GB, Japan, West Germany and the USA since 1945*, Gloucester: Edward Elgar.

Sugden, R. (1990b) 'Strategic industries, community control and transnational corporations', *International Review of Applied Economics* 4 (1), 72–94.

Sugden, R. (1993) 'Why transnationals? The significance of divide and rule', in G. R. Krishna (ed.), *Human Resource Management in Multinationals*, Delhi: Kanishka.

Tempini, N. (1989) *Multinational Enterprises and the EEC*, London: PNL Press.

Tempini, N. (1992) 'Multinational enterprises and competition policies', in V. Lintner and S. Mazey (eds), *The European Community: Economic and Political Aspects*, London: McGraw Hill.

Thomas, A. L. (1969) *The Allocation Problem in Financial Accounting Theory*, Studies in Accounting Research 3, Sarasota, Florida: American Accounting Association.

Thomas, A. L. (1974) *The Allocation Problem, Part 2, Studies in Accounting Research*, Sarasota, Florida: American Accounting Association.

Thomsen, S. and Nicolaides, P. (1990) 'Foreign direct investment: 1992 and global markets', *Royal Institute of International Affairs Discussion Paper*, 28.

Tinker, A. M. (1980) 'Towards a political economy of accounting: an empirical illustration of the Cambridge controversies', *Accounting, Organizations and Society* 5 (1), 147–60.

Tinker, A. M., Merino, B. D. and Neimark, M. D. (1982) 'The normative origins of positive theories: ideology and accounting thought', *Accounting, Organizations and Society* 7 (2), 167–200.

Tinker, T. (1985) *Paper Prophets: A Social Critique of Accounting*, Eastbourne: Holt, Rinehart & Winston.

Tinker, T. and Neimark, M. (1988) 'The struggle over meaning in accounting and corporate research: a comparative evaluation and critical historiography', *Accounting, Auditing and Accountability Journal*, 1 (1), 55–74.

Torem, C. and Craig, W. L. (1968) 'Control of foreign investment in France', *Michigan Law Review* 669–720.

Tucker, D. (1984) *The World Health Market*, London: Euromonitor Publications.

Turner, L. (1987) *Industrial Collaboration with Japan*, London: Routledge.

United Nations (1978) *Transnational Corporations in World Development: a re-examination*, New York: United Nations.

United Nations (1983) *Transnational Corporations in World Development, Third Survey*, New York: United Nations.

United Nations (1985) *Transnational Corporations in World Development, Third Survey*, London: United Nations/Graham & Trotman.

United Nations (1988) *Transnational Corporations in World Development. Trends and Prospects*, New York: United Nations.

United Nations (1991) *Transnational Business Information. A Manual of Needs and Sources*, New York: United Nations.

US Committee on Government Operations (1980) *The Adequacy of the Federal Response to Foreign Investment in the US, House Report No, 96–1216*, Washington DC: US Government Printing Office.

US House of Representatives (1978) 'The operations of Federal agencies in monitoring, reporting on and analyzing foreign investments in the United States', in *Hearings before a Subcommittee of the Committee of Government Operations*, Ninety-fifth Congress, Washington DC: US Government Printing Office.

US Senate (1975) 'The regulation of foreign direct investment in Australia, Canada, France, Japan and Mexico', in *Hearings Before the Sub Committee on Securities of the Committee on Banking, Housing and Urban Affairs*, Ninety-fourth Congress, Washington DC: US Government Printing Office.

Wallace, C. D. (1982) *Legal Control of the Multinational Enterprise, National Regulatory Techniques and the Prospects for International Controls*, London: Martinus Nijhoff.

Whittington, G. (1984) 'Accounting and economics, in B. V. Carsberg and T. Hope (eds), *Current Issues in Accounting* (2nd edn), Deddington: Philip Allan.

Williamson, O. (1975) *Market and Hierarchies*, New York: Free Press.

Wilms-Wright, C. (1977) *Transnational Corporations: A Strategy for Control*, Fabian Research Series 334, London: The Fabian Society.

Young, S., Hood, N. and Hamill, J. (1988) *Foreign Multinationals and the British Economy. Impact and Policy*, London: Croom Helm.

INDEX

Abel-Smith, B. 122, 123, 128, 163
accountability of transnationals:
   corporate reports, use of 87–9;
   financial 80–2; form of 79–99;
   traditional, criticisms of 82–6 *see
   also* financial accounting; social
   accounting
Accountancy 116
accounting professionals in British
   Centre 95
Adams, R. 95
advertising, by Glaxo 123–4
Alexander, K. J. W. 163
Ames, W. L. 30
Anell, B. 93
annual report: excluded
   information 82, 85–6;
   information disclosure in 87;
   typical contents 81
annual report (Glaxo) 105; contents
   of 106–7; forecasts in 115–16;
   segmental information in 117–19
Aristien, P. 206
Armstrong, A. A. L. 113
Arnold, J. 87
Atlantic Richfield 108
Averyt, W. F. 25, 27
Avon companies 141, 143;
   donations by 159; value added
   per employee 166; women and
   disabled in 148–9
Ayres, M. 43

Bachtler, J. 62–3
balance of payments issues 71–3;
analysis of 193–4; in Glaxo case
   study 149–55
Bale, H. E. Jr 42
Baran, P. A. 1, 186
Barwise, P. 83
basic issues 71–3
Bauer, R. A. 93
Beaver, W. H. 87
Behrman, J. N. 34
Benston, G. J. 91
Bérégovoy, P. 36
Bergsten, C. F. 27, 41
Berle, A. A. 4
Bernstein, D. 162
Bertin, G. Y. 34
Birembaum, D. 27, 28, 29
Boddington, S. 92
Boothman Committee 82, 116, 153,
   174
Booz, Allen and Hamilton 30
Bougen, P. D. 97
Braithwaite, J. 123, 128
Breugel, I. 94
British Centre on Transnational
   Corporations (proposed) 53;
   agenda for 75–8, 222–3; attributes
   of 56–9; benefits of 57–9; and
   form of account 79–99; future
   strategies from 57–8;
   government, relationship with
   63–4; information needed by 57,
   79; monitoring in Britain and
   Europe 220–2; operation of 61–5;
   outline of 55–6; purpose of

102–3; transnationals' behaviour and 58, 62–3

British transnationals 3–6; attitude to in Britain 11–12; deindustrialisation by 12

Buckley, P. J. 1, 207

Bull take-over attempt by NEC 37, 47

Business Week 121

Canada: foreign ownership, concern over 60–1

Carey, A. 95

Casson, M. 1

Caves, R. E. 7

charitable donations 159–60

Chemical Week 127

Chemical Weekly 128, 157

Cherns, A. B. 98

Chetley, A. 180

Chubb, J. 43

Clarke, Kenneth 20

Clarke, Sir Richard 20

Clift, R. C. 88

co-operation: between countries 197–215; monitoring strategy for transnationals 206–12

Coalite Companies 141, 143, 167

Coase, R. H. 1, 208

Committee on Foreign Investment in the United States (CFIUS) 23, 39–46, 49, 95

Committee on Government Operations (USA) 39, 40, 48

community relations, Glaxo 158–61

Companies Acts (UK, 1985, 1989) 80, 111, 145

competitiveness issues 71–3; analysis of 189–90; in Glaxo case study 114–29

control 71–3; analysis of 188–89; in Glaxo case study 108–14

Cooper, D. J. 79, 86, 89

corporate reports, use of 87–9

corporation tax, Glaxo 169–72

cost accounting, historic: and economic reality 84; excluded information 82, 85–6; and future benefits 83; and price changes

83–4; and social costs 86; subjectivity of 82–3, 85, 94

cost accounting model 81, 82

Cowe, R. 121

Cowling, K. 1, 2, 12, 19, 185, 209

Craig, W. L. 32, 33

Crane, P. 201, 202

Cresson, Edith 30, 37

Cripps, F. 86

cultural issues 71–3; in Glaxo case study 180

Daily Telegraph, The 121, 129

Davidow, J. 43, 44

Day, J. F. S. 88

de Marsac, X. T. 33

Dearing Committee 79

Defense Science Board 45

Dicken, P. 7, 17, 23, 69

Dierkes, M. 93

Dilley, S. C. 93

disaggregation, in Glaxo case study 117

disinvestment, Glaxo 161–2

Dow Chemicals 108, 160

Drew, J. 204

drug companies, relations between 127

Dunning, J. H. 1, 5

Dunston Community Workshop 93

economic and social accounts 89; by British Centre 222–4; construction of 193–5; as externalities 90–2

economic policy 71–3; in Glaxo case study 156–8

economic reality in historic cost accounting 84, 92

Economist, The 103, 122, 124, 169

efficiency issues 71–3; in Glaxo case study 163–8; in social accounting 94

employment, General Motors (USA) 146–7

employment in Glaxo case study 139–49; changes in 144; conditions of 142; equal opportunities 145; exploitation, rate of 141–2; health and safety of 142–4; involvement of 145–9; job quality 144; job quantity 144–5; remuneration 139–41

employment issues 71–3; analysis of 191–2

environmental impact 71–3; analysis of 194; in Glaxo case study 102

Estes, R. W. 90, 93

ethical drugs, patented 120

Ethical Investment Research Services (EIRIS) 140, 162, 180, 182

Euroforum 204

European Centre on Transnational Corporations (proposed) 198, 203–4, 209, 212

European Chemical Business News 121

European Chemical News 121, 138

European Community: and French investment policy 35; member states, attitudes of 200–3; monitoring by 203–6; previous concerns 199–203

European Management Forum 201, 202, 203, 207

Evening Standard 138

Exchange Control Act (UK, 1947) 13, 15

exchange rates, Glaxo on: 125

Exon-Florio amendment, Omnibus Trade Act (USA, 1988) 43–6, 218

exploitation of employees in Glaxo case study 141–2

external accounting 82, 83, 84

fairness issues 71–3; in Glaxo case study 179–80

FASB (Financial Accounting Standards Board) 79, 80

Fayerweather, J. 18, 20

financial accountability of transnationals 80–2

financial accounting: corporate reports, use of 87–9; R&D in Glaxo case study 131; traditional, criticisms of 82–6

financial data in Glaxo case study: financing operations 153; for forecasting 115–17; research and development 131–6

Financial Times, The 121, 123, 139, 173

Fischer, W. A. 34

Ford, President Gerald 39

forecasting, financial in Glaxo case study 115–17

foreign direct investment *see* inward investment

Foreign Exchange and Foreign Trade Control Law (Japan, 1949) 24–6, 217

Foreign Investment Review Agency (Canada) 40, 53, 59–61

Foreign Investment Study Act (USA, 1974) 39

foreign ownership 71–3; analysis of 188–9; in Glaxo case study 108–14

France: attitude to transnationals 31–8; contrast in attitude with Britain 46–9; issues of concern 69–75; liberalisation of investment policy 33; transnational regulation 201

Fry, E. H. 61

funds, flow of in Glaxo case study 149–52

Gaffikin, F. 12

Geddes, M. 89

General Motors (USA): employment 146–7; and government regulations 176–7; taxation 175

Gereffi, G. 128

Gerowin, M. 38, 39

Gillespie, R. W. 32, 33, 69, 75

Giscard D'Estaing, V. 34

Glaxo, description of 104

Glaxo case study 100–82; annual report, contents of 106–7; approach 105–8; background to 100–8; board and structure 113–14; core accounting issues 108–55; disaggregated performance 117; discussion of 183–96; market shares 125–8; patents 120–1, 136; political issues 155–62; purpose of 100–2; random issues 162–83; reasons for choice 103–4; subsidiaries 112, 114, 150–2

Glaxonews 142, 149

Glaxoworld 161

Globerman, S. 11, 59, 70

Gniewosz, G. 88

Gorz, A. 92

government: and pharmaceutical industry 128; relationship with British Centre 63–4

government, in Glaxo case study 128–9; grants by 173; relations with 173–8

Gowland, D. 206, 207

Graham, N. A. 13, 17, 18, 20, 201, 202, 204, 210

Gray, R. 90, 93, 95, 96, 108

Gray, R. H. 84, 98

Gray, S. J. 7, 117

Gray Report (1972) 60

Great Britain (*see also* British Centre): British transnationals, attitude to 11–12; constraints on policy development 54–5; contrast in attitudes with others 46–9; Glaxo R&D staff in 130; manufacturing employment 5–6; manufacturing employment, share of 5–6; manufacturing sales 3–5; monitoring by 220–2; overseas transnationals, attitude to 12–21; transnationals and 3–6

Griffiths, I. 83

Guardian, The 174

Haberich, K. O. 5

Hamill, J. 13, 14, 15, 16

Hamilton, F. E. I. 201

Hamilton, G. 97, 194

health and safety: analysis of 194; of employees in Glaxo case study 142–4

Held, D. 2, 185

Hellman, R. 17

Hennart, J. F. 1

Her Majesty's Factory Inspectorate 143

Herzel, L. 43

Hines, R. D. 84, 85, 86, 87, 92

Hodges, M. 10, 13, 15, 16, 17, 18, 20, 57

Hood, N. 2, 7, 13, 14, 15, 16

Hopwood, A. 86, 92, 97

Horst, T. 27

Howe, Sir G. 113

Hymer, S. H. 1, 19

industrial policy issues 71–3; in Glaxo case study 156–8

industrial relations 71–3; analysis of 192–3; in Glaxo case study 139–49

Industry Act (UK, 1975) 13, 14

information disclosure 71–3; in annual reports 87; and investors' needs 194–5; needed by British Centre 57, 79; on transactions in foreign currency 153–5

information disclosure, in Glaxo case study 181; segmented information 117–20

Inouye–Culver Bill (USA) 38–9

International Trade and Industry, Ministry of (MITI, Japan) 24–9

Invest in Britain Bureau (IBB) 16

Investment Canada Act (1985) 61

investment data, segmental, Glaxo 157

investment policy, Britain: constraints on 54–5; information for, lack of 55

inward investment: British attitude to 17–19; in France 31–2, 35; in Japan 24–5; in USA 38–9, 42

Ishizumi, K. 29, 30

Japan: attitude to transnationals 24–31; contrast in attitude with Britain 46–9; issues of concern 69–75; liberalisation of investment policy 25–8, 217

Jenkin, Patrick 12, 14, 16

job quantity, R&D in Glaxo case study 144–5
Johnson, C. 24, 26
Jones, D. T. 19

Kaplan, R. 84
Kassarjian, H. 70
Kindleberger, C. P. 1
King, Tom 202
Knee, J. A. 44
Krandsdorff, A. 83

Labour Party 10, 12, 70, 95, 185
Lea, S. 34, 38
Lee, T. A. 80, 81, 128
Levey, M. M. 28
Liebenau, J. 163
Linowes, D. F. 93
Locate in Scotland (LIS) 17
location policy, Glaxo 161
Lynn, M. 114, 122

Mail on Sunday, The 103
manufacturing: employment 5–6; employment, share of, UK 5–6; sales 3–5; sales, share of, UK 4
Marglin, S. A. 2, 185
market concentration and share, Glaxo 125–8
market price and social accounting 93–4
marketing, Glaxo 121–5; expenditure on 122–3
Mason, S. 88
Maunders, K. 93, 108
McDermott, M. C. 201
McMonnies, P. 84, 116
McSweeney, L. B. 7, 84
Means, G. C. 4
Medawar, C. 98, 123, 128, 180
Merino, B. D. 84
Miliband, R. 95
Miller, J. 93
Minebea take-over attempt by Trafalgar 29
Moizer, P. 87
monitoring strategy for transnationals 53–67 (*see also* British Centre); attributes of centre for 56–9; background considerations for 53–5; co-operation over 206–12; by EC 203–6; effects of 6–7; experts, role of in 95; form of account *see* accountability; in Great Britain and Europe 220–2; investment policy *see* investment policy, Britain; operation of 61–5; outline of 55–6; possibility of 1–9; as unique approach 59–61
Monopolies and Mergers Commission (UK) 13–14, 65
Moran, T. H. 27
Morgan, G. 85, 86, 92
Morgan Stanley 172
Muller, M. 180
Mulroney, Brian 61
Murray, R. 172, 185, 186

National Audit Office 62, 225
national competitiveness issues 71–3; in Glaxo case study 175–8
national/local resource issues 71–3; in Glaxo case study 178
Neimark, M. D. 84, 92, 98
New York Times 123
Nickson, A. 12
Nicolaides, P. 201, 202
Northern Echo 138
Northern Ireland's Industrial Development Board (IDB) 17

Observer, The 124
Office of Foreign Investment in the United States (OFIUS) 23, 40–1, 49
Ogden, S. G. 97
Organization for Economic Cooperation and Development (OECD) 10, 23, 27–8, 33, 59, 69
outward investment: from France 33–4; monitoring of 59
overseas transnationals, attitude to in Britain 12–21; description of 12–17; reasons for 17–21
Owen, D. 93, 108, 158
ownership *see* foreign ownership

Parker, J. E. S. 116
patents, Glaxo 120–1; challenges by 121, 136
patriotic issues 71–3
Pearce, D. 91, 94
Pearl, A. R. 24, 25, 26, 47
Pharma Japan 127
Poggi, G. 85
political donations 181–2
political issues 71–3
Power, M. 83, 95
Preston, L. E. 93
price changes in historic cost accounting 83–4
product liability, Glaxo 136–8
product shares of Glaxo, by country 127
productivity issues 71–3; economics of, Glaxo 167–8; in Glaxo case study 163–8
profits, retention of (Glaxo) 116
promotions, by Glaxo 124
Prudential Portfolio Managers 111
Puxty, A. G. 91, 95, 97, 194

quality control, Glaxo 138

Raby, J. 61
Rananathan, K. V. 90, 98
regional policies 71–3; in Glaxo case study 158–62
remuneration, R&D in Glaxo case study 139–41
research and development in Glaxo case study 71–3, 129–39; analysis of 190–1; development expenditure 137; exploratory development 132–3; financial data on 131–6; full development 134; pipeline status 135–6; product liability 136–8; and productivity 163–4; programme 131; quality control 138; staffing 130; training 138–9
Robinson, J. 17, 199, 201, 202, 203
Robock, S. H. 24, 27, 42
Rootes take-over by Chrysler 15–16, 49
Rowntree take-over by Nestlé 11, 20

Safarian, A. E. 11, 13, 15, 28, 29, 37, 42, 60, 69, 70
sales, Glaxo 125, 157, 167
sales force, Glaxo 123
Schott-Stevens, P. 43, 44
Schreuder, H. 98
Scrip 124, 129, 157, 162, 167
share capital (Glaxo) in financial forecasts 116
shareholders: annual reports, use of 87–8; and financial accountability of transnationals 80
shareholders, of Glaxo 109–13; directors' shareholdings 111; size and value 110
shareholdings, in Glaxo 108–10
Shaw, J. B. 7
Shepro, R. W. 43
Sherer, M. 79, 86, 89
Shinmura, T. 29
Silverman, D. 85, 123, 128
Simmonds, K. 24, 27
Sklair, L. 1, 186
social accounting 89–90 (*see also* British Centre); appropriate measures 94; calculations of 92; construction of, lessons for 193–5; economic accounting *see* economic and social accounts; experts, development of 94–5; externalities in 90–2; financial approach to 93–4; in Glaxo *see* Glaxo case study; in Great Britain 222–4; and market price 93–4; scope of 96; subjectivity in 94; theoretical framework for 96–7
Social Audit 96, 97, 141, 143, 155, 165, 167
Solomons, D. 82, 84, 85
Spinelli Report 200, 204
Spondex take-over by 3M 36
staffing, in Glaxo case study 129–30
Steuer, M. D. 15
Steward, F. 92
Stopford, J. M. 5, 11, 12, 13, 14
subsidiaries, Glaxo 112, 114, 150–2
Sunday Telegraph 129
Sunday Times 103

suppliers, Glaxo 158
Sweezy, P. M. 1, 185

taxation 71–3; in Glaxo case study 168–78; and transfer pricing, Glaxo 172–3
technology issues 71–3; analysis of 191–2; in Glaxo case study 129–39
Tempini, N. 199, 200, 204
Thomas, A. L. 83, 117
Thomsen, S. 201, 202
Times, The 138
Tinker, A. M. 163
Tinker, T. 82, 84, 91, 92, 96, 98
Torem, C. 32, 33
Trade and Industry, Department of 17, 36, 37
trade flows, Glaxo 153–5
training, R&D in Glaxo case study 138–9
transfer pricing, Glaxo 172–3
transnationals: financial accountability of 80–2; and Glaxo case study 185–7; issues of concern 69–75; and manufacturing employment 5–6, 216; and manufacturing sales 3–5, 216; monitoring in Britain *see* British Centre; overseas, attitude to in Britain 12–21; ownership and control, analysis of 188–9; performance and impact, analysis of 186–93; power of 185 *see also* British transnationals
Tube Investments 143, 168; donations by 160
Tucker, D. 123, 124, 127, 128

Turner, L. 11, 12, 13, 14, 30
turnover, Glaxo: segmental information 117–19; therapeutic analysis 119, 126
Tweedie, D. P. 81

United Nations 23, 28, 30, 34, 43, 50
United States: attitude to transnationals 38–46; contrast in attitude with Britain 46–9; issues of concern 69–75; national security concerns 43; ownership of Glaxo shares 110–11, 114
United States House of Representatives 40
United States Senate 24, 25, 26, 69

value added in manufacturing, Glaxo 164–7

Wales Investment Location (WINVEST) 17
Wall Street Journal 43
Wallace, C. D. 15, 30, 49
Webley, S. 34, 38
Weygandt, J. J. 93
Whittington, G. 81
Williamson, O. 208
Wilms-Wright, C. 2, 185
women, in Avon companies 148

Young, Lord 11, 18
Young, S. 2, 7, 13, 14, 15, 16

Zackula, S. K. 27, 28, 29
Zwick, J. 24